Memoirs of a (Highly) Political Economist

Jan Winiecki

Memoirs of a (Highly) Political Economist

PETER LANG
EDITION

Bibliographic Information published by the Deutsche Nationalbibliothek
The Deutsche Nationalbibliothek lists this publication in the Deutsche Nationalbibliografie; detailed bibliographic data is available in the internet at http://dnb.d-nb.de.

This publication was generously supported by the University of Information Technology and Management in Rzeszow.

Library of Congress Cataloging-in-Publication Data
Names: Winiecki, Jan, author.
Title: Memoirs of a (highly) political economist / Jan Winiecki.
Description: Frankfurt am Main ; New York : Peter Lang, [2015]
Identifiers: LCCN 2015034748 | ISBN 9783631668795
Subjects: LCSH: Winiecki, Jan. | Economists–Poland–Biography. | Economics–Poland. | Poland–Economic policy. | Poland–Economic Conditions–1945-
Classification: LCC HB114.W56 A3 2015 | DDC 330.092–dc23 LC record available at http://lccn.loc.gov/2015034748

ISBN 978-3-631-66879-5 (Print)
E-ISBN 978-3-653-06242-7 (E-Book)
DOI 10.3726/978-3-653-06242-7

Peter Lang Edition is an Imprint of Peter Lang GmbH.

Peter Lang – Frankfurt am Main · Bern · Bruxelles · New York · Oxford · Warszawa · Wien

This publication has been peer reviewed.

www.peterlang.com

Contents

Part I:
Communism: Between Horror and Political Cabaret

Chapter 1: An Inquisitive Youngster in the Stalinist World

My earliest reminiscences, going back to 1945, were associated with travels from central Poland, where my family lived during the war, to my birthplace, Sopot, on the Baltic coast. My father went ahead of us during the last months of the war, intent on helping to establish Polish administration there, and we joined him in the spring of 1945. The trip of less than 350 km took in these very uncertain times about a week.

The uncertainty did not end upon arrival, either. The so-called *Ziemie Zachodnie* (Western Lands), allocated to Poland at Yalta by the great powers as a compensation for the loss of almost half of the pre-war Polish territories to the Soviets, were at the time something of a Wild West. There were overlapping Polish and Soviet administrations here and there and the balance of power was very uncertain, indeed.

One day a group of Soviet soldiers arrived and started robbing house after house on our street of whatever movable goods they hoped to take with them back to the Soviet Union. Local Sopot authorities, where my father worked, alerted the Polish security police and we observed a real battle between the Russians and Poles along Kosciuszko Street, where we lived. Interestingly, Poles won, took away the booty from the Russians, but never bothered themselves to return them to their rightful owners…

I saw many times on railway wagons, transporting Russian soldiers or Russian booty, carried from Western Poland and Soviet-occupied zone of Germany to Soviet Russia, a scrawled sentence:

> "*Wezcie zegarki, wezcie rowery*
> *i idzcie do jasnej cholery*"
> [Take our watches, take our bicycles,
> and go to hell, where you belong]

A relevant story at this point is a 1960s official literary competition under the pretentious title: "The First Day of Freedom," which was to mean the day we were "liberated" by the Soviets. In fact, one totalitarian dictatorship superseded another, with the difference that the communists had their own Polish offshoot. A writer from Cracow, Jacek Stwora, later also a co-founder of one of the best Polish political cabarets (a Polish specialty in East-Central Europe!) wrote a very short, to-the-point, story and sent it to the competition committee. It ran approximately as follows:

> In the early morning it looked just like any other day. I shaved myself, took a bath, put my clothes on, and had my (meager) breakfast. At about 9:00 a.m. I decided to leave my apartment and take a walk. At about 9:30 a.m. I met the first Russian soldier. I was able to buy my next watch three years later…

I do not need to add that Mr. Stwora did not get any prize for his story in the literary competition.

Some months later, in early 1946, my family experienced another display of Wild West patterns, combined with the growing communist lawlessness. As it soon turned out, a neighbor living on the first floor in the same house as ourselves was a ranking communist security police officer. As such he felt he was above the law. So, when some radiators in his apartment broke he simply ordered workers to disassemble some radiators … from our apartment and reassemble them in his own. My mother called father who came in and threw the workers out. The neighbor came furious to our apartment, but my father kicked him down the stairs as well.

Hours later, however, my father was arrested and kept for 48 hours under interrogation at the Gdansk security police headquarter. Yet, even the communist lawlessness had some limits, and this type of plain robbery was not a good advertisement for the new regime. So, my father was freed after extensive interrogation, but it was he (not the security policeman!) who was charged with "petty hooliganism" and given a six months suspended sentence.

The whole story had its cabaret side as well. The sentence was published in a local newspaper, but with a surprising twist. Due to a printer's error, a part of the sentence shifted from one column on the newspaper's page to the neighboring one, as it happened devoted to the commemoration of some anniversary of the Soviet military. So, the readers were surprised to learn that my father got "six month suspended sentence for petty hooliganism to commemorate the anniversary of the Red Army."

Increasingly, however, my family – as well as most other Poles – experienced more and more cases of pure communist horror. Without cabaret. A distant relative received in 1947 a life sentence for an alleged sabotage act made at the behest of the British intelligence service. He was an engineer and a production manager in a Gdansk factory, whose general manager was a semi-literate communist party *apparatchik* (popular word also in Poland, although born in Soviet Russia). This *apparatchik*, in order to increase production, ordered workers to raise pressure in the boiler above the safety level. The boiler exploded and the relative in question, not the *apparatchik,* was charged with sabotage.

He was put in the special room, full of water, in the building of the Gdansk office of security police. They told him to sign an admission of working at the instigation of British intelligence. He refused, so they left him in the room, standing in water up to his chest. The next step of pressure was to put in the same room his wife and their small son, whom they carried in turn on their arms. At a certain point his wife said she cannot keep the child above water anymore and would soon collapse. So, he knocked on the door and said to the guard that if they free his wife and a child, he would sign what they wished. After the end of Stalinism he was freed in 1955 (having spent 8 years in prison anyway).

The foregoing was, so to say, a kind of general education of a youngster living under communism. A sad joke was popular at the time: "What was the safest answer to the question – put to a child – whom he or she loves more: his father or his mother?" The safest answer was that she loves most "Uncle Stalin"...

As far as economic education was concerned, I received it primarily from my mother. She was to me a source of knowledge that made a stark contrast with the propaganda, with which I and other youngsters were bombarded at school and elsewhere about the country and the world – and inevitably about the superiority of the communist present over the pre-communist past.

So, for example, I came one day from my elementary school and informed my mother that we were told that a janitor in a building earns now 600 zlotys, while before the war he earned only 60 zlotys per month. The implication was that earlier he must have been obviously worse off.

My mother put her arm around me and gently suggested to take a place at the table. She took a pencil and a paper and said: "If they say so, they are quite probably right. But let us see how much such janitor could buy then and now. I still remember pre-war prices."

She put on paper, in two columns, the respective prices before and after the war for basic food products, clothes, shoes, prices of some services, such as a visit to a barber, added respective rents for a small, one bedroom apartment, and summed everything up. "You see," she said, the janitor could buy roughly the same amount of goods and services before and after the war. Maybe a bit more in the earlier period. Clearly, not only wages, but also prices went up considerably in the meantime." This is how I got my first lesson in the economics of a representative basket of goods and services, as well as the first sensible signal on the nature of inflation.

My mother was not an economist; she had a general secondary education only. But she had an advantage of being a daughter and a granddaughter of business managers, each with an engineering degree. In such an environment she learned a lot. Besides, she was a stickler for details and endowed with a large dose of common sense.

Maybe the most important intellectual lesson I learned from repeated encounters of that sort with my mother was her underlying message, namely the need for critical inquiry to be applied to any subject under consideration rather than for an unreflective acceptance of whatever information (or *dis*information) was presented to me. In a world of purposeful mendacity, one of the persistent features of communist rule and its propaganda, it was a particularly timely and important message.

Given the debt I owed to my dear mother, it should not surprise readers that – decades later, of course – I dedicated one of my books [*Political Economy of Reform and Change*, 1997] to my mother, with thanks for teaching me to how to differentiate between right and wrong, as well as between right and wrong economics.

Given my family background, it is not surprising that a preference for private ownership was something that came natural to me. This conviction had early spillovers. A classmate of mine from elementary school complained once – a bit frightened (after all it took place at the height of Stalinism!) – to my mother: "Why Janek always says loudly in a [state-owned – JW] grocery that dry or rotten carrots, or other vegetables, are the outcome of state ownership. For if a grocery were privately-owned, its owner would keep them in good condition. Otherwise he would not be able to sell them at all. And private owner depends on what he sells, in contrast with the state employee who depends on what he tells (those above him)."

Theoretical conviction in the superiority of private property apart, the business association of my family with private ownership was coming at that time to a close. With the passage of time, the pressure on private owners of shops, workshops, or whatever, was becoming stronger, discrimination was rampant, and taxes and arbitrarily imposed surtaxes multiplied. The end came with the fraudulent change in the monetary system in November, 1950. All private savings, including the working capital of private firms, on their private bank accounts were exchanged at 3:1 rate, meaning that two thirds of them were confiscated. Since firms' debts continued at an unchanged 1:1 rate, most private owners went broke. And, like my father, they had to pay their debt years after closing their firms (in the case of my father, a construction firm).

The family decided to leave the Wild West and move back to Warsaw, where my father joined the state transportation company to run its construction division. My skirmishes with the surrealistic system continued at secondary school as well. I remember our tutorials with the Latin teacher for whom it was his last year in school before retirement. Maybe for that reason, he was more frank with us than his younger colleagues who had much more to lose in this 1951/52 school year, at the height of Stalinist terror.

At one of his tutorials, he was asked by one of us about the availability of meat, always a delicate issue in Poland and in other communist countries (as I was to learn, first, as a consumer and, next, as an economist). Our colleague's question was the following: "I read in the newspaper that the meat output increased last year by 14%. And, yet, after classes, I go as told by my mother to a state butcher's shop nearby, stay there in a queue until my mother comes from her job, and then I go home to do my homework. She remains in the queue, at times joined later by my father. But they come home – more often than not – empty-handed. No meat was available."

"The Tomato," as we called our Latin teacher due to his round, pink cheeks, replied in all outward seriousness: "Dear children, from your physics' classes you should know that one and the same material object cannot be found at the same time in two different places. If meat is in the newspaper, then it cannot be in the shop." Even the principles of physics, usually not much attractive for children, could add some color to life in those dreary years!

One of the systematic exercises in mendacity we experienced in Stalinist times was the creation of new politically correct communist inventors. In all textbooks of physics, chemistry, and other natural sciences you would find new, generally Russian, inventors who "invented" everything 10, 20 or more years earlier than the Western inventors everybody knew about for ages. Yet another hallmark of invented Soviet inventors was that they had proper class credentials. They were usually ingenuous handyman, peasants (more rarely industrial workers who in Tsarist Russia were few and far between).

I remember one physics class at the elementary school when our teacher was talking about electricity and in the context of a light bulb mentioned Thomas Edison. One of our very few brainwashed classmates, always wearing a green shirt and red tie (communist youth organization's uniform) protested: "Professor! In the textbook they say that the light bulb was invented by Lodygin (a Russian)!" – "Yes, indeed – answered our teacher – But it did not light up well and had to be reinvented."

Classes in Polish language and literature were conducted by a teacher from the family with long literary tradition. His sister was a known author of children's books. During one of the classes, when various literary forms were considered, a classmate inquired, facetiously, whether it is a good example of an epigram:

"Here is the tomb of Vincent Pstrowski.
He took part in the 'socialist rivalry' racket
Poor miner exceeded all work norms
And kicked the bucket."

Socialist rivalry was invented by propaganda as a communist response to the much criticized competition in the capitalist economic system. It was to be spontaneous and prove its superiority with much better economic outcomes. Both spontaneity and outcomes were a propaganda-organized fiction. Pstrowski was one of the early heroes of "socialist rivalry," who fulfilled daily norms in 1000 percent. Inconveniently, however, he died at the age of 43. Since Poles were always quick to react by inventing jokes, somebody wrote the above epigram.

The epigram query by a classmate, clearly with ironic undertones, was nonetheless a problem of sort for our teacher who was under the specific security surveillance. He served in the parachutist brigade in the Polish army in the West, decided to come back to communist Poland after the war and suffered a lot of persecution and simple indignities throughout the whole Stalinist period. One of such frequent indignities was periodic interrogation sessions pursued by the communist party secretary at our secondary school. The party secretary was by occupation not a teacher, as one might expect, but a night janitor (believe me, a real troglodyte!).

Pupils observed what had been happening there and many were (quietly) indignant at the treatment meted out to our much-liked teacher. One day a few older, higher class pupils prepared a trap. Upon noticing that the communist party hack in question walked to school from his cubicle in another building and back, they dismounted the door from the men's room on the second floor and threw it from the toilet window on the passing guy. He had his shoulder broken and suffered a concussion. There was a secret police inquiry, but to no avail. No one saw anything.

Apart from the specific act of vengeance, it is also worthwhile to consider a more general idea of such a communist arrangement like a party leader from the lowest rungs of the society thrust against the much better educated school personnel. Such a relationship between the communist party and the school teachers was also a painful reminder for the latter of who was the boss at the time.

However, on a personal basis, 1955 was a crucial year for me as I was approaching the end of secondary education and had to decide upon my future career. The post-Stalinist thaw began. Soon the change in question brought in Wladyslaw Gomulka, less bloodthirsty head of the *politbureau* than his predecessor Boleslaw Bierut, and the foregoing developments created some opportunities, closed earlier for those without politically correct social background like myself. I decided to apply to the foreign trade department of the Main School of Planning and Statistics (SGPiS) in Warsaw – and was accepted. As I learned soon from an English language teacher at that school, with the daughter of whom I was flirting at the time, I had one of the worst diplomas, but wrote the best paper on the subject of foreign trade. My secondary school diploma was not that bad (although, to be true, I did not overwork myself at the secondary school!), but those trying to get to the Foreign Trade Department of SGPiS were the *creme de la crème* of all those vying to land at the best university of economics in Poland.

After all, completing such a study gave a chance to work abroad, see something other than the communist world, and maybe earn some real money, that is foreign exchange (dollars, etc.) that in contrast with communist monies could be exchanged for everything, including some much desired, but domestically unavailable, consumer goods. With the reigning communist political correctness, however, the proper answer before the examination commission as to why a candidate decided to apply to study at the foreign trade department was that he or she wanted "to help the country to earn precious foreign exchange."

Having been accepted, I made another important – as it turned out – decision, although I did not have at the time the slightest idea that it would be such an eye-opener on the economic reality of Polish collectivized agriculture. I simply decided to earn some money during the vacation period and got drafted into the so-called town-country cooperation linkages at my new place of study. I would spend the summer working – as many did, often under obligation – at one of the state farms (Polish abbreviation: PGR, a state agricultural firm). Apart from earning some money in return for helping the state farm to fulfill its plan target (clearly, they had problems of doing that on their own!) I also hoped to become acquainted with the students who already studied at the same department and learn more about the study I was soon to undertake.

Thus, on a July day, about two dozen SGPiS students landed at PGR Mazany, near Ketrzyn (not far from the Hitler's Prussian headquarter during his war with Soviet Russia). This was my first encounter with the state farm and I looked at everything in amazement.

First of all, the place seemed to have been crowded with people. How was it possible that they needed so many extra hands from outside? After a few days there I learned that the staff of that particular agricultural farm exceeded 80 persons, while the land under cultivation did not exceed 300 hectares (less than 750 acres)! Disorder and filth were the norm. Agricultural implements, once workers came back from the fields, were thrown in the nearest shack and left there until the next use. Besides, the feeling we had was that that we were watching the film in slow motion. Everybody seemed to be moving around at a snail's pace. Coming from an entrepreneurial family and brought up in the appreciation of the superior private property, I could – and did – expect lesser care and lower productivity in the state farm. But not -t-h-a-t -m-u-c-h lower!!

The only place where state farm workers displayed some care were the tiny private gardens each family was allowed by law to cultivate. Much, much later

I learned that, for example, in the Soviet Union such tiny plots supplied between one fourth and one third of all vegetables and more than half of all fruits produced by Soviet agriculture!

Our student group was allocated to weeding, a labor intensive activity, clearly shunned by locals working in Mazany. Cucumbers, cabbages, red beets – all badly needed weeding. However, we learned that daily norms were so low that we fulfilled them usually after 3–4 hours. And we were newcomers to such work! Since we were paid a daily rate rather than a piece rate, we tried to be on the safe side and exceed the norm by, say, 20–30% in terms of the weeded area and then called it a day. Usually, we took a walk to the forest at the borderland of our farm and looked for some fruit, mostly raspberries and blueberries.

Fruits are a good source of vitamins, but they could not solve all our food problems at Mazany. There was a mid-day soup offered by the farm management to all workers and beyond that we were on our own. Permanent PGR workers had their families (also working there), so they prepared breakfasts and dinners at home. But we were there alone. Besides, the question arose soon what to prepare our meals from?

The shop in PGR Mazany was opened one hour in the morning and two hours in the afternoon and in most cases there was nothing there one could safely eat. Bread was delivered there 2–3 times a week and had one feature that I never found elsewhere throughout my whole life. Namely, it was always musty from the inside!! The next shop was 1–2 hours from Mazany (by a local bus). The situation looked hopeless. We inquired among the state farm workers and they, reluctantly, admitted that there was a *kulak* (large scale private farmer – an ideological enemy in Stalinist times) nearby who produced extra food beyond the need of his own farm and it just might be possible to buy something there if we wished to do so.

A small group, including me, went there and we were delighted with the contrast. It was a family of six: the farmer and his wife, her parents, and two teenage children. They had maximum land allowed under the communist rule, that is, 100 hectares. The land was kept in excellent condition. Their grain was bigger and thicker than in the state farm, vegetables were weeded, farm animals looked much better (and cleaner!) – and all this was done by a small family. And yet the family had one third of the land of the state agricultural farm and one thirteenth of its personnel! Even in quantity terms (leaving immeasurably higher quality aside) private farm's productivity was many, many times higher.

Additionally, from our perspective of half-starved college students, they produced for themselves milk, butter, cottage cheese, eggs, baked their own bread, and even made their own sausages. At a price they were ready to sell us some of their fresh and tasteful products. We were saved and could survive the remaining almost three weeks of our stay.

Some readers might argue that it was a case of bad luck and things were undoubtedly better in some other state farms. With the benefit of hindsight I would argue the opposite. Mazany were quite close to the miserable average, above which were mostly those – always present – showcases of communist propaganda. I remember from later times one such place: PGR Manieczki, which was usually shown to other communist leaders, coming on "brotherly" visits. Manieczki were mentioned a number of times, for example on the occasion of Soviet leader Nikita Khrushchev's visit in late 1950s.

Only decades later, after the fall of communism, I learned from somebody's reminiscences that the *sovkhoz*, that is PGR, in Manieczki was performing so well because the agricultural authorities appointed as a manager of that state farm a former landowner, whose land was nationalized after communist takeover. He apparently knew what farming was about and besides must have had an iron hand in managing those working on the farm. Such cases were not so numerous, though, at the time, when ideological purity and "class struggle" mattered more than professional performance.

To shift for a moment to the political cabaret, the "brotherly" countries, "brotherly" leaders, "brotherly" visits, etc., gave rise to another series of jokes. There was once a discussion at my school about countries that are particularly friendly, well disposed toward Poland and Poles and a female teacher asked pupils to name such a country or countries. Various were mentioned: France, Hungary, Sweden, etc., but the teacher was not satisfied. She was expected from the higher-up propagandists to elicit a "politically correct" answer that first of all such country was the Soviet Union. So, she pressed on the pupils to think about yet another, really very friendly country.

Pupils did not oblige, though, and did not deliver the "correct" answer. Thus, she gave up the pretence and said that such a very friendly country was the Soviet Union. And then, one of the pupils protested and said that the Soviet Union was not a "friendly," but a "brotherly" country. "But what difference does it make?" she asked, a little baffled. "A great one," answered the pupil. "You can choose your friend, but you cannot choose your brother."

The next encounter with the economic reality of communism took place during the next vacation period. Although it belonged already to my university years, I regard it as a part of my earliest experience with the world of work under communism. This time I found a job for two summer months not on a state farm, but in a state industrial enterprise, in Warsaw itself. It was a firm producing prefabricated road and construction materials, and I was hired for two months as a quality controller. I supervised the quality of output of two working parties, consisting of eight workers each.

After a week or two I recognized the pattern of work and – with a few conversations on the side – found an explanation. Formally, they should work from 7:00 a.m. to 3:30 p.m., with half an hour's lunch break. In reality, they usually started at 8:00 a.m., worked for about two hours, then made a long break until 1:00 p.m. They either left the factory area for a drink, or, more often, found a place to sleep nearby (there was some bush and grass there, and a lot of unused machinery, to find a reasonably comfortable place in their shadow to sleep). They returned at about 1:00 p.m., worked until 3:00 p.m. and then headed home.

A brief digression. Readers should not treat their sleeping-on-the-job habits as something unusual in communist factories. Some years later I visited on business a furniture factory in central Poland. After entering the area I noticed a group of sleeping workers, while walking to the building of factory management. The political cabaret side of this story was that they slept in the shadow of a very large billboard, with the – undoubtedly true – statement: "Only high productivity of labor leads to higher living standards."

But let us go back to my first encounter with communist industry. Since the workers I dealt with were paid by the week, I soon noticed that they tried not to earn more than 2700–2900 zlotys on a monthly basis (at that time about 50% more than the average wage). I learned from them why. Working by piece rate, they could earn more, they said. But if they produced more, their quota would be increased, but not their wages; they would still earn the same 2700–2900 zlotys, while working longer hours than before.

The only other factor affecting the length of their real, not statutory, hours of work was me. If they were more negligent than usual, I rejected a larger percentage of defective pieces and they had to work, say, five hours instead of the usual four to produce the average daily output of a minimal acceptable quality. Since this happened quite often, they decided to try diplomacy *cum* incentives in dealing with me.

They learned somewhere about my own (fixed) salary of 900 zlotys, about one third of what they earned. But, allow me, again, yet another digression. Paying supervisors of all sorts less than piece rate workers was a norm rather than an exception under communism. In early 1960s I had a highly informative conversation with a young engineer in an agricultural machinery factory in the very old city of Plock. Seeing somebody of a similar age, he confessed that the quality of work is abysmal in the factory. "But how it could be otherwise?" he said. "I am a production manager on a shift, but they disregard all the orders and recommendations I make. They know I make 1800 zlotys per month, foreman that nominally supervises the working group earns 3000–3500 per month, while they earn, working so badly that half of them should have been fired long ago, up to 5000 zlotys per month." As a quality controller I had at least some measure of influence; the helpless production manager had none. Thus, if one knew something about the abysmal quality of output under communism, this story about the structure of incentives explains a lot.

Readers most probably suspect what was coming. A delegation of two from the teams approached me when I was leaving factory after work and invited me to a nearby bar. There, they suggested that they know I am a poor student working to earn money for the next year of my studies. "So, what?" I asked cautiously. "Well," they said, "we will pay you another 900 zlotys if you don't reject so much of our output." They would still earn roughly their 2700–2900 zlotys as before, their sacrifice would be small (some 50 zlotys per worker), while I would earn twice as much as I was getting.

The offer was tempting and fitting well into the surrealistic world of work I was to enter in the not too distant future. However, I could not accept it for more fundamental reasons. But rejecting the offer with indignation out of hand did not seem – even to a youngster like myself – a good strategy, either. It could exacerbate the relations on the job, with unpredictable (as it sometimes happened) consequences.

I said that if they work in such a way that the rate of rejected defective pieces was at or near the norm they would still be able to work their four hours a day and earn their "safe" level of wages, with just a bit higher regard for the quality of what they do. And if they work that way till the end of this month I would consider their generous offer for the next month.

Surprisingly, a bit of moralizing mixed with a bit of diplomacy helped somehow. They worked a bit less carelessly than before, I was not a stickler for details, where it was not necessary – and the quality was roughly kept at the (very low) level required by the norms. By the end of the next month, however, I was to be approached with an extra envelope, a situation that I tried to avoid. Thus, I agreed with the respective section in the administration office that I'll leave my monthly report a day earlier, take my pay and say good bye. Of course, a year later I had to find another place to earn extra money during the vacation period.

Maybe, to close the reminiscences of my early youth, I should add a conversation I remembered from late 1940s, while we were still living at the Baltic coast in Sopot. For I think it is characteristic of certain illusions about communism that so many decent and educated people held at the time – maybe less frequently in Poland and other countries afflicted then by real-life communism, but much more often in Western Europe and elsewhere.

There was among the friends of my parents, one pre-war communist. A highly educated, cultured man, he continued to believe in communism even after the imposition of communist rule in Poland. He was not blind to terror and lawlessness and – I remember – he was at times at the butt of criticism during the social gatherings at my parents' Sopot apartment.

But what I remember most vividly – even after all these decades – was his conversation with my mother I overheard and the explanation he gave of the problems of communism in Poland, as well as elsewhere in our part of the world. "You know, Helen (my mother's first name), the drama of communism in this country stems from the fact that it came from the barbarous East, rather than civilized West. Had it arrived from the West, our life would have been much different – and undoubtedly much better."

My mother did not seem to have been convinced for the topic came back on a number of similar occasions. Decades later I asked my mother why she was not convinced. She answered it was an instinctive rejection by a person from a family with a managerial and entrepreneurial tradition. And, looking at the issue from historical perspective, it could not have been otherwise. After all, many understood even then that communism was both evil and inefficient to boot. Coming from the democratic West, it could presumably lose its evil characteristics as my parents' friend assumed in late 1940s. However, the inefficiencies of collectivist arrangements based on collective ownership were not yet proven at that time beyond any reasonable doubt. Especially in the cases of voluntary introduction of such arrangements.

Not known at the time, for example, was the much later research conducted by Joshua Muravchik, then from American Enterprise Institute, who studied small groups, earlier of religious and later of socialist origin, who upon arrival to North America between the seventeenth and nineteenth centuries opted for collective ownership and egalitarian distribution of the produced wealth.[1] He studied the records of almost three hundred of such communities. Their histories had one thing in common. Namely, the collectivist arrangements broke down in -a-l-l cases and sooner or later members of a given community shifted to a private ownership-based arrangements.

Clearly, regardless of whether under duress, as under communist rule, or undertaken voluntarily by some religiously or ideologically motivated communities, collectivist arrangements were inefficient to boot. Thus, my mother was right. As she used to explain (and I repeated it so often), if carrots are sold in the state shop, the probability that they rot, dry, or otherwise become wasted is very much higher than in the case of those sold in the private shop.

Chapter 2: Studying and Working under Communist Orthodoxy

In the second half of 1950s I moved – for personal reasons – from the Main School of Planning and Statistics to Warsaw University, where I joined the School of Law and Administration. At the time, with no business school on the horizon (even as an idea), the latter school accommodated to some extent business administration issues. It, thus, came a bit closer to the reality than what passed as economics at the time. Besides, studying at the latter school gave me much more spare time in which to earn money (to help my family that unfortunately had fallen on hard times).

I was a bit older than most of my new colleagues and, moreover, had previous experience with economic studies. And my new colleagues had some serious problems – as it transpired – with economics that was also a part of the study of law and administration. Leaving aside the quasi-philosophical subject called "Marxist-Leninist philosophy," it was the *political economy of socialism* that disturbed them more than anything else.

Readers should keep in mind that those who decide to become lawyers are usually serious, no-nonsense young people, predisposed to logical thinking and trained in that direction during their years of study. Maybe it was their intellectual predisposition that prodded them to look for logical answers to economic issues they faced and they hoped that I might help them in finding such answers. "Listen," they pleaded. "We managed somehow to cope successfully with an earlier subject: the *political economy of capitalism*. We did not believe much in what we read, but at least we could understand the flow of argument and memorize it" (at least until the end of the exam's time).

I could easily understand their skepticism with respect to the political economy of capitalism as taught in communist times. A standard textbook consisted of a half a dozen chapters saying what Marx said about the capitalist market system hundred years earlier, then a few chapters saying what Lenin said about monopoly and finance under capitalism fifty years earlier.

The two final chapters of the textbook dealt with "modern capitalist developments." One, under the heading of "state interventionism" dealt, crudely, with Keynesian macroeconomic demand management. The other chapter – on the so-called less developed, or developing, countries of Asia, Middle East, Africa, and Latin America – offered students a Marxism-cloaked propaganda on the exploitative Western colonialism of the past and the pernicious contemporary (no less exploitative) "neocolonialism" of the present. More often than not students did not believe what they read, but they could parrot the text for the exam. And if they forgot something, reconstructing the crude criticism was not all that difficult.

No such easy way out existed, however, in the case of the political economy of socialism. Marx's musings about the future socialist system of happiness and plenty were few and far between. The general idea was "production for use, not for profit" and the associated idea of the abolition of money.

And victorious Bolsheviks decided in 1917 to graft these ideas onto the living body of the Russian economy and society. Thus, industrial workers were supposed to produce on the basis of a mere promise that their needs for food would be satisfied by the peasants and other needs by fellow workers. Peasants, in turn, were supposed to deliver food to the cities in return for the promise of delivery of the industrial goods they needed. The system did not envisage any economic incentives and assumed the dominance of "revolutionary consciousness and selflessness" of the masses. The foregoing ideas were in stark contrast with what Adam Smith wrote a hundred years earlier than Marx that it is not from the benevolence of the baker that we obtain our daily bread.

The ideas – unsurprisingly – did not work. Both industrial workers and peasants noted that their demands are not satisfied and refused to deliver (in the case of peasants in spite of confiscatory raids on the villages by ruling communist administrators). When the Lenin-led *politbureau*, the top political body, called off the Marxian utopia, the Russian economy was a disaster. Industrial output in 1921 amounted to about 10% of what Russia produced at the beginning of World War I in 1913, while agricultural production shrank so much that 2–3 million people died of starvation.

Having learned the lesson, the next communist economic system introduced in 1928 used classic Marxian ideas more as ideological beacons than specific economic and organizational recommendations. And it was the latter system, best known in English language literature as a *command economy* (or centrally planned and administered economy) that the lawyers-to-be – and everybody else – tried to cope with.

The system willy-nilly accepted the existence of economic incentives for managers and workers. And for incentives to have an impact they had also to accept the existence of money (something the earlier utopia rejected). Money was for the most part a unit of account in the command economy, but at least in the consumer goods market money gave consumers some – often quite limited – measure of choice among goods and services that communist planners cared to include into the production plan (and, more importantly, state firms cared to deliver!). It was a far cry from the consumer sovereignty in the capitalist market system, but some limited choice had been offered nonetheless.

In more general terms, leaving aside the consumer goods market, the system started with the political monopoly, then established the dominance of state ownership and, next, ensured bureaucratic, top-down coordination of economic activity. It started with the communist *politbureau* as the top decision maker with respect to fundamental proportions of the plan, then charged government and the central planning bureau with the plan preparation and control of its implementation. A typical pyramid emerged, with the planning bureau at the top of the economic bureaucracy, giving commands to ministries, ministries to associations of state firms, and the latter to state firms. Then, the firms were to implement the plans, handed down from above, and report results of implementation upwards (as the planning theory had it).

Two features of such a system added most to the puzzlement of those trying to understand its workings. The first was the lack of financial constraints. Simply speaking, state firms were not threatened with bankruptcy in a command economy, regardless of how bad their financial performance was.

Such an unspoken rule meant that firms could demand as much production inputs as they wished, ask their superiors for as much investment as they wished, and demand as many workers as they wished to fulfill plan indicators, regardless of the fact that the incurred costs might have exceeded value of their output. And to round out the picture with the term known in economic theory as *informational asymmetry*, their superiors could not evaluate whether state firms' claims were legitimate (meaning: really needed to fulfill plan targets) or not, because they did not know the details that firm managers did.

Besides, state firm managers learned quickly that for their superiors – planners at the higher levels of the pyramid - output quantity was almost all that mattered. Not only output cost mattered little, but also output quality was usually accorded a very low priority. Firms were rewarded for producing greater quantity at as low quality as was acceptable (see my experience at the firm producing construction materials in Chapter 1 above!). All the foregoing features created a completely unbalanced economy, where demand persistently exceeded supply and the imbalances were additionally aggravated by the uncertainty as to whether supplies – if and when they arrived – were usable (that is of minimum acceptable quality) or not.

I was not able to explain the foregoing puzzles in their entirety to my younger colleagues from the School of Law and Administration. I mastered myself a more complete knowledge on the subject of command economy later, although bits and pieces of the puzzle (low productivity, abysmal quality, etc.) I noted or sensed intuitively already at the time.

What students had to cope with in the textbook on political economy of socialism were, then, a few utterances of the Marxist classics, completely useless as a guide to understanding how the planning and administration system really worked. What use students could make, for example, of Lenin's statement that management was a simple activity and any cook, able to add, subtract, multiply, and divide, could manage a firm without much difficulty? A thoughtful student would rather side with Ludwig van Mises, one of the leading lights of the so-called Austrian school of economics, who poked fun at Lenin, saying that the statement in question was written by someone with the mentality of the filing clerk.

Thus, the textbook was an uncertain compromise between a few utterances of Marxist classics and numerous – but confusing – elaborations of contemporary Marxists economists on how the system should operate in theory. Finally, some cautious confrontations of the model with the real-life centrally planned and administered economy were offered. Such confrontations with the reality had to be cautious, however, because the discrepancies between the model and the reality could not be shown to be too large. Otherwise, textbook authors would be accused of "revisionism" and other mortal sins against the communist ideology and system.

Yet I was intermittently pressed to tell my younger colleagues how to approach the subject of the political economy of socialism from a purely utilitarian (that is examination-centered) perspective: "It does not make much sense! Are there any tricks one could learn to pass the damn thing?" they inquired. I was skeptical, as far as shortcuts were concerned. "There are no miraculous prescriptions," I warned. "But I can, at the very least, suggest the following. If you are sure you remember what the textbook says on a given topic, say so. But if you are not, use an inverted logic. Think calmly what would be the logical sequence of cause and effect – and say something that is opposite to what you would regard as logical."

However unusual, intuition-inspired were my suggestions they seemed to have satisfied my younger colleagues' demand for the time being. I forgot about the whole story, but was reminded of it more than a decade later. To my surprise I learned from a young university graduate from the same School of Law and Administration that the "Winiecki's prescription" still circulated among students, coping with the same problem of the illogic of the political economy of socialism. The prescription might have been forgotten later, but when I looked (to verify my suspicions) at the textbooks on the subject in mid-1980s, just a few years before the collapse of the communist system, I discovered the same tired nonsense offered by the same – or younger – generation of (opportunistic) authors.

Leaving aside my encounters with some irritated law students, a student of economics in any communist country – and Poland was by no means the worst! – could after graduation safely forget what he or she had learned over the years. To retain in his or her memory the content of all these textbooks would be more a hindrance than an advantage. Yes, statistics, econometrics, input-output analysis, and all the math could help, no matter where such a graduate would later find a job. But the "high theory" could become a real hindrance if treated seriously, both at the state firm and state bureaucracy level. Only if a graduate decided to stay at the university he had to memorize the "high theory," maybe elaborate it a bit to make it more digestible for the students and then pass it on to a (rather confused) younger generation.

Economics was special in social science in the sense that the gulf between the real life and theorizing on political economy of socialism, planning theory, and what not, was the largest among social science disciplines. Even under communism, theorizing in sociology or psychology had not been infused so much with the ideological wishful thinking as was economics.

We all learned this special status of economics the hard way in the early years of study. In his writings, Marx differentiated between the "base" of his system, that is the economy, and the "superstructure" (the polity, society, etc.). According to Marx's musings, the causation ran from the – most important – base to the superstructure. So, for example, Marx thought that the economy would evolve under the capitalist market system in the direction of the ever greater concentration of capital and – in his view – at a certain stage it would consist of a few very large firms, ripe for nationalization after the successful anti-capitalist revolution of the proletariat.

In reality, however, the change was taking place in the -o-p-p-o-s-i-t-e direction. Communist takeover, that is the change in the superstructure, came always first, and once communists were firmly in the saddle they nationalized thousands (not a few as envisaged by Marx!) private firms – large, middle-sized, and small.

Thus, an inquisitive student interested in learning how the communist economic system came into being and operated in practice was on his or her own in the search for an answer. The contrast between theory and reality was too large to rely on the former. Not that there were any strong incentives for him or her to start such an independent inquiry. In fact, they could spell trouble if such student started thinking independently. The trouble would multiply if a part of such an inquiry were an absorption of the Western Sovietological literature (even if a larger part of it was sympathetic to communist ideas, although not necessarily to the real-life communist arrangements).

The use of pure logic at a wrong time and place, combined with what one already knew of the practical operation of the system, could get an explorer into trouble. I remember a training course in the place where I worked in the mid-1960s (production and technology department of the Central Council of Trade

Unions – CCTU), where a high ranking planner from the Planning Commission presented a few shockingly unrealistic opinions. First, he maintained that plans were generally well prepared, internally consistent, balancing supply and demand, but when they were put into operation "people twisted and turned them, generating various distortions." Clearly, the planner neglected the existence or rejected the importance of such a fundamental issue as incentives. A standard action-reaction model predicts what happens if incentives tell the player how to react and these incentives are not positively correlated with implementing the (handed down) plan targets.

But the main thrust of his lecture was even more surrealistic. He waxed lyrical about the expected monumental progress in economic planning, forthcoming due to the use of computers. The mania started in early 1960s, a period I dubbed later the "comrade computer age." Since balancing the plan numbers through the successive approximations ("iterations" in the computer scientists' jargon) was extremely time-consuming, the rapidly growing computational capability of computers was thought to be at the time a panacea for various planning ills. Even such a socialist celebrity in economics as Oscar Lange wrote shortly before his death something similarly foolish to that effect.

Foolish, because the main problem continued to be the clash between macro-level planning goals and micro-level incentives of managers and workers in state firms. Moreover, the informational asymmetry allowed firms and subordinate levels of the planning hierarchy to doctor – by and large with impunity– plan implementation reports sent to their superiors. Therefore, during the discussion that ensued I challenged the planning apparatchik to explain what difference it would make if falsified data were sent via a computer terminal in a state firm instead of being sent more slowly by a messenger or by mail. Getting distorted numbers faster did not look to me like a great step forward, I opined. And I suggested it would be more efficient to start thinking how to change the incentives firms have to cheat in their reports to associations and ministries.

As the readers might have guessed I did not get a sensible answer from the planner in question (in fact I did not get any answer!). However, the silence with respect to serious answers did not mean that there were no reactions at all. There were. I was wrong in assuming that the repressive regime, even if a slightly relaxed relative to the Stalinist era, would accept the criticism of the fundamentals. Clearly, computers did not belong to fundamentals, while the structure of incentives in a communist command economy presumably did.

So, I was called to appear, in turn, before my superiors and before the communist party committee in the CCTU. Both expressed their displeasure with respect to my "destructive criticism." I defended myself that it was a case of "constructive criticism," acceptable in principle by the system. After all, I suggested an alternative to the reliance on computers in cases, where computers did not solve the problem at hand. But my defense was not well received. I was passed for promotion for two years in a row and deprived of usual quarterly bonuses for about the same period.

I learned in secrecy from a friend that firing me was seriously considered. What saved me were not my professional economic skills (which, as it happened, turned out to be more a hindrance than an advantage!), but rather my journalistic, that is writing skills. No one else in the department could write reports with similar ease, clarity, and speed. So, the deputy chairman of the Central Council in charge of economic affairs decided – in his own interest – to bear with me. What I wrote for them, however, was more thoroughly scrutinized than before…

I continued nonetheless with my learning process not only through such encounters, but also through reading normal (meaning: Western) economics literature. The major problem was the poor state of economic libraries. In fact, there was only one relatively large such library at the Main School of Planning and Statistics. But even that library held only a few and incomplete sets of Western textbooks that one should confront in search of basic economic knowledge. Besides, the textbooks available belonged to authors of different theoretical persuasions, were associated with different teaching programs, apart from different sophistication levels. So, to complete the minimum knowledge on the subject I had to supplement textbooks with many theoretical contributions of particular authors.

In consequence, the edifice of my knowledge was not necessarily built from the foundations up. Sometimes, I was laboriously trying to build the second floor, while foundations were barely finished, to say nothing about the first floor. My accumulation of economics knowledge proceeded at an uneven and halting pace…

In any case I learned that those intellectually curious like myself were, to my surprise, a minority – even among academic economists. To explain, let me enter a time capsule and move for a while forward by about a quarter of a century – to 1990. A small team of four economists (including myself) was then asked by the Polish branch of the George Soros Foundation to prepare a report on the state of academic economics.[2] In an analysis prepared for the final report I classified academics into four categories:

<1> Those who believed in what passed as economics within the framework of the officially approved teaching programs. These people rarely if ever in their later career reached intellectually beyond the boundaries of that kind of economics. They did not feel the need to look at what others wrote

(mostly in the West) on the subject called economics, even on the subject of political economy of socialism and its more detailed derivatives.

<2> Those who did not believe that officially approved economics was the pinnacle of professional knowledge, but were convinced that communism was here to stay forever – or at least for their lifetime. They opportunistically, or cynically if you wish, concluded that a thorough learning of normal (meaning: Western) economics would be a waste of their time, because they could not use that knowledge, either in teaching or in doing research. I evaluated that the group 2 was the most numerous among all four.

<3> Those who did not believe in the economic sense of officially approved economics and decided to learn normal economics (note, that normal economics was taught before communism also in East-Central Europe). They decided, however, that they did not want to clash with the ruling communist system and kept their acquired knowledge close to themselves. They certainly were not ready to give a lecture in a state-owned grocery about the inferiority of state ownership that I delivered while still at the secondary school!

<4> Those, not very numerous, economists who did not believe in the economic sense of officially approved economics, learned normal economics and tried to use it in their teaching and/or research. The most difficult part of it was to apply normal economics to the problems of the centrally planned and administered economy.

Some in that last – and most interesting – group had an advantage over others. And it is at this point that the story of Aleksy Wakar should be told, moving in the time capsule backwards about half a century to the time of Bolshevik revolution and civil war in Russia that ensued. Wakar, at that time already with a Ph.D. in economics, was a "white" Russian who fought communists in the civil war and after the defeat luckily escaped to the reborn Poland. There, he took the job at the then Main School of Commerce (after World War II renamed into the Main School of Planning and Statistics), wrote his post-Ph.D. thesis (habilitation), and became a chaired professor there.

However, after the war and the imposition of communist rule, the Soviet NKVD, the dreaded secret police, claimed Wakar with their Polish equivalent, UB, and Wakar was sent to the Soviet Union. He was sentenced to the stay in the concentration camp and expedited to Siberia. However, with the death of Stalin and the Khrushchev's "thaw," many people were freed from the camps, including Aleksy Wakar. Another repatriation effort of Poles from the Soviet Union was then under way since late 1956, and Wakar, having Polish citizenship already in the inter-war period, was covered by the agreement between Polish and Soviet authorities. He returned in 1957, was offered his former chair and resumed teaching and writing. A history one in a million – and confirming the saying that Poland was the merriest barrack in the whole socialist (concentration) camp.

Upon his return Wakar discovered that his young assistants had dramatically limited knowledge of normal economics. Well trained in classical and neoclassical economics, from Adam Smith to Alfred Marshall (after all, normal economics was taught also in Russia before 1917!), Wakar decided to systematically train his assistants in normal economics. The seminars, where assistants produced papers presenting step by step the developments in economics' knowledge, lasted a few years, but they paid off handsomely. Articles and books coming from the Aleksy Wakar's circle were the most interesting applications of normal economics to various areas of command economy. Whether on economic equilibria (or, rather, permanent disequilibria) under central planning, or on inflation, or the (disruptive) nature of investment processes within the command economy, or on other topics, articles and books by Wakar's ablest assistants, such as Janusz Beksiak, Urszula Libura-Grzelonska, and others, dominated economic writings on command economy in Poland for about two decades, since early 1960s till early 1980s.

To balance the good fortune of those who encountered Aleksy Wakar on their professional path with the bad fortune of those who were viciously maltreated by the communist authorities for what they wrote, I have to mention another older colleague of mine, who – like myself – taught later (in 1980s) at the only university not controlled by the communists, namely the Catholic University of Lublin.

Professor Stefan Kurowski published in 1963 his excellent post-doctoral thesis on the historical process of economic growth.[3] He concluded there that the industrialization of Russia, which accelerated since 1880s, if proceeded along these lines, would have achieved the same level of development in late 1950s that it did actually achieve under the command economy. The "subversive" implications of the story were somehow missed by the censors, most probably overwhelmed by dozens upon dozens of tables and graphs, and in consequence the idea that the Soviet experiment was not the superior achievement in economic history of mankind was presented there with all the empirical evidence then available.

The reaction of communist authorities was delayed as a result of limited knowledge of the censors, but once they understood the implications of Kurowski's reasoning, it was delivered with a vengeance. Kurowski's post-doctoral degree was retroactively (!!) annulled, and he was fired from the Institute of Economics of the Polish Academy of Science. Nonetheless, it was Poland, not the Soviet Union. So, Stefan Kurowski landed not in Siberia, but at the chair of geography at the Warsaw

University (with an accompanying ban on teaching economics). The barrack was -s-o-m-e-w-h-a-t merrier, after all.

The (limited) degree of merriment spilled over to politics as well. And here I would like to present my own test of the degree of political control with respect to (pseudo) elections we had. We often discussed among friends in private conversations to what extent the communist party *cum* security apparatus controlled the electoral process. The most interesting – in fact vital – question for us was whether they knew who voted against the-one-and-only list of communist party-approved candidates.

We knew controllability was possible. The official propaganda demanded that those who support the so-called "party line" do not enter the voting booth, but – upon identifying him or herself and receiving the list of candidates head straight to the ballot box, stuff the list in, say "good bye" and leave the office. Those who decided to use the voting booth – to reject some or all candidates – were seen by authorities as those voting against.

In early 1960s, upon beginning to work in the production and technology section of CCTU, I decided to discover how it worked in reality. Thus, at a right pre-election time I volunteered to work in the ground level electoral office and, upon being accepted, volunteered to take the least attractive, because most time consuming and labor-intensive, role of a gate-keeper. That is, I was the first person whom the would-be voters approached, presenting their documents. Only upon being found on the list of eligible voters and of showing their proper IDs, they were shifted to one of the other stands, where they received the list of candidates. From there they had two options: head for the ballot box or demonstrate his or her opposition by entering the voting booth.

The catch was that if the party or security apparatchiks on the staff of the commission wanted to know who – personally – went into the booth they had to come to me and ask for the name of the person who had just entered the voting booth. There was no other way.

However, nothing of the sort happened. I looked around for some time and finally realized how the control system worked. There was yet another stand, where a delegated commission member marked only the number of those who entered the voting booth. These numbers, as I learned later during the day, were phoned to a higher level electoral commission a number of times – the last time after the closing of the commission's work. It was an important piece of knowledge because it revealed that one could with impunity vote against (if he or she was not known personally to some commission member!). As the readers might have guessed I used that knowledge myself and spread the information to my relatives and friends. Besides, I reduced the attendance at elections substantially.

Usually I attended them to check from time to time whether the arrangement I noted continued to be in use. And, fortunately, it did.

The late 1950s and 1960s were the treadmill years in the Polish economy (later I was to learn that in other communist economies as well). The limited reforms of late 1950s did not help much, while *ad hoc* tinkering did more damage than help. Therefore, the Polish economy sputtered along with ever greater difficulty, plagued by disequilibria, shortages, inability to compete internationally, etc. Daily life, which improved somewhat with the end of the extreme waste of the Stalinist period, began again to be difficult to cope with in a deteriorating domestic economic environment.

Besides, an increasingly despotic communist leader, Wladyslaw Gomulka, step by step chipped away the limited freedoms brought in by the end of Stalinism. Moreover, every politically mature individual understood very well that Poland was not an island, and we should be acutely aware of what the trends in the center of the Soviet empire, the Soviet Union itself, might mean for its dependencies. Thus, when the news about the massacre at Novocherkassk during the food riots in 1962 filtered through to Poland it was treated as a sign of tightening the screws in the Soviet Union with possible implications also for "brotherly" dependencies.

Only much later – and from another geographic direction, via radio *Free Europe* – I heard another kind of a comment, the one by Winston Churchill, about the Novocherkassk implications. Although he was approaching ninety, his wit was as sharp as ever. "I thought I would die of old age," he commented. "However, upon learning that Russia, which in the past fed half of Europe, is now buying grain in the West, I realized that most probably I'll die of laughter."

Of course, Soviets had at that time also their days of glory, not only of shame. However, Polish – unofficial – reactions were not sympathetic even on such occasions. For instance, the proudly announced successful orbital flight by Yuri Gagarin two years before Novocherkassk was met with a battery of jokes. The best of them, I think, is the interaction between the foreman and one of his workers on the construction site. The worker in question was sent (surprise, surprise!) to the nearest shop selling liquor. He soon appeared running toward the group, bottles in hands, but also shouting something in excitement.

> "Foreman! You know, Russians flew into cosmos!
> – he shouted once more,
> upon joining the group.
> Foreman, looked at him quizzically and asked: All of them?
> No, just one! – the worker answered.
> So, why bother? – commented foreman and reached for a long awaited bottle…"

Individuals interested in the world at large and considering probable or even only possible political and other consequences for their own country under Soviet domination, concentrated – for obvious reasons – on the Soviet Union. But that kind of strategic thinking had to be accompanied by a more systematic learning. I tried, then, to learn as much as I could from the economic literature and from the real life economy. For also the latter supplied me with a lot of interesting insights.

Thus, I had yet another eye-opening experience as an economist in 1965. One day it turned out that both the head of my department and his deputy were out of Warsaw and I was ordered to attend the next meeting of the managing board of the Planning Commission as a representative of the Central Council of Trade Unions. It was one of the series of preparatory meetings leading to the formulation of the next (i.e., 1966–70) five-year plan.

There were a few items on the agenda, but I was shocked by developments that took place with respect to the role of technological change in the formulation of the plan. Some specific technologies that were planned to be introduced in a number of important (meaning: large) state firms were accepted without any queries, let alone a debate. The temperature in the meeting room rose only when proceedings turned from various specifics to a general issue: namely, to the assessment of the aggregate annual rate of savings to be achieved on the material inputs to production during the forthcoming five-year plan.

Some of those present stressed the past experience and suggested that the rate should be somewhere between less than 2.0% and 2.5% annually, while others – including the chairman of the Planning Commission, Stefan Jedrychowski – opted in favor of a much higher rate (4.0% annually). The chairman closed the exchange of views by ... forcing a vote on the issue. "Who is in favor of the 4.0% *per annum* rate?" – asked, raising his hand. There were a few abstentions, but nobody raised a hand against the preferred rate chosen by the chairman.

I was astonished, but not by the voting behavior of the planners. As a person living and working under the communist regime, I understood why so many decided not to vote against the head of the Planning Commission. Moreover, he was not only Planning Commission's chairman, but also a member of the top political body, that is the Polish communist party *politbureau*.

What I could not understand was the meager analytical support for -a-n-y opinion presented on the subject during the meeting whether for or against the chairman's position. My theoretical Sovietological knowledge was still limited at the time – it became much fuller in the 1979–82 period – but I learned enough already in order not to take seriously the soundness of theoretical foundations and truthfulness of official statistics. So, it was clear that the vote was based on purely subjective preferences, but my problem was that I was not sure about the motives behind such a preference for a higher rate of material savings as against the lower one. I inquired here and there, raising the question with some planning practitioners. And discovered what was the nature of the intellectual trick that was played before my eyes.

As I stressed earlier, the fundamental characteristics of the system resulted in the emergence of a highly unbalanced economy – and unbalanced one way only, that is generating persistent excess demand. Figure 2.1 presents the stylized dynamics of such persistence.

Figure 2.1: How persistent excess demand had been reproduced within the communist centrally planned and administered economy

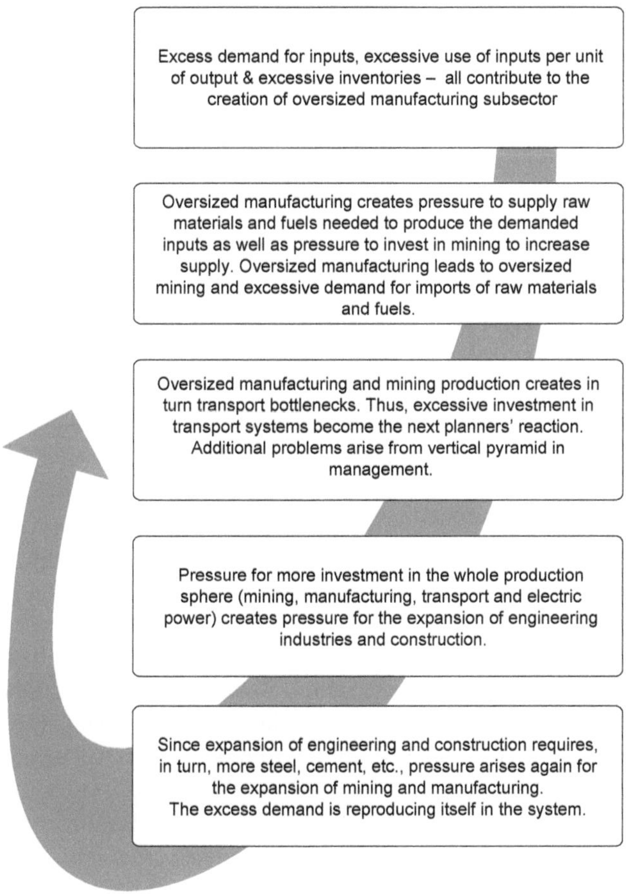

Obviously, the consequences of such an unbalanced system appeared already at the period of plan formation. After all, plans should in principle – as well as in practice – be balanced, inputs should equal outputs! Moreover, communist economies were semi-autarchic units and imbalances could not be easily alleviated by international trade. However, with demand exceeding supply by a large percentage, balancing was out of the question. And one trick used to create an appearance of a balance was to assume high rate of material inputs' savings. When unit material costs of output decreased with the technological progress, demand quantities looked "miraculously" smaller, closer to supply quantities. The whole show was all fiction, of course, but it routinely saved some faces in the planners' world.

It must have been obvious that those numbers had to be corrected during the plan implementation, when the material intensity of output did not decrease as planned, or did not decrease at all, but by the 1960s nearly everybody in the planning world accepted already the lasting discrepancy between plan numbers and reality. In Soviet Russia, for example, about 40% of annual input allocations were changed during the implementation year. Another trick tried in all communist countries by their planners was to decide to physically allocate some 70–80% of supplies planned for a given year and decide on the reminder only when planners were reasonably sure that these supplies – so far remaining on paper only – did physically exist.

Some readers would be tempted to protest. After all why not sensibly admit that the planned high rate of economic growth was unrealistic and reduce that rate to the rate, where demand would balance supply. There were two reasons why this was an attitude central planners did not want to take in the planning process. The first was systemic and the second – more important – political.

Firstly, even with the best intentions, planners did not know – due to the informational asymmetry and resultant doctored statistics – what was an actual and forthcoming level of supply. And second more important reason was that the economic growth rate was a political variable set by a political body: the communist party's *politbureau*.

With the passage of time all the promises of the world of happiness peopled by the "new socialist man" (called ironically *homo Sovieticus* by anti-communist dissidents) were increasingly wearing thin. Thus, the remaining rationale for the totalitarian dictatorship was the promise of higher material living standards than those already achieved in the West. Some leading socialist economists did believe in such an outcome as late as the early 1960s. For example, Oscar Lange wrote then that soon Western powers would be busy to erect the new Iron Curtain in order to hide the fact that workers in the communist part of Europe would soon enjoy higher living standards than their equivalents in the West (*sic*!).

Paul Samuelson did not go that far but was more persistent in his predictions. In the successive editions of his famous textbook he devoted one chapter to comparisons of economic systems and in each edition was coming to conclusion that, given Soviets' higher economic growth rate than the American one, the Soviet Union would at a certain date reach a higher GDP per capita than the United States. What changed from one edition to another, was the future date of such a reversal in the world's economic leadership. The nonsense was removed by the author only in the 1989 edition. The irony of the timing was that 1989 was a year of the disappearance of communism in East-Central Europe, followed in two years' time by the disappearance of communism in the Soviet Union – and the disappearance of the Soviet Union itself.

Whether Westerners believed in such prospects or not mattered less than the fact that the leadership in communist countries just had to use these arguments, whether they still believed in their validity or not. For during the 1960s they increasingly found that they could not find another – or even accompanying – rationale for their rule.

While reminiscing on my living and working in 1960s, two important developments should not be neglected. The first was by and large a national one and the second international (especially with respect to its consequences). To begin with the primarily national one, the 1968 anti-Semitic campaign in Poland and events that triggered the campaign are worth considering. The apparent trigger could, in actual fact, be interpreted as much in the political cabaret framework as a sinister plot.

The seven days war in the Middle East and the successes of the Israeli army against Egypt and other Arab neighbors (armed and trained by the Soviet Union) generated almost an euphoria among Polish intelligentsia. And not only among the – not so numerous – Polish citizens of Jewish ethnic origin. However complicated were ethnic Polish-Jewish relations in the past, as well as mutual sympathies and antipathies, by the time of the 1967 Israeli *Blitzkrieg* in the Middle East one thing was certain. On average, Poles undoubtedly disliked the Russians much more than the Jews. At the same time, given the large pre-World War II emigration of Jews from Poland and smaller migrations afterwards, emigrants from Poland played important roles in the Israeli politics and its army.

An unexpected psychological side effect of these developments was a near universal sympathy and satisfaction among Poles that "our" Jews gave a thorough beating to "their" (meaning: Russian) Arabs. People organized liquor parties, often in public restaurants, where toasts to the Israeli successes were a common feature. I remember that my tennis partner, Mietek Wilczek, whose turn was that day to pay for our playing at the club, turned to club's secretary with the words:

"Paying today is on me! After all, we won the war. The receipt should be written for *Wilczek* [his real name, meaning in Polish "a little wolf – J.W.], formerly *Wolf* [a coded signal he was Jewish, as Jews, when they decided to assimilate into the local society, changed sometimes their names into locally familiar ones]." The crux of the matter was that my tennis partner was not of Jewish origin; it was just his way of showing how he enjoyed the occasion!

Unfortunately, however, there was an earlier subterranean political warfare waged between different factions within the apparatus of the Polish communist party, in the government and the army. It went on for a number of years. One of those factions, so-called "partisans" decided after 1967 to play openly an anti-Semitic card. Taking the lead from the Soviets – pursuing their virulent anti-Israeli propaganda campaign after their protégés lost the Middle Eastern war – the partisans' position became stronger, and they started a campaign to eliminate from the public life those in other communist party factions who "betrayed socialist principles." Translating these words into communist political reality, the "betrayal" meant in this particular case little more than an insufficient enthusiasm for Soviet-supported Arab dictatorships.

The ruling despotic – but by then politically enfeebled – party leader, Gomulka, decided to join the anti-Jewish crusade and demanded that Poles, regardless of ethnic origin, should have "the one and only homeland" to which they should remain loyal. No divided loyalties were allowed. These developments prompted the response from a poet – and a superb polemist – Antoni Slonimski, who commented (in private, of course!): "I understand that a Pole should have just one homeland, but I cannot understand why this homeland should be Egypt, of all places."

Nonetheless, the hate campaign was officially unleashed and hundreds of families of Jewish descent were forced to leave the country. Since the anti-Semitic campaign ran parallel to anti-intellectual campaign, academics, writers, and journalists not necessarily of Jewish ethic origin were made also a part of that emigration. Economists, present in both groups, were affected by the exodus as well.

As it sometimes happened in communist internal convulsions, those viciously criticized economists, kicked out of their jobs and often forced to emigrate – as in the Polish 1968 case – were often sincere reformers who still believed that the performance of communist system could be improved. As it was formulated at the time, they believed in the *reformability* of the system. In consequence they tried to show in their writings how economic management could be modernized to make the economy perform better. The net outcome of such vicious campaigns against reformers ("revisionists" as they were called in the official propaganda) was that – after the exodus of reformers – active believers in the socialist economic system among those left in Poland were less numerous than before – and less numerous than those who were skeptical about the success of reforms.

Similar were the results of cleansing the Czechoslovakia of "revisionists" after the Soviet invasion on that country in 1968 to prevent the emergence of the market-oriented reforms and, even more importantly, to prevent the emergence of the wider reforms intended to create *socialism with a human face*. Clearly, the whole idea was offensive to the Soviet guardians of communist orthodoxy, implying – and rightly so! – that theirs was socialism without a human face.

But it is not my intention to dwell upon the story of Prague Spring, as these developments became known throughout the world. Within the framework of my memoirs of a political economist living and working under communism, I would like to stress the economic implications of the suppression of Czechoslovak search for both an efficient and humanely decent version of the system. Honest, but futile search, but a search nonetheless.

The message of what was then called "the Brezhnev doctrine" of the Soviet intervention if and when a similar search were to be undertaken was well understood within the realm of the Soviet empire: both at the center and in the dependencies. Earlier reforms, beginning with Hungarian and Polish ones in mid-1950s and ending with Soviet and East German reforms in early-to-mid 1960s, aimed at alleviating the most costly systemic distortions, did not eliminate any of the major deficiencies bedeviling the system.

In retrospect it was obvious why. Sources of these major distortions were embedded in the fundamental communist political-economic institutions: state ownership, bureaucratic (top down) coordination of the economy, as well as political control of the economy through the symbiosis of the state apparatus and that of the communist party. No reform was allowed to go that far.

Now, with the implications of the far reaching Czechoslovak reforms already clear to the communist leadership, the Soviet ruling elite lost appetite for major overhauls of the centrally planned and administered economy. Communist elites in the dependencies accepted the message emanating from Moscow: "Tinkering, yes! Major reforms, no!" and followed suit. The wasteful, highly resource-intensive, anti-innovative economic growth, producing persistent excess demand and structural distortions continued unabated.

As for the poor Czechs and Slovaks, the level of repression in intellectual life in general and in economics in particular far exceed what happened in Hungary and in Poland after communist imposed upheavals in these countries. Although a majority of Czech economic reformers emigrated from the country, those who remained were expelled from their jobs and often had to earn a living as manual workers.

Thus, for example, Vaclav Klaus (after the fall of communism a prime minister and, next, president of the Czech Republic), but then one of the leading lights of the younger generation of economists in Czechoslovakia, was more fortunate than most because he had the luck to get a white collar job as a low level clerk in a bank. He was kept at a distance from bank's research department, but at least he had access to the library and, accordingly, to the professional economic literature (such as it was available in the bank's library).

The degree of intellectual control was such in Czechoslovakia that all doctoral and post-doctoral theses were sent to agreed Soviet academic institutions to be reviewed there. One need not add that a negative review on ideological grounds disqualified the thesis (and, worse still, the author).

An extra piece of information is needed, I think, at this point about what was available in professional libraries throughout the communist world. When I complained earlier about the shortages of Western books, textbooks, and researchers' books alike, I did not stress that these books were – after all – widely available to all academics and students there. What was prohibited, and lent only upon receiving a special permit, were Western books about communism and communist countries, usually referring to history and contemporary politics rather than economics. Such a "stunning" degree of freedom existed only in Poland and – since 1960s – in Hungary. In Soviet Russia and communist East Germany, for example, special permits were required with respect to all Western books and academic journals.

Coming to a close with my story of living and working during the last period of communist orthodoxy I should make a confession, concerning the biggest error of judgment that I ever made with respect to economics-politics interaction and its consequences. Upon learning about the Soviet invasion of Czechoslovakia I exclaimed to my friends I was with at that moment: "I am afraid, that will set back a clock for any meaningful change here for at least a decade!!"

And yet barely two years passed between August 1968 invasion and the toppling of the Polish head of the *politbureau*, Gomulka, in December 1970. His successor, Edward Gierek, was an ex-miner with an extensive experience of working in the West – in France and Belgium – in the interwar period. Besides, more importantly, the 1970s were to reveal a number of new developments concerning the communist system's performance that were noted with a lag – and even then by a small minority of insiders in communist countries and Sovietologists outside.

Chapter 3: *Mane-Thekel-Fares*: The (Still Barely Visible) Writing on the Wall

The surprising change in my country was not surprising as a fact. After all, the 1956 change, an earlier – post-Stalinist – shift in the communist leadership, was a manifestation of the same syndrome: the urge to correct an erroneous course. Quite obviously, to change course within the confines imposed by communist rule and subordination to the Soviet Union. Surprising was, however, the style in which the change was taking place. Edward Gierek, who superseded Wladyslaw Gomulka, in December 1970, was the first Polish communist leader using the everyday, normal language of an average worker, not an Orwellian "newspeak" of communist party leaders and *politbureau* communiques.

Professor Michal Glowinski, a noted linguist, remarked in his unpublished diary of the period[4] that Gierek in his first speech used, for example, the term "reality," stating that the principle of our economic and social policy must always take the reality into account. However minimalistic was the program of that sort, noted then Glowinski, it was at least a commitment not to build castles on the sand promised by earlier communist leaders.

In his successive public appearances Gierek indirectly criticized the behavior of the communist party and confessed that the answers to the question of why things happened the way they did would be "difficult (for the communist party – J.W.)." Also, the party faced the task of "rebuilding trust." The contrast with the speeches of his predecessors since 1945, where the communist party – in contrast with particular individual *apparatchiks* – was presented as omniscient, omnipotent, and always right, was refreshing. The language of his speeches was – for a communist leader, of course – relatively non-ideological. This was something new and offering a (modest and cautious) hope for the less ideology-intensive future. Maybe, it was this ability to talk to common people in their own language, which was at the roots of Gierek's success of his early appeal: "*Pomozecie*? (Will you help?)" at a meeting in Gdansk, after all the turmoil following the most recent massacre of workers in December, 1970. Quite a few of those present were then ready to give Gierek the benefit of doubt.

In consequence, the 1970s, under the impact of the new style of leadership, evolved also into a period of decline in the intense ideologization of everyday life. The change was most clearly visible with respect to the authorities' attitude toward young people and their perceived entertainment and other needs. Reorganized communist youth organizations continued to exist, of course, and produced the usual string of ideologically correct slogans, but their impact upon the life of school children and students shrank considerably. The practice of organizing young people's lives through the (forced) participation in social activities, production commitments, mass meetings, creating visual propaganda pieces, etc., was gradually weakening.

And, since nature abhors vacuum, its place was filled with the exploding fascination with the Western mass culture: from youth music to youth clothing. Incidentally, the latter applied not only to Poland. When I visited Moscow in mid-1970s on an academic occasion, I was asked a number of times by the personnel in the hotel where I stayed whether – by any chance – I had pairs of blue jeans for sale. However, the extent of the freedom of the Western mass culture was undoubtedly the greatest in Poland at the time. The de-ideologization of the life of grown-ups was not proceeding as smoothly as that of the youth, but a degree of pressure was also reduced, compared to the earlier period's orthodoxy.

There is an obvious temptation for an economist to jump into the then economic theory debates, as well as economic strategies pursued by the Gierek's team (or, more realistically, economic tinkering with the system and naive groping in the dark, which passed as strategic thinking at the time), and then link strategies with economic outcomes.

However, I would like first to say a few words about my own pursuits in 1970s. The turn of the 1970s was for me a period of important events and decisions. First, I completed my doctoral dissertation in 1970, while still working in the production and technology department of the CCTU, and was conferred the LL.D. title in 1971 at the Warsaw University. The topic was, consciously, as politically neutral as I thought possible ("Technical Assistance in the UN System"), far away from the (highly contentious) issues of performance of the socialist economy and its theoretical underpinnings.

The topic itself was dictated by the choice I made some years earlier. My decision was that I preferred to live in Poland, no matter how mean the communist regime of the day might become and how unattractive was the living under the conditions of "institutionalized boredom" (to borrow a phrase from one of Zbigniew Brzezinski's books). I was reluctant to accept the costs of being uprooted by emigration because my relationships with family and friends would of necessity suffer as a result.

The choice I made counseled prudence in choosing the subject of doctoral dissertation and, in the longer run, the choice of the specialized research area. I chose international economics: foreign trade, foreign direct investments, capital flows, foreign economic and technical assistance, etc. I realized that all choices one made had in communist times their consequences. Under communism, a totalitarian regime, I could not say, as under an authoritarian regime, that "I am not interested in politics."

It was clear that under a totalitarian regime, even if gradually mellowing with the passage of time and its repeated failures to create the promised world of happiness and plenty, *politics was interested in me, and in everybody else.* Thus, one could not avoid an oversight from institutionalized politics: from the omnipresence of the communist party, from watchful eyes of the secret police, or from censors intervening in one's publications. There was, however, an opportunity to reduce the level of that oversight.

After a short stint in the economic information gathering institute of the patents office, I had some luck and obtained a position in the department of international trade and finance (international economics) in the Polish Institute of International Affairs. It turned out to be a lucky choice. The issues I dealt with as a researcher allowed me to – by and large – write and say what I really thought on the issues of international trade, trade policies, foreign investment, etc. And the topics were so far away from the most suspect areas of the economics of planning and administration that they rarely, if at all, raised the level of vigilance of either my superiors or external censorship. The years in the institute were the relatively most peaceful and, more importantly, intellectually productive. They were also a period of highly intensive self-education and the next, momentous choice I was to make (more about it toward the end of this chapter).

Although, given the choices I made, I avoided major clashes with the system, little skirmishes were unavoidable from time to time. The one worth mentioning took place in 1976, when problems with economic growth were superseded by growth of economic problems under the Gierek leadership. The head of my department asked me to prepare a comment on his presentation of the issues associated with the 1976–80 five-year plan for the economy. The comments I made then at an open communist party meeting in the institute were some years later elaborated in articles I wrote about investment cycles and other disturbances under centrally planned and administered economy (but that was in 1980s, a completely different era!). Here, I limited myself to a number of comments and predictions that I assumed would be understandable for non-economists who made a majority of institute's researchers and administrative staff.

First, I outlined the dynamics of investment within the framework of the multi-year planning. I stressed that such plans start with the hidden imbalances between supply and demand, with demand partly hidden from planners by the nature of the plan formation process (see above, chapter 2, on informational asymmetry). Since planners did not know by how much demand exceeded supply, they reacted only when the imbalances visibly grew relative to the average level of imbalances in the past. Usually such imbalances reached the peak in the third year of the five-year plan and it was only then that planners began to realize, which investment projects were very much over the budget and/or which investment projects' implementation was very much delayed (after all, overspending and delays were a norm)! Only at that point they froze, postponed implementation or (rarely) outright cancelled some projects. In consequence, the economy – growing much more slowly – returned to a lower level of imbalances than at the peak of the problems during the middle years of the plan. I added, then, that historically the same pattern was being repeated from one multiyear plan to another, both in Poland and elsewhere in command economies.

Next, I explained that the 1970s were not a typical planning era. Instead of 2–3 years of faster growth rate of investment and a traditional reversal later, investments in the Polish economy grew rapidly throughout the whole 1971–75 period, also due to foreign borrowing. Imbalances accumulated for a longer period and were much larger as a result.

Then, after an explanatory part, came a predictive one. I said that the scale of adjustments, usually made in the middle of the five-year plan, would accordingly have to be also larger and longer lasting. Economic growth would be subdued – I said – till the end of the 1970s' decade, throughout the whole period of the then present five-year plan.

In fact, the period of low and negative economic growth rates lasted till 1982. But the comments of mine were found interesting not only by some colleagues from the institute, but also elsewhere – and for different reasons. On such occasions like the meeting in question, usually an *apparatchik* from the district office of communist party was present to check whether some subversive ideas were not aired at a meeting. Such a comrade was also present at the meeting in my institute. The consequences were – in line with the less ideologized era – milder than before. Both the communist party secretary of the institute and the head of my department were called to party's district office and lectured about the importance of inculcating optimism about the future among party members and in society at large. The *apparatchiks* who instructed them said also that such opinions as mine should not be too widely disseminated. Certainly not at communist party meetings! They would be acceptable at a maximum in internal working papers of the institute – they consented graciously. No punishment of me for my comments was demanded, though, as I learned afterwards. A limited, although welcome, change from Gomulka times!

Soviet Russia was, of course, different. In 1977 I was for the first (and last) time on a weekly visit in that country in the Institute of World Economy and International Relations. Academics in the USSR wrote really awful, primitive propaganda pieces that passed as books on economic affairs (in other areas of social sciences the story was not much different). However, while preparing papers for their superiors in the communist party or the government, they dropped the propagandist tone and expressed their opinions on the same issues differently, both in tone and – interestingly – in substance.

Thus, when writing for the public about the capitalist market economies, they repeated, monotonously, the same incantations about the "present stage of the crisis of capitalism." The word "present" was used obligatorily in each period to describe often different economic developments. It was to stress that there is nothing new in the situation of capitalism, which, by definition, must be at some stage of the (everlasting) crisis.

Having befriended one of the Russian analysts during his earlier stay at a conference in Warsaw (I helped him to make a trip to Czestochowa to buy some religious items for his Catholic wife), he suggested when I arrived in Moscow that I could read their recent report for the foreign affairs department of the Central Committee of the Communist Party of the Soviet Union. It was a forecast for Western Europe on economic growth in the 1970–85 period.

I accepted his offer with alacrity for I was curious of the academic value of their unpublished studies. The report was prepared quite decently in methodological and statistical terms. It had its analytical weaknesses, the most important being a near complete neglect of the demand side determinants. The report was a purely supply side-based venture, a typical product prepared by those who did not think much about preferences of consumers or users.

An interesting feature of the report was its high expectations of economic growth in Western Europe, higher on average than in Western projections of similar type! Another – this time quixotic – feature concerned the sharp difference between the substance of the report for communist authorities and the substance of the book on the same topic for the public. So, Western economic growth in the secret report was expected to be high, while in the published books on the same topic there were predictions of crisis and decline.

When I pressed my friend and – in one-to-one situations, over a bottle of vodka – also some other Soviet academics they admitted with disarming cynicism: "You know, we have to write such things (*i.e.*, propaganda pieces). But we do concentrate on real research. The life must go on." Knowing well the viciousness and repressiveness of the Soviet regime, always much greater than that of the Polish one, who I was to cast the first stone?

Interestingly, the repressiveness and control applied not only to relations with the "suspect" Westerners, but also with academics from "brotherly" countries. I was invited one evening by another colleague whom I met earlier at a conference of young economists from "brotherly" countries in Visegrad, Hungary. My colleague was a Georgian, married into a musicians' family of Polish descent; this was probably a motive behind the invitation. I spent a delightful evening surrounded by very friendly people and very beautiful paintings of Polish and Russian artists, collected by the head of the family, a well known musician.

I learned on that occasion also that wines in Soviet Russia were differentiated not in accordance with traditional characteristics, but according to political criteria. When I commended a red wine I was offered during the dinner and inquired about its brand, I was surprised to see that it was the wine that I already drank in one of the restaurants. And there it tasted much worse. My Georgian friend smiled and explained to an uninitiated that they do not change labels, yet there are three levels of quality under the same label in the case of Georgia wines. The best quality is sent to various republican central committees of the Soviet communist party, the next best – the one I was drinking – was sold only in Georgia (and he got the bottles straight from his family there), while the remaining lowest quality wine with the same label was sold to state wholesalers in Russia and other republics.

And, finally, on our way back to the hotel my Georgian friend told me, a bit embarrassed, that they are not allowed to invite home even colleagues from "brotherly" countries. In consequence, if I were ever asked by his colleagues from the institute where we had our dinner, I should mention a Moscow restaurant. I was shown that restaurant on that same return trip from their apartment.

Since the wine issue has popped up, let me note one more feature of life in the Soviet Union, that is the heavy drinking as a way of life. I learned the hard way that it starts early in the morning. On the very first day of my week-long stay, I was met at breakfast at the hotel by a delegation from the host institute. They immediately ordered a bottle of Armenian brandy and greeted me officially in the name of the (absent) institute's director. Each person of the group of three stated his own slightly differently formulated toast to our future fruitful academic cooperation. I understood that I should reciprocate. I duly expressed a similar hope for the fruitful cooperation and the opening was made. Drinking and talking continued.

It was not surprising. In the Soviet Russia there was a saying that drinking without toasts was the reprehensible *pjanka* (drunkenness pure and simple), while drinking with toasts was the acceptable *mass-politicheskaya rabota* (political propaganda activity). Thus my hosts were on the safe side with their drinking. Incidentally, they ordered yet another bottle of brandy before the breakfast ended…

Some years later the Soviet drinking issue came to my rescue in a conversation in my institute. In late 1979 I received an invitation from Pittsburgh University to teach there for a semester, and it was accepted by my authorities. It was my second visit to America in just three years and it raised some envious musings. During one coffee break at the institute a communist party secretary wondered how it happens that Professor Winiecki went again to the US to teach, but did not teach (surprise, surprise!) in the Soviet Union.

I had to react somehow and answered that there are two reasons. The first was that I did not get an invitation to teach from Soviet academic institutions. And, the second was that even if I were to get such invitation, I would have to refuse. "But why?" asked quickly the party secretary in the hope that she could report something on me to her communist party *cum* security superiors (security, too, as her husband was a high ranking officer in the Ministry of Interior). I answered that academics drink so heavily there that my kidneys would not stand more than a week or two of such life style. The tension was defused; drinking was not politically objectionable.

What I gained professionally from this visit to the Soviet Union was not just the knowledge of what analysts there thought about the performance of the Western economies. No less interesting were the impressions from bits and pieces of various conversations comparing the respective Polish and Soviet economies and from my systematic overview of Moscow's shops to compare prices of a "representative basket" of goods in both countries (knowing the nominal wages in Poland and the USSR).

The Russian economy did not look impressive at the close of the 1970s. Ballistic missiles were (presumably) in good shape, but bread, butter, and meat were in a (visibly) worse condition. Worse even than in Poland, where in late 1970s, at the phase of growing adverse consequences of Gierek team's haphazard fumbling which passed for an economic strategy, the supply of consumer goods was deteriorating visibly from one year to another in both quantity and quality.

Maybe the one innovation helping consumers in Moscow was what had been observed by a colleague of mine who visited Moscow a year earlier. She stood there in a long queue to buy a fur cap for her husband. Suddenly somebody appeared before her and commanded her: "*padajtie ruku*" (give me your hand). Without much reflection, she did and the guy spit on it and wrote a number on her palm with an indelible pencil.

She was shaken for a long while, but – coming from another communist country, where queuing was also an everyday's activity – realized that it was a useful solution to the problem of all those who queued, while formally being obliged to work (or at least stay) in their offices or factories. Having a number meant that he or she could go back to the office or factory, stay there for some time, and later come back and take the same numbered place in the queue. There was, of course, a small question of hygiene, but undoubtedly a minor one from the perspective of those simultaneously queuing and working.

I tried to signal so far a changing atmosphere in Gierek's time. It was a marked – and welcome – change. But people expected also economic change in the sense of moving away from what a well-known demographer, Jerzy Holzer, called then the "society of minimal needs"[5] to long desired mass consumption. These increasing expectations for consumer goods were reinforced by the stories of those who visited the West.

Here, however, problems multiplied. Gierek and his team undoubtedly had a lot of good intentions to raise the living standards of their countrymen. They accepted, for example, automobile production for private use, something the previous head of the *politbureau*, Gomulka, was strongly against throughout his long rule.

These were, however, largely case studies of such good intentions, while room for maneuver was rather limited, both externally and internally. The lesson from Czechoslovakia, stressed in the preceding chapter ("Tinkering – yes; major reforms – no!") was as valid in the 1970s as it was at its birth in 1968. Unsurprisingly, then, the commission called into being early in Gierek's period to reform the state and the economy did very little in either area.

Thus, they limited, for example, the number of indicators that state firms were obliged to fulfill and/or take into consideration in plan implementation, introduced vague institutional recommendations on the establishment of large state firms (touted, mistakenly, as a panacea for the persistent difficulties with interfirm cooperation issues), as well as gave – informally – a measure of freedom to managers of state firms. The improvements were again mostly in the economic climate – and, as such, of transient nature.

There were, however, some attempts to consider the rise in living standards from a systemic perspective and relate it to expected economic performance under the national economic planning system. The idea was to ask for professional evaluation by outstanding economists. Thus, for the first (and last) time in communist period in Poland, a group of professionally competent advisers was created at the central committee of the communist party (Polish acronym: PZPR) who were to make relevant recommendations.

I stressed the transient nature of the economic climate, since the traditional model of centrally planned and administered economy resisted change, especially market-type change. Usually, under pressure from the planning hierarchy and communist party *apparatchiks*, the operation of the economic system tended to revert to its original model – if not in form, then at least in substance. Thus, reforms tended to be short-lived or, even more often, distorted.[6]

An excellent graphic example of the foregoing characteristic was offered by a Polish economist who had studied changes over time in the number of plan indicators in the 1945–1981 period [see Figure 3.1.]. Although it was a case of one industry (engineering) in one country, it was typical for the system as a whole. After each phase of – more or less extensive – reforms, usually accompanied by the reduced number of plan indicators, their number inexorably increased, sometimes dramatically.

Figure 3.1: *How economic reforms repeatedly failed in the communist economic/political system? After each reform apparatchiks and planners reintroduced as much as possible of the pre-reform regime as shown by the example of reintroduced numbers of plan indicators (data from Polish engineering industry in the 1946–1981 period)*

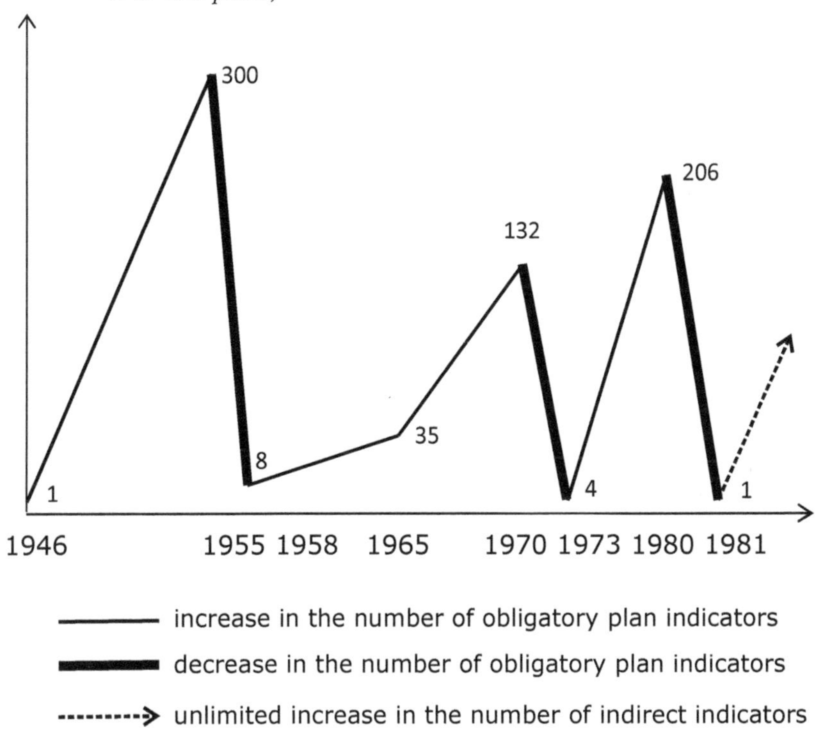

Source: W. Jermakowicz' study, 1984

General policies in the early period of Gierek's leadership included a number of highly desirable changes. They included a much greater openness to the West. For example, the number of citizens allowed to travel westward multiplied to hundreds of thousands, or even more. It is sobering to remember that in Stalinist times, for example in 1952, only 12 (I repeat: twelve) private passports were issued, while in Gomulka's times these numbers annually did not exceed tens of thousands at most.

What also changed were somewhat altered commodity structure of imports, with a greater concern displayed by the authorities about the supplies of some domestically unavailable consumer goods, like tea, coffee, cocoa, etc., as well as a greater readiness to accept the expansion of domestic production of consumer durables (I already mentioned the initiated for the first time production of passenger cars for private use).

All this was welcome, but as far as economic strategy was concerned, what passed as a strategy was in reality a combination of good intentions intertwined with wishful thinking, and combined with the hopelessly amateurish knowledge of economics by Gierek and his team (unfortunately not upgraded by the – largely neglected – opinions of the otherwise competent advisers I mentioned above).

An older colleague of mine who worked at the Planning Commission learned first-hand what some people from the Gierek team thought about knowledge, professors, and professorship as such. Listening to the evening TV news he learned the previous day that his top boss, a certain Mr. Pyka, was nominated as a professor of economics. Before coming to the Planning Commission, he held the post of economics secretary in Upper Silesia's regional PZPR (communist party) committee, the region Gierek came from. An earlier collaboration of Gierek and Pyka in Katowice (the region's capital) were probably the strongest credentials, explaining Pyka's appointment to the top planning job.

It just happened that the colleague in question met his boss at the entrance to the commission's building, while arriving at the office. After the exchange of greetings, the colleague offered his cautious congratulations. Pyka had laughed, slapped my colleague in the back, and explained: "You know, it does not really matter! But the professorship has one important advantage. If you are kicked out from a real job, the professorship allows you to land afterwards in a peaceful and quiet place, where you do not need to overwork yourself."

But let us move back from the *apparatchiks*' perception of academia to their perception of the existing international capital markets. A greater availability of capital in 1970s (the result of the inflow of petrodollars from oil exporters) created new opportunities for substituting Western credits for serious modifications of the economic system. Borrowing for the purpose of increasing consumption is always a bad idea in the long run. Presumably, Gierek and his team wanted to create a good social climate for the planned "great (investment) leap forward." Usually investment effort under communism augured badly for the level of consumption. This time it was to be different. Both consumption and investments were to increase.

However, one should keep in mind that the increase in the investment/output ratio may bring positive effects (of greater output per worker in the future) only under the condition of availability of production factors and other resources that are complementary to the borrowed capital. To borrow capital from abroad was not enough. Construction capacity to build physical structures, complementary technologies, skilled labor force required for a given project, based on imported technology and machinery, were also required. Yet we should keep in mind that communist economies were shortage economies, where -e-v-e-r-y-t-h-i-n-g was in short supply! Since this was a problem not only of Poland, but of all communist economies, I am going to deal with it later. Here, I would like to concentrate on the effects of reckless borrowing on Poland.

Clearly, increasing year after year an investment growth rate, without commensurate higher productivity effects of such investment, aggravated the already existing imbalances, not only on the producer goods market, but – through spillovers – also on the consumer goods market. People rapidly got more and more money, while the supply of consumer goods supply increased, but at a relatively much slower rate. Inflationary pressures intensified, although in the world of rarely changed list prices they appeared primarily in the form of longer queues. The socio-political climate began visibly to change for the worse by the middle of the decade.

With the little changed structure of incentives, with the unchanged institutional arrangements of planning and plan implementation, and with aggravating imbalances due to the large – and growing from year to year – investment program, the level of performance of the Polish economy began to decline sharply, even below that of the earlier, on its own, highly unsatisfactory level. Half-hearted tinkering by the authorities with consumer goods prices in the face of growing imbalances between supply and demand resulted in strikes – and intensified the dissatisfaction throughout society. The dissatisfaction was probably disproportionally high relative to the level of negative changes (especially compared with the pre-Gierek's past!), but it was – I suspect – proportional to the collapsing hope for better future, so palpably visible in the early Gierek's era.

There were some purely negative developments as well. The mismatch between effort and effect in terms of material rewards might have increased in the 1970s. I tended to look at the construction sector in earlier chapters as an indicator of extremely low quality of performance resulting also from the demoralization of the labor force. Since shortages were a norm under the communist economic system, shortages of labor were a part and parcel of the system in question. And if one's labor is in high demand regardless of one's work effort, then the depth of the Marianas Trench might have been the lower limit, as far as labor demoralization was concerned. With dramatically declining labor effort, the consequences for economic effects were devastating, indeed.

There were famous stories, repeated from one period of communist economy in Poland to another. Three of these are my family stories as well. In the late 1950s my father was working in the state construction firm, where his task was to make final check-ups of the recently finished apartment blocks and to decide whether they were ready to be turned over to the housing administration and, then, be assigned to people who had been waiting for years in state-approved queues. However, in one of the buildings he found – along with other, less grave malfunctions – that the central heating system did not connect. Some pipes were, most probably, stolen and sold on the side, and the workers who sold them simply bricked up the unconnected pipes in the wall!! There was about 8–10 meter gap between the two ends of the pipes. In the late autumn, when the water would be poured into the heating system, the wall would have simply collapsed.

Another case from the Stalinist era was an apartment block designed by a married couple of architects, known pre-war communists. That they designed a block without even one staircase was somewhat understandable; after all, what is a staircase in comparison with Marx, Lenin and Stalin's ideas. Less understandable was that construction workers and their supervisors did not care to warn their superiors what they were ordered to build! Maybe, they were too drunk to notice. There was a popular saying in the construction sector about the "bricklayers' Monday," when one could find hardly anybody (or at a minimum anybody sober!) at the building site.

In the period of Gomulka's orthodox drudgery, such stories were not different. In one of the apartment blocks workers bricked up a concrete-mixer in the wall because they did not want to be bothered to carry it down from the third floor of the building as at that moment the lift was not yet operating. Also, in the late 1960s my uncle, an accounting specialist, worked in the builder cooperatives association, in the financial control section. At one time he was controlling one such cooperative, constructing apartment buildings for the military. All the papers he went through were in ideal order, something that very rarely happened under communism in real life. He smelled a rat and decided to take a walk through the housing estate. And he discovered that there was, after all, a difference between the documentation and reality. There were only six apartment buildings instead of seven as accounted for in the construction cost documentation! The construction materials and all the equipment (bath tubes, toilets, gas stoves, etc.) for the seventh disappeared into the thin air.

Gierek's times were not different. In 1975 an apartment building, where my mother lived, was 25 years old and already urgently needing renovation. The team from the state construction firm came and started renovating, or rather making mischief, throughout the building. A small building, after all, just three floors and three staircases, was renovated for more than 18 months. My mother from time to time could not stand the drunkards messing around in her little apartment and called for my help. I could not be of much help but was coming there nonetheless (as a good son should) and tried to sensitize an engineer who supervised the renovation works. I pleaded with him that my dear Mother had her second stroke not so long ago and her irritation with his subordinates might cost her dearly. I repeated such a visit after each call from my mother.

But the best part of the story was yet to come. At one moment my mother discovered that a worker painting her bathroom was so drunk that he fell into the bath tub and could not get out on his own. My mother, a frail person, with a serious heart condition, did not try to help the drunkard, but went directly to the little cubicle of the supervisor, appealing for help. This time she was not seeking to speed up the renovation process, but just to ask him to pull the drunken worker out of her bath tub.

After some more months my mother became irritated again – and again appealed to me for help. Without much hope for success, I nonetheless duly visited the supervisor. And he told me something that ended my visits there. "You know, after this drunken worker fell into your mother's bath tub, I decided to fire him. However, over the period of three months I could not find anybody to take over and, finally, rehired the bloody s.o.b. When he is less drunk, he does some painting, after all." I answered that I pity my dear Mother but I pity him as well and left him alone.

Having read the small sample I offered above, readers may understand why a first class Polish humorist, Jacek Fedorowicz, wrote at that time a book, in which he was trying to send a message that under communism the central heating system that works is an anomaly. Central heating that is out of order is the norm. The book, a collection of his humorous weekly stories aired on the radio, appeared under the tongue-in-cheek title: "*In Principle – Yes*".[7] His stories were sending an exactly opposite message to the title, of course, but it should be obvious that a book with the title: "In Principle – No" would not stand a chance of being approved by the censor's office. Actually, the fact that it was published at all – even under the misleading title – was a signal that also censorship became somewhat milder in Gierek's time than in the earlier periods.

However, as signaled already, the combination of aggravating economic problems, created largely by the incompetent tinkering by the ruling team with economic policies, and social reactions to these fumblings eroded the atmosphere of hope from early 1970s. Nasty police reactions to workers demonstrations in 1976 in two cities in central Poland, Radom and Ursus, and subsequent further persecutions, generated additional tension. In that period of an increasingly tense atmosphere, a number of developments and one-off events created a specific energizing atmosphere that produced important – because institutionalized – consequences.

Firstly, some intellectuals decided that it is time to stop being dissidents, that is, individuals protesting against evil because of their moral convictions. This was the time for the next stage, one of beginning to become oppositionists, that is, to organize themselves for a chosen type of action. This self-organization began along two lines. One such line was to educate society through the creation of underground journals and the so-called "flying university" that would discuss sensitive issues, either avoided by the censored press or presented there in a distorted manner. Another, more practical line of action – highly political at the same time – was to come with material and legal assistance to persecuted workers, who lost their jobs after 1976 strikes and were suffering further unpleasant consequences. The rudiments of the (underground) civil society were beginning to take shape.

Secondly, the harsh, snowy winter of 1978/79 showed the complete indolence of the state bodies in organizing employees to orderly cope with the above average, but not catastrophic, meteorological phenomenon of such a winter. There always was in communist countries a tendency of the official propaganda to lay the blame for various failures upon meteorological anomalies. There was even a joke repeated often in Poland, asking to name the four riders of the Apocalypse? The answer was: spring, summer, autumn, and winter. Putting usual excuses aside, the above average incompetence in dealing with one of the riders of Apocalypse, that is winter, made many Poles look with contempt on the country's rulers. Another humorist, Jan Pietrzak, the creator of the best post-World War II political cabaret, called *Under the Aegis*, introduced himself to the audience in the following manner in the 1978–79 season:

> "What I am doing here maybe described in a nutshell
> That I make a laughing stock of myself and am paid for that.
> It is a very important distinction
> Because many people in this country

Make a laughing stock of themselves,
But they are paid for something else..."

I suspect that the mental attitudes of that sort might have made at least some people more ready to challenge the system than before. Finally, last but certainly not least, the election of the "Polish Pope" in 1978 and his visit in 1979 to Poland was an energizing event for Poles. It somehow created in many people the feeling that change for the better was not a mirage, but something possible, almost visible on the horizon. Besides, the emergence of the numerous organizers appointed by church authorities in cities visited by John Paul II, who were working efficiently alongside the police to maintain order among hundreds of thousands of those taking part in encounters with the Pope, suggested the emerging ability of a self-organization of the society – and on a large scale at that. And, let it be noted, it contrasted with the indolence the ruling communist displayed during the preceding winter.

On a personal level, I must confess that as the second half of 1970s progressed I increasingly felt an intellectual discomfort. My professional career proceeded satisfactorily, given the obvious general constraints. I completed my post-doctoral thesis (habilitation) and the road to full professorship was thrown open. Publications on various aspects of international economics piled up; some of them were accepted for publication in Western professional journals (without incurring – for the time being at least – the protests from the home country censorship and party overseers).

And, yet, I had a strong, and growing, feeling that I missed something very important, not with respect to the developments in Poland, but more generally with respect to the communist world as a whole. There was a film, years earlier, about the man who watched the trains go by. I had a similar feeling about the train of history. Which train? Going where? By late 1970s I harbored no doubts, as far as the answers to both questions were concerned. It was the train of communist economic system (in fact, the entire communist system, due to symbiotic links between politics and economics). And that train, according to my intuition – rather than already a fully fledged knowledge that would come somewhat later – was going downhill. The period I lived through looked increasingly to me like a watershed, a period of the reversal of direction: from wasteful, but nonetheless economic growth to no less wasteful stagnation and maybe even decline, due to the accumulating inefficiencies displayed by the system.

The intuitively perceived watershed demanded I react. If the system was– as I sensed – in decline and there were prospects that it might disappear altogether, the "resigned realism" I displayed over the preceding decade should be abandoned.

I should change my research priorities and start learning in earnest the intricacies of the communist system, as well as polishing my knowledge of normal, that is, capitalist system, because such knowledge might become useful in the future. I needed to be aware of the probable consequences, but with systemic change possible – even probable – I should take a calculated risk.

I made, then, in 1979, another decision, reversing the earlier one of staying as far away as possible as a theorist from the crazy – and dangerous – world of centrally planned and administered economy. But the starting point of such a change should begin with my earnest working on closing the knowledge gap between my intuitions and the thorough knowledge about the operation and the (declining) performance of the system. And I had to be able to analyze it from a comparative perspective standpoint.

I was fully conscious of the probable political consequences for me (and, in turn, for my family), but I decided to free myself from the time-and-place imposed constraints and become an independent analyst of the communist system. I did not change jobs. There was no place for independent analysts in the academic institutions of the communist world anywhere! I simply committed myself to accelerate my research of the system and start publishing the results abroad, that is in the West. The years of 1979–82 were the ones when I absorbed all the domestic literature, comparable literature from some communist countries, as well as Western comparative systems and Sovietological literature.

Interestingly, I learned no less (and at times more), in terms of empirical knowledge, from Polish and other East European literature than from Western sources. Even inputs to my theorizing were at times greater from what I read in Polish, Hungarian, and earlier (pre-invasion) Czechoslovak sources. At the beginning of my accelerated research I regarded that as an anomaly that I learned less from the free uncensored literature, but soon I realized where my surprising conclusion came from. The reasons of major analytical errors found in Western comparative systems and Sovietological literature stemmed, largely, from the ideological disposition of the majority of writers, as well as from the grossly erroneous attitude toward the communist official statistics.

To begin with the former, communist or, more narrowly, Soviet studies were in the West a marginal branch of economics. The best and the brightest usually looked to intellectually greener pastures. To specialize in comparative systems or Soviet studies (Sovietology), individuals had to display some specific interest in that study area. The first and most often found specific interest was the sympathy for socialism and consequently the socialist economic system and its workings.

But Westerners, also those of collectivist, or more narrowly socialist, persuasion, had been brought up in the environment of freedom and that created problems in their approach to various despotic, totalitarian regimes. They knew, of course, that all governments overstate their case. Some of them might have suspected that such regimes like the communist ones stretched the truth farther than democratic regimes.

However, it was too difficult for them to accept the naked truth that communist official statements at times might not have possessed even a grain of truth and that these statements might have been issued for the specific purpose of making the search for the truth more difficult. Next, they had problems with accepting the fact that such official statements were a part and parcel of the mendacity principle treated as the foundation of an information – or disinformation – strategy. The foregoing was often too much for the sympathizers of socialism in the Western world studying communist system and specific countries.

In actual fact, it continues to create problems for Westerners dealing with such despotic regimes as Putin's Russia and totalitarian regimes such as North Korea and Iran. It does not matter that North Korea is a ghostocracy (with the ghost of the "immortal" Kim Il Sung being the eternal president of the country) and Iran is theocracy. Mendacity as a principle in dealing with both the internal and, even more, external image of their respective countries has been, practically speaking, one of the founding principles of their policies.

Clearly, any strategy or policy assessment based on uncritically accepted official statements emanating from communist countries, must have, inevitably, generated a distorted picture of whatever these official statements dealt with at the time. There were other analysts with a specific interest in the communist world. They were *émigrés* from these countries who had a first-hand experience with policy making *cum* propaganda in their respective countries. They had fewer illusions about the reality. However, they were quite often not free from their sympathies to socialism, even if not Soviet-style socialism, as a preferred collectivist idea.

Of course, apart from these two specific – and large – groups of academics there were rare intellectual figures such as Gregory Grossman, Charles Wolf, Jr., Philip Hanson, Michael Ellman, and others, who were neither sympathizers nor *émigrés*. Reading their books and articles was a sheer joy of discovery. I was an avid reader of their sophisticated explanations of important workings of the system. There were also some *émigrés*, who did not share the socialist sympathies, yet contributed mightily to my knowledge. Their works, such as, e.g., two monumental studies on Soviet planning by Eugene Zaleski, were sometimes real eye-openers. The somewhat later publications of Ljubo Sirc and Igor Birman also added to my Sovietological knowledge.

Adverse intellectual and political consequences of the credulity of a large part of Western socialist-leaning academics dealing with the communist world, were compounded by their similarly uncritical attitude toward official statistics. As I stressed earlier, communist statistics were indecipherable. Arriving at the true numbers was not possible because they were doctored both from below, by enterprise managers, and at times from above, by central planners on their own initiative or on orders of their political masters from the *politbureau*.

Besides, even without doctoring, some statistics in a different economic environment should be interpreted differently, in line with the impact of informal rules of the game influencing economic outcomes. Without understanding the systemic differences between the world of the plan and the market, empirical studies yielded at times nonsensical conclusions. Such as, for example, articles by a well known British economist who discovered the excess supply regime on the consumer goods' markets in East European communist economies!

My attitude toward the official communist statistics or, more generally, all numbers emanating from these countries, could be compared to that of an archeologist rather than a traditional economist. The former dug out, for example, bits and pieces of an ancient vase and from these tiny fragments tried to describe the shape, the pattern of ornaments, the color of the vase, etc. Traditionally a Western economist was, in turn, usually certain of the data he or she obtained from official sources or, second-hand, from various empirical studies of his or her colleagues.

By contrast, as a Sovietologist, I behaved on many occasions more like an archeologist. Given the prevailing statistical secrecy of communist authorities, as well as the prevalence of doctored statistics, I often collected bits and pieces of quantitative information from various sources, and then selected those numbers, which for some reasons I thought to be true (or close enough to be believed). And, next, on the basis of economic linkages between those, true – or truer – numbers, I tried to draw some conclusions on a particular issue under consideration.

Let me illustrate this, highly atypical, attitude for an economist with a real-life example from the Soviet literature. A group of Russian academics from Novosibirsk worked on the recalculation of Soviet GDP, by using more reliable methodology than that used in official statistics. They came to the conclusion that economic growth nearly stopped in the middle of 1970s, falling from 3.2% annually in 1971–75 to bare 1.0% in 1976–80 and even less, 0.6%, in 1981–85. Then, from a piece in a Soviet economic journal, I learned that thousands of kilometers of oil pipes had to be replaced every 2–3 years (!) because of corrosion due to their very low quality. Conclusions? First, it was clear that costs of producing oil were high and getting higher under the circumstances. Next, if so large volume of pipes went to Soviet oil industry, there must be less left for other industries and services – particularly in the near-stagnant economy (see the first piece of the foregoing information).

The "archeological" type of conclusion was applied to the third component of the collected pieces. From yet another article in the Soviet press, this time on the state of the metropolitan infrastructure in the Soviet Union, I learned that the breakdowns in trunk pipes of the central heating systems there increased between 1976–80 and 1981–85 from very high 40 breakdown cases for every 100 km of trunk pipes to mind boggling 100 breakdowns! It was obvious to me that for Soviet authorities earning foreign exchange money from oil exports was more important. Therefore, the proper conclusion was that the repairs of the municipal infrastructure would be limited and the infrastructure would become increasingly decrepit. The conclusion would apply not only to central heating, but one should expect similar developments also in other components of that infrastructure: water pipes, sewage pipes, etc. Thus, my efforts differed little from those of an archeologist.

Readers should not be under the impression that I was an exception. Living under the mendacity-based propaganda for decades, made people in the East much more skeptical about whatever was officially announced or presented in the press and electronic media (radio and TV only at that time). In Poland and elsewhere in East-Central Europe I heard the same joke about three types of news coming from the communist media: *true*, that is obituaries, *probable*, that is weather forecasts, and *the rest*.

In actual fact, rumors concerning forthcoming obituaries elicited jocular reactions as well. I remember one such rumor that a Polish Prime Minister died suddenly, but the authorities do not want to announce it yet for some reason. There was an official communiqué that he had an accident. The reaction from the public was immediate. A joke was then circulated that he, indeed, had his arm broken – when they were carelessly putting his body in the freezer.

My skepticism with respect to both theorizing and statistics, combined with what I learned already about the communist economic system, allowed me in late 1970s to formulate, so to say, an "informed guesstimate," diagnosing the past and forecasting the future.

(1) First of all, the operating principle of the communist system, reinforced by the Brezhnev doctrine, allowed me to assume that no serious reforms would be undertaken in the foreseeable future ("Tinkering – yes; serious reforms – no!"). Thus, the usual self-reproducing pattern of wasteful output growth would continue unabated.
(2) Second, the palliative to reform in the form of borrowing capital and technology in the West would increase, not decrease the imbalances in the economies pursuing such policy. The generalized shortage of everything would ensure the emergence of such an effect. And, since nearly all East-Central European

communist economies pursued such policy to a greater or lesser extent, all would be adversely affected. Why adversely? As I signaled earlier in this chapter, imitation, like original innovation, also required the availability of complementary factors and resources. Thus, construction capacity must be available to build new factories, using imported technology. Even so-called "turn-key" projects could not do without local support.

(3) Third, the level of technological sophistication of imported technology was generally higher than that applied at the time in communist economies. The inability to supply higher quality building materials, higher quality local inputs to imported products, etc., added to the length of the period between the beginning of an investment project and reaching the planned level of production. Output quality would also be adversely affected.

(4) Fourth, a more or less heavy borrowing by smaller, East-Central European economies, coupled with delayed production and lower quality of licensed output augured badly for the external balance of these economies. And it should be remembered that the 1970s were also a period of the so-called mineral resources crisis, with prices of industrial minerals and fuels going up sharply in the earlier part of the decade and those of fuels exploding over the whole decade, in fact until 1980/81. Thus, import cuts and even debt repayment crises became a distinct probability (they did happen in Poland and Romania, while Hungary and communist East Germany suffered as well, but were supported respectively by international financial institutions and by democratic Federal Republic of Germany).

(5) Fifth, an intriguing piece of a puzzle was the Soviet Union itself. It should also be remembered that – in contrast with its smaller dependencies – the Soviets were among the major beneficiaries of the fuel price explosion. And, yet, that was not visible when one scrutinized the Russian consumer goods market or leafed through the Soviet press. In late 1979 I did not have the knowledge of the Novosibirsk economists, working in 1980s, whose recalculated data showed that in the second part of 1970s Soviet GDP growth rate fell to a stagnation level (see above). My intuition was, however, the same. That is, in spite of windfall benefits of higher world market prices for Soviet mineral exportables, the economy was by the mid-1970s in a rather bad shape.

The next step was to generalize on the above considerations. European communist economies must have exhausted their possibilities of economic growth along the path of the – extremely wasteful – model of centrally planned and administered economy. The refusal to even think of a major systemic overhaul condemned them to stagnation and decline. The 1970s were, then, the watershed between two periods. The road ahead was only in one direction, that is downward.

Personally, as a next step, I had to solve a methodological and presentational dilemma. Since I decided to become an independent analyst, publishing primarily in the West, my writings should be intelligible for those Westerners reading the Sovietological and comparative systems literature. While going through the East European literature I realized that the not so numerous publications of East European economists (*i.e.* those from East-Central Europe and from the Soviet Union) in Western languages, primarily in English, were often not only written in bad English, but – worse still – were unintelligible for more fundamental reasons. They mixed the Soviet planning terminology with normal economics' terminology used in Western literature, often with confusing results. There were some, very few, exceptions, Janos Kornai, being in a class of his own. He invented his individual, distinct terminology that was both understandable and to some degree accepted in the international discourse on the Soviet-style command economy.

I decided differently. Exceptions apart (*e.g.*, adopting some Kornai terms, such as "shortage economy," "soft budget constraint" of state firms, etc.), I decided to try to present my ideas on the communist economic system in the language of the mainstream economics as it was taught in the West. One of my Western friends, Prof. Andrzej Brzeski from the University of California, Davis, once described me as an economist sitting comfortably on the fence between East and West and telling Westerners what he saw in the East in the language Westerners could understand – and the *vice versa*.

I was not willing to quarrel with the rather flattering description, except for the adjective "comfortably". Firstly, sitting on the fence is rarely comfortable in the longer run. And, secondly, I was sitting on the communist part of the fence. I had no doubt that – once my critical studies began to be published and quoted in the West – the clash with the communist overseers was inevitable. It might have serious negative consequences for me and my family. But at that point in my personal history I was ready to face such challenge.

Moving back from the personal to the general Polish history, the latter galloped again in 1980. Another series of workers' strikes in summer 1980 accelerated the change at the top of the communist hierarchy. Edward Gierek and his team were removed from power at the end of August 1980. It was both a less turbulent and – more importantly – bloodless change, in contrast with the ouster of his predecessor, Wladyslaw Gomulka in 1970.

I had observed these developments, while sitting proverbially on the suitcases, with air tickets in the travel bag. I was to go to the US to both teach and pursue my research (for obvious reasons it was to be, first of all, research on the communist system). I was accompanied by my son, while my wife did not get a passport and stayed at home as a hostage of sorts. I left for Washington, D.C., on the third day of the fast spreading strikes, when their outcome was not yet decided. Since the promised economic paradise of communism was by that time the only kind of legitimacy the regime could count upon, the disappearing prospects for economic betterment were seen by many Poles as the end of the road. The scale of the disappointment was very high at the time.

In Washington, quite by chance, I had a long conversation with the then Polish ambassador to the United States. A colleague of mine from the institute married a daughter of Ambassador Romuald Spasowski and asked me to deliver a letter from his wife to her father. I was not much surprised that – upon learning about my arrival – the Ambassador invited me to his office. Clearly, he was interested in the first hand news from home country – not filtered by the official propaganda that the embassy was stuffed with through official channels from the ministry of foreign affairs.

I was asked by Ambassador Spasowski to give him a "frank" opinion about the current situation. As professionally as possible, I presented my views on the economic underpinnings of the present eruption of dissatisfaction, on distortions characterizing the centrally planned and administered economy and these distortions being endogenous to the political-economic system, and completed my overview with a forecast that this time the change will not – in all probability – end with the simple substitution of one first secretary of the communist party by another. The societal malaise was deep, manifestations of economic problems very serious and manifold and, therefore, some significant changes are in the air.

By the standards of the, usually superficial and insincere, contacts within the officialdom in the communist world, my overview offered to the ambassador was, most probably, much different from what he had been accustomed to. Nonetheless he listened attentively without interrupting me in any way, with a slight frown on his face, without giving an inkling of what he had thought himself (that is what diplomats are trained for, after all!). To ease the rather tense atmosphere of our conversation I told him a political joke I had heard just before leaving Poland. "Question: What is the difference between Gomulka (toppled about 10 years earlier) and Gierek (at the time of our conversation to be toppled in a matter of days)? Answer: There is none. Only Gierek does not know about it yet." I had the feeling that telling jokes, even anti-communist ones, was more acceptable for officialdom than intellectually well grounded and systematically presented critical views of the system.

In actual fact, Spasowski turned out to behave very decently during the Solidarity period. In his attempts to help to defuse tensions around Poland, resulting from Soviet and other communist pressures, he often cooperated with the State Department and with the head of the National Security Council of President Carter, Zbigniew Brzezinski. When the political/military leadership under general Jaruzelski imposed martial law in Poland, Spasowski decided to defect.

As far as my academic progress was concerned, the year in the US was extremely profitable. It was during the subsequent stays at the University of Maryland, College Park, Md., University of Pittsburgh, Pennsylvania, and finally at the University of Southern California, Los Angeles, that the first drafts of some important future papers of mine were written. Thus, I was not only loading my batteries, but also using them very intensively. Most of my early papers on the macroeconomics of socialist political economy, on disruptive investment cycles, on the endogenous nature of persistent imbalances, as well as those on the hidden inflation were written between September 1980 and early June 1981, during my stay in America.

Chapter 4: "Solidarity Picnic" and Its Aftermath

Readers may wonder why I used so light-hearted, almost flippant, title for this chapter. I would not have used such title right after coming back from America in June 1981. Nor, certainly, after the imposition of the martial law on December 13, 1981. But from a historical perspective, after seeing what I saw since June 1981 and what I read afterwards, the term "picnic" seems justified.

Let me explain, as usual, by beginning with an example. On the second or third day after my return from the States I spotted a youngster in a T-shirt that had a printed inscription: *Nie lubie ruskich* ... ("I do not like Russians ..."). When he passed me by, I turned my head and read the rest of the inscription on the back of his shirt: ... *pierogow* ("...dumplings). In Polish it sounded even more linguistically precise as the disparaging term: "*ruskie*" (instead of: Russians) – in plural – could be grammatically applied both to people and dumplings.

Also in June 1981, I attended an annual nightly review of political cabarets in Opole (a tradition started in 1973, in the Gierek's era) and enjoyed the near complete freedom of expression compared with the past. The already mentioned cabaret performer, Jan Pietrzak, reminded the audience that our previous leaders wrote Russia into the Polish constitution, stressing our eternal friendship with the "brotherly" Soviet Union (a very unfortunate method chosen by Gierek to demonstrate Poland's attachment to the "big brother," while at the same time developing stronger economic ties with the West!). Pietrzak, then, added: "Let us hope that Russians will not reciprocate and write Poland into their constitution!" There was a roar of laughter from the audience who understood the allusion; after all, they wrote Lithuania, Latvia, and Estonia into their constitution after annexing these republics in 1940.

One noticed the offshoots of freedom flowering everywhere. People, after decades of censorship and other constraints, were clearly testing the limits of what was possible under the evolving circumstances, where no clear demarcation lines seemed to have been set. In fact, these lines were barely visible in the summer of 1981.

While still in America, and absorbing the knowledge on comparative systems, Sovietology, etc., I nonetheless looked all the time with intense interest and hope, combined with no less intense anxiety, at the developments in Poland. My earlier, late 1970s intuition about the sprouting islands of organized (yet underground) civic society turned out to be true. More to the point, the spontaneous emergence of local leaders and the very rapid creation of the social movement with strong political overtones, which wisely took the brand of a trade union, to whom allegiance was offered by about 9.5 million of working Poles, was an unbelievable organizational success.

My anxiety, associated with the emerging and evolving Solidarity movement, had historical roots. For the preceding one hundred and fifty years Poles and their reactions were out of step with the rest of Europe, to say nothing about the three empires that partitioned Poland in the eighteenth century. Disastrous uprisings, undertaken at the politically and militarily wrong moment (as the 1830–31 uprising), or without the slightest prospect for success (as the 1863/64 uprising), or the most devastating 1944 Warsaw uprising, all turned the bad situation in Poland in each case into a still worse one. We had no allies, no sources of external support in Europe or elsewhere for our dramatic moves. An unmitigated disaster had been awaiting us at the end of each episode.

Thus, I was afraid that the Solidarity movement – if taken over by some radical activists – might bring upon Poland yet another similar disaster. Disaster on a great scale, given Poles' penchant for fighting the losing battles. For we, just as Hungarians in 1956, certainly could not expect any military help coming from the West.

In the preceding chapter my analysis suggested that by mid-1970s the economic decline began to be visible across the Soviet dependencies and the Soviet Union itself. But it looked like a long-term process, not a rapid collapse, generating systemic change as its outcome. With an attempt at forcing the rapid change in Poland alone we might be, once again, out of step with the rest – this time with the rest of losers on the East side of the East-West divide. The Brezhnev Doctrine could be invoked and applied, again, with much more devastating effects than in Czechoslovakia in 1968.

One of my best friends, at the time a ranking Solidarity activist, told me recently that he had the feeling, while talking with me in the summer of 1981, that I regarded him then as a dangerous radical. I could not protest that it was not the case. As most Poles, I wished Solidarity a political success in their "self-restraining revolution" and associated efforts to peacefully modify the repressive nature of the system. But what was perceived at that time as the maximum possible change?

In 1980–81, during the "Solidarity picnic," a Finlandization of sort looked more like a dream than a – barely attainable – maximum. As in Finland after 1945, the maximum that could be attained were economic freedoms, civic freedoms, maybe also a multiparty system with a pro-Soviet party as an anchor of every governing coalition at home, with continued subordination to Soviet military and foreign policy goals in international affairs. Obstacles to such a (dreamed up) maximum change were enormous and manifold.

Geographically, and therefore strategically, Poland's location in 1980 was far more important for the Soviets than was that of Finland in 1945. Soviet leaders expected unimpeded movements of their troops between the then Soviet Russia and communist East Germany. Thus, the Soviet resistance to Finlandization in Poland would have been much stronger than to Finlandization in Finland.

Moreover, it seemed that the Soviets in 1980–81 were not yet ready to accept a far reaching arrangement of that sort. There were, however, some new factors to be taken into account that could make Soviets somewhat more ready to compromise. But neither I, nor many others, knew about the extent of the cancerous effects of the unwinnable Afghan war on the thinking of Soviet leadership. In fact, even now, with the benefits of hindsight, the attainability of such a dreamed-up maximum seems to have been in 1981 extremely low.

Apart from Soviet Russia's unpreparedness for such a move, there were important internal factors making the attainment of such an arrangement very difficult, if not downright impossible. The whole apparatus of the communist party would be dead set against the internal part of any Finlandization-type arrangement. The apparatus of repression would be against civic freedoms, restraining dramatically their power, while the economic apparatus would be against shifting the economy in the direction of the market. In the market economy there is no place for the communist party-appointed managers, and – above all – no place for the bureaucratic coordination through planning and administration pyramid. Economic *apparatchiks* would quickly become redundant, once market reforms started – just as they indeed become redundant after 1989.

It is worth noting that the foregoing considerations concerned so far only the communist side of the puzzle. Professionally, as an economist, I had also reservations with respect to Solidarity's approach to economic issues. To put it mildly, trade unions around the world nowhere seem to offer sensible answers to difficult economic questions. And a trade union from behind the communist iron curtain, so separated from normal economic thinking, was in an even worse position in this respect.

The political aims of the Solidarity movement were generally formulated by learned intellectuals, with numerous linkages throughout the West, who were thinking along these lines for years if not decades. The economic aims and means seemed easier to grasp for trade union activists. Or so they thought. Therefore, they were often ready to come up with their own (usually incompetent if not downright silly) proposals.

Besides, the tradition of the Polish non-communist workers activists' thinking was emotionally and ideologically associated with the nonsensical Yugoslav idea of state-owned firms run by workers' self-management arrangements. For someone well acquainted – like myself – with both the theory of property rights and the Yugoslav practice of the workers' self-management since its introduction in 1974, the collectivist arrangement of that sort was a cure no better than the disease.

Moreover, with a passage of time during the 1980–81 "Solidarity picnic" period, a range of more or less specific proposals were formulated by some influential Solidarity activists, concerning economic strategy at the macro level, operations of the economic system, as well as the evaluation of the state firms' performance. Most of them raised serious objections from the standpoint of basic economic knowledge and – as it, unfortunately, turned out – also from the rules of sensible debate. Worse still, economists were more polarized than before in the 1980–81 period. And the divisions run not necessarily along the lines of being for or against central planning and administration of the national economy. I discovered that upon my arrival from America in June 1981.

Almost immediately I was invited to join a seminar on economic reforms at the Institute of Planning. I accepted the invitation with great interest, looked impatiently to the first debate, only to listen with amazement to the discussion, when the debate took place. Nobody sounded as if he had been interested in fundamentals of such reforms. There seemed to have been no agreement – even declared in principle, let alone in details – that "more market economy" was a path to follow.

The subject that absorbed most attention at that first seminar I attended, about two weeks after coming back from the States, was the stabilization program. I had no quarrel with the specific subject selected for a given debate; the restoration of even the semblance of balance in so deeply unbalanced, shortage-ridden economy was both legitimate and important. My objections concerned the substance of the proposals, displaying the ignorance of economic realities.

The proposals, prepared by an evidently poorly educated Solidarity-leaning economist, ran as follows. The first task was to balance the consumer goods market. So far, so good; in politically tense periods consumer satisfaction tends to reduce the level of tension and strengthens the probability of reaching some sensible, negotiated settlement.

However, the means for the attainment of the aim in question revealed the lack of understanding of communist economic weaknesses in their interactions with the international economy. The proposals assumed increased exports of intermediate inputs and capital goods to the West. Both were to be made available as a result of cuts in the oversized investment program. With foreign exchange earned from these exports, imports of consumer goods would help to balance or at least markedly reduce the very large scale of excess demand on the consumer goods market. The first step would, then, be accomplished.

However, command economies were inefficient to boot and unable to produce manufactured goods at competitive prices for international markets. To sell any manufactures in the Western markets they had to offer deep discounts. Moreover, such discounts stood a chance of success primarily with respect to light consumer goods and standard semi-manufactures, but rarely with respect to the intrinsically more sophisticated investment goods. Therefore, most of the goods targeted for exports to the West would find no buyers in the West (as communist planners learned many times in the past). As a consequence, with little, or much less, foreign exchange earned, the opportunities for large scale imports of consumer goods would be nonexistent. The deeply unbalanced consumer goods market would not register the expected rebalancing effect. The proposal was, clearly, a non-starter.

I then took floor and, cautiously, as a newcomer to these debates, explained the unavoidable problems that assured an inevitable failure of such a proposal. Besides, I added, we should start thinking about reforms in order to avoid repetitions of such grave imbalances in the future. I was shocked, however, when another – influential as I learned later – Solidarity economist, Mr. Bugaj, frankly without known academic credentials, did not rise to the defense of the presented stabilization proposals by adding some convincing arguments in their favor (not that there were many!). He just declared that "there is no sense to debate the proposals, such a program should be quickly implemented – that is all."

I knew such mental attitudes from my own skirmishes with communist *apparatchiks* in the past. Solidarity activists present at the debate were wearing the colors of a different, opposing organization, but their mental attitude seemed to have been of the same sort. A Polish sociologist, Professor Jadwiga Staniszkis, once compared the mentality of the communists and the Solidarity activists to the head and tail of the same coin.

The foregoing confirmed some suspicions, which I harbored, while looking at Polish political-economic developments from America. A substantial share of those, who joined the nearly 10 million strong trade union, were the people whom I defined years later, in my 1992 article, after the fall of communism, as "anti-communist Bolsheviks." They withdrew their support for communists and joined the Solidarity movement not because they realized that the system was both inefficient and demoralizing, but because it promised the pie in the sky – and did not deliver. Now, they thought, it was the Solidarity's turn to deliver (the undeliverable).

They did not care either for substantive rationality of arguments or for liberal rules of debate. The more specific ideas of markets, free prices, profit-and-loss account, private property, entrepreneurship, and competition were light years away from their thinking. In actual fact, I clashed intermittently over the next three decades in general with our "anti-communist Bolsheviks," abundantly present in Polish debates, but also specifically with the particular Solidarity economist who was in favor of imposing the obviously defective stabilization strategy, without any serious debate and arguments in its favor.

But the above was the problem for the future. In summer 1981 I had a different problem, one of allegiance. I am by nature a loner, a thinker, not an organization man. And, yet, upon my return to Poland in June 1981 I was toying with the idea of joining the Solidarity to contribute to the pool of knowledge they undoubtedly – in fact, sorely – needed in the discussions on economic reforms. Yet, skirmishes like the one described above were discouraging me from doing so. Moreover, economically exotic proposals, emanating increasingly from the Solidarity side, were becoming more and more numerous as the first congress of Solidarity was getting closer and its economic program (for all it was worth) was being prepared.

On the other hand, I was even less ready to join the economic officialdom on the other side of the fence. At the turn of 1980s I did not believe in the "reformability" of the communist political-economic system and my accelerated learning of that system since 1979 suggested that the system had no future in the longer run (see the preceding chapter).

In the end I was offered a King Solomon's type, middle ground solution. Namely, a small, autonomous trade union emerged, positioning itself in between the communist side and Solidarity. It had mostly corporate rather than individual members: accountants, lawyers, and other professional organizations created a core of its membership. They also needed economic competence to evaluate various reform proposals and turned to me with an offer to become their volunteer adviser. I accepted this offer, which was to be but a brief interlude between my summer decision and the end of the hope for a possible political compromise.

How much willingness to compromise was on the communist side was unclear. In the late summer of 1981 a press spokesman of Jaruzelski's government was asked at one of the party activists' meeting about the meaning of the term "social consultations," declared to be held by the government. He answered the question in following terms: "Consultations are not a referendum; they are even less a national election. They should be seen as *a way to inform society*" (of the forthcoming decisions of the authorities). A humorist, Jacek Fedorowicz, commented about that statement in his radio program *Sixty Minutes Per Hour* by saying that if an anchorman of a TV station reads the news that Legia (a Warsaw football club) won with Wisla (a Cracow football club), he is -c-o-n-s-u-l-t-i-n-g the public with respect to the outcome of the game…

So, there was to be no compromise. On December 13, 1981, tanks (Polish, not Soviet this time) rolled in, thousands of Solidarity activists were detained, and martial law – declared by the leadership headed by general Wojciech Jaruzelski – ushered in a completely new phase of communist rule, a phase without the earlier ideological pretensions that the communist party was the "vanguard" of the working class. The real vanguard, that is Solidarity activists, however intellectually misguided on many (economic and other) issues, was then locked away in the detention camps.

The imposition of martial law changed little in my (self-proclaimed) status of an independent analyst. I still worked on a number of important articles on various features of the system and their economic outcomes. I intended to continue to do so regardless of martial law. And martial law did not change my intentions of publishing them mostly in the West.

However, the new situation demanded some short term reactions and longer term adjustments. Some friends were fired from their jobs while others were incarcerated, like for example the friend who sensed that I had regarded him as a dangerous radical. They and their families needed help.

Some help came also from outside Poland. Barely a few weeks passed since the imposition of the martial law, when I received a big package from a German professor from Dortmund I had met earlier at some conference. Knowing the dramatic food situation in Poland, he sent about 10 kg of various products, barely attainable in Poland at the time. There was no accompanying letter, which dear Prof. Boehm must have regarded as more dangerous for me from the vantage point of the martial law authorities then the food itself!

I did not need the assistance at the time. After a year in the States I had the wherewithal to survive with my family even if I were fired from my job (which I was not at the time). But others needed help right away. I decided to write a letter to him, express my appreciation and my – relatively safe – position for the time being, and ask him whether he would be ready to help two others persons in need I began helping on my own: an unemployed journalist from the closed rural Solidarity weekly (a mother with a dependent child) and an incarcerated political sociologist, a ranking Solidarity activist. I added that I divided the package and passed half of all he sent to each of the two families in question. If he sent another package I would conclude that he approved of what I did and was willing to help these two families.

The problem was how to communicate with him. Telecom lines were taped, letters to the West were ordered to be sent open, with one side of the envelope cut out to make censorship faster. I decided to send a letter to one of my Hungarian friends for I learned that letters to "brotherly" countries were left uncensored. I sent him a letter informing that I am alive and well and working in Poland (a signal I was neither incarcerated, nor fired from my job so far) and added, without any comments, three other letters to some colleagues in the West, including the letter concerning food assistance, written to the already mentioned German professor from Dortmund. My Hungarian friend, Zoltan Krasznai, accepted my roundabout way of communication (at some risk to himself, let me add!) and for about two years became my intermediary in postal contacts with the West.

My academic colleague from Dortmund got my letter and responded positively. The next food package arrived a month later – and so did further packages for about two-three years. Let me add for the benefit of readers who have not been acquainted with the intricacies of post-martial law aftermath that it had been Germans who turned out to be most sensitive to the plight of Poles under the Jaruzelski regime. Others helped, too, making at times embarrassing mistakes.

I remember a conversation with an American professor in Helsinki; Finland was the first country I was given passport to visit (after a string of refusals). He admitted that he and his wife, too, decided to help Poles suffering from the harsh regime and transferred every month a hundred dollars to the Polish consulate in New York. I smiled and said that he was actually helping the regime, not regime's victims. For all the money and food sent to official state organizations was later distributed to the army and the police. I saw them – I added – stopping and checking up cars at various crossroads or surrounding the more rebellious cities, with their pockets full of Western sausages, Western sweets, as well as American cigarettes. He and others, making the same mistakes, were helping to keep their morale high. They did not feel the shortages so painfully as the rest of the population.

I do not need to add that he promised to stop their cash transfers right away. Also, a decent chap, he inquired by what channels they could help the really suffering side of the conflict; I gave him a few names and addresses of mostly catholic church-associated charity organizations or those Solidarity-associated, but nonetheless pursuing their assistance under the umbrella of this or that parish church (run by some brave priest, ready to face various pressures from the communist security apparatus).

Some longer-term adjustments demanded my decisions as well. First of all, I started thinking about changing my place of work. First of all, my views were quite well known even before martial law (remember the skirmish on the occasion of the presentation of five-year for the 1976–80 period?). Besides, I learned on an occasion that the institute's leadership was passing information on me to the security police. So, I could expect to be fired sooner or later.

How did I learn that? After a string of refusals to travel abroad I decided to appeal a third or a fourth such adverse decision in 1982 and in due time was invited to the passport bureau's officer in charge of such appeals. I noticed that he had a letter on his desk. He looked at me and declared in a grave voice that my prospects of obtaining passport were dim, indeed. Firstly, I maintain contacts with some undesirable individuals. And, secondly, my brother – an applied graphic artist who worked on a contract in Germany (West Germany of course!) – renounced in protest against martial law his Polish citizenship and returned his passport to communist authorities (a mortal sin!).

At that moment some superior of the officer in question called him on the phone and the latter tried to explain some issue or decision. I did not listen because I was busy reading the letter across the desk; my eyesight was much better in 1982 than it is now! The letter was sent by one of the directors of the Polish Institute of International Affairs (his signature was unintelligible from my side of the desk) and informed the Ministry of Internal Affairs, of which the passport bureau was a part, that Professor Winiecki maintains contacts with some suspect foreigners and underground Solidarity activists.

It was time to change jobs – I quickly thought – for under such circumstances it was better to leave on my own then be fired. I was ready to leave the passport bureau once the officer ends his phone conversation. To my surprise, though, it was not to be the end of the story. The officer turned to me and said that I could regain my freedom to travel if I were ready to help them to obtain various confidential economic materials during my visits in Western research institutions and universities. The dumb cluck really believed, presumably together with his superiors, that there exists something akin to the philosopher's stone that makes the capitalist market economy tick! And, if stolen therefrom, would do the same for the communist planned economy.

I decided to play a game of an academic innocent who offers his – unsolicited – economic advice on the basis of his professional knowledge. I said that academic pursuits during my visits abroad, like those of any of my colleagues, were routinely reported by me to my institute's authorities. There was nothing secret there, just the reports on what conferences I attended, what papers I presented at seminars and what I researched.

Moreover – I added – it was an intellectual error on the side of his superiors to think that there were some secrets allowing capitalist market economies to perform better than communist planned economies. The reasons why they perform better are rather well known – at least among experts on comparative economic systems. Instead of searching for the nonexistent secrets of West's success, it is better to consider the weaknesses of communist economic system. If his superiors were willing to listen, I would be ready to give for free a series of seminars at the Ministry of Internal Affairs to explain what are the real problems and what should be changed in terms of institutions and policies in order that the Polish economy could start performing decently.

I do not know what he thought about my proposal (I suspected he thought it was a display of *hutzpah* on my side), but he said he would pass on my proposal – and the visit ended. Unsurprisingly, I did not get my passport for some time. Nor, in fact, did I get an invitation to teach security *apparatchiks* some normal economics...

At about the same time I learned that the Polish Academy of Sciences established a new unit, a management science institute, and decided to apply. I was accepted in principle and now it was the time to say good bye to my workplace since 1973. I decided also to say good bye to the communist party. I joined it quite late, in 1964, after it became clear that the freedoms of post-Stalinist era had been shrinking fast and it would not be possible to do anything sensible outside the framework of the ruling party. And decided to leave the party during the martial law in late 1982, when it became obvious – to me at least – that opportunities for doing something sensible outside the ruling party have clearly reemerged, martial law or no martial law being imposed on society.

In the new outfit, which I joined at the beginning of 1983, its head wanted to be useful to the political/military authorities talking about (but not acting upon) economic reforms. Accordingly, I was asked to present my opinions on various aspects of the present economic situation and suggest some ideas on policy improvements. While presenting bits and pieces on various partial issues, I signaled to the professor in question at the helm of the outfit that I would like to write a larger, more comprehensive analysis, combined with a range of probable scenarios: from those leading nowhere to those, which could result in the desired change for the better. In a fit of absentmindedness – I suspect – he agreed and I duly presented such a paper in late autumn 1983.

The longish paper first diagnosed the situation. I explained that an inefficient centrally planned and administered economies like Poland, using two to three times more resources than market economies to produce one dollar of gross domestic product, do not stand a chance not only to catch up with the West (and old dream of communist authorities since Stalin's time!), but even to keep the present distance from the level of income per capita in market economies of the West. All the known distortions of the communist economies tend to have cumulative effects, decreasing performance and increasing the distance to countries we historically tried to catch up with. At a certain point in time it will become impossible, given the unavailability of the required volume of resources, to continue the "business as usual" by the unreformed centrally planned and administered economy. What will be left, then, would be two remaining scenarios: (1) the shift to a fully fledged market economy or (2) a more or less steep economic decline. Considerations were supported by a diagram, showing the probable options, as well as the improbable one of the continuation of the present institutional and policy framework (see Figure 4.1).

Figure 4.1: Communist economies, using 2-3 times more resources to produce the same amount of GDP than capitalist economies would face at some point a strong barrier to further economic growth. The figure presents available alternative scenarios upon reaching such a threshold (based upon the relationship between energy use and GDP per capita level)

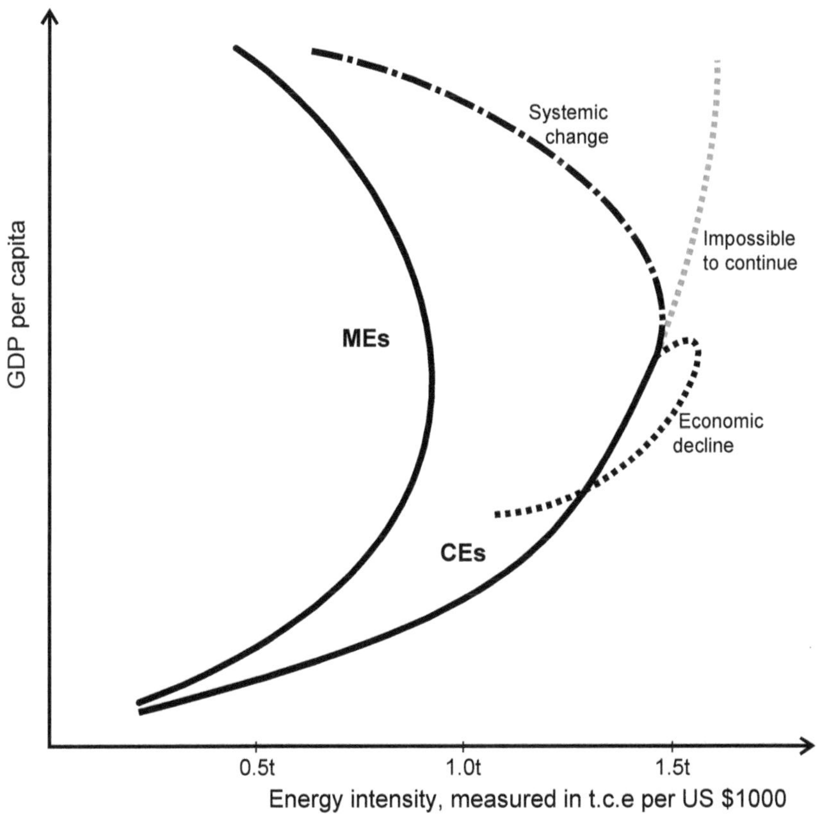

I suspect, however, that what was most objectionable politically were my scenarios for the future, especially two of them. The first assumed that the ruling stratum of the system (the party *apparatchiks*, the bureaucrats, the military, and the police) would become "softened" over time. Increasingly tired, seeing more and more duties and less and less privileges from their position, they would be at some point willing to forgo their support for the communist system and negotiate the systemic change.

The second was no less objectionable and also closer to the actual Polish post-martial law reality. I drew a scenario based on the difference in the ways various segments of the ruling stratum under communism benefited from the system. The military and the police benefited – like in autocracies – primarily from their access to best paid positions in their respective hierarchies. By contrast *apparatchiks* and bureaucrats, apart from appointments in their respective hierarchies, benefited even more from their ability to impose – formally or informally – the non-market distribution of goods and services in short supply in favor of themselves.

Accordingly, the military and the police are keen primarily on the continuation of the *political* system, while the latter two are also keen to preserve the *economic* system of command economy (regardless of the fact that it is utterly inefficient). Thus, at some point the military, alone or in cahoots with the police, would be ready to abandon the highly inefficient economic system, leaving *apparatchiks* and bureaucrats without much of their power to appoint themselves and their cronies to well paid positions in the planned economy and, no less importantly, without the benefits from non-market distribution. And in Poland in early 1980s it became increasingly visible that party *apparatchiks* had less and less say on economic, as well as other issues, while the military overshadowed the party. Thus, the scenario in question sounded, indeed, ominous for the former.

After I presented the paper at the outfit's seminar, the head of the institute clearly became frightened and decided to get rid of me as quickly as possible. He wrote a letter to the head of the Academy that he wanted to constructively assist Polish economic reforms, while I was excessively critical and, therefore, interfering in the institute's works with my far-fetched ideas about change (rather than acceptable reforms). Let readers note that the lack of the "constructive" position on my side was, again, brought against me, just as in 1960s (see Chapter 2).

The President of the Polish Academy of Sciences, a dignified old professor of medicine, but a political and moral weakling, wanted to live in peace and quiet during his term in office. He obviously was not interested in defending some unruly academic economist against the communist party *apparatchiks*. I was duly fired in winter 1983/84 and – interestingly – I was informed that during the months until the end of the legal dismissal period I need not appear at the institute.

Thus, I had something like three months in early 1984 without any duties and decided that I was going to write a book – in English – on the future of communist economies, based on the paper that generated such panicky reactions. As a comparative systems analyst, I decided, however, to write a parallel story on the West. This is how my first book in English: *Economic Prospects: East and West. A View from the East* was born.[8] There were some complications afterwards. The proofs of my text, sent from London and sent back by me, after I made the corrections, did not reach the publisher (they must have been impounded by the postal censors!). So, they had to be sent again from London and sent back by me (this time by a safer route than the communist mail!) to the publisher. Finally, it appeared in London in the book format with a long lag in spring 1987.

On the occasion of its publication I had at least the opportunity to poke fun at the ideological watchdogs of the Polish Academy of Sciences. I did it in the acknowledgments' part of the preface to the said book. Thus, I thanked the authorities of the Academy for their decision to free me "from those bureaucratic and pseudo-scholarly activities typical of academic institutions in the Soviet system." Their decision of not wanting to see me at the institute – I wrote – turned the dismissal period into a "highly desirable fellowship of sorts: I could devote most of my time to writing which enabled me *inter alia* to produce these essays. For this service, however inadvertently rendered, I do wish to thank the ideological policemen in the Academy of Sciences."[9]

It is worth noting that the fact of the growing role of the military did not mean that the system worked any better. Obviously, military officers by the very nature of their job are more accustomed to take decisions and then to implement them (or at least to try to implement them). Party *apparatchiks* had more experience in "taking stand" on issues and explaining them in ideological-propagandistic terms. However, when it came to take decisions based on economic knowledge, and more generally economic logic, both groups were, in fact, helpless.

I may add at this point that in the 1981–83 I attended yet another seminar. A group of scholars from various disciplines attended the seminar called – in loose translation - "crisis management seminar" (an original Polish term used an impossible to translate adjective: "crisisological").

The seminar was an initiative of a professor of psychology, Janusz Reykowski, who brought in representatives of various academic disciplines from humanities to social sciences to economics, in order to debate the manifold manifestations of the Polish crisis. Taking into account the political polarization of the period, it is worth mentioning that there were more academics closer to communist establishment and less those who did not take sides during the "Solidarity picnic" period and later, and almost none close to "Solidarity."

Reykowski was in an interesting academic – and indeed political – position, knowing and advising some *politbureau* members, including the most important individual, namely Jaruzelski. So, listening to a variety of opinions was beneficial for him not only in the scholarly sense. Frankly, I did not see anything politically objectionable in his use of our opinions as inputs in his advisory role. All participants were very frank in their – often critical and varied – opinions. I thought that if something sensible reached sometimes the top policy makers of the regime, it might even turn beneficial for the public.

Such expectations were, however, too optimistic, I am afraid. Reykowski sometimes – not very often – said something, in evident frustration, about his interactions with the "high and mighty." At one point, talking about the ability of policy makers to link their political, social, or economic ideas with actual decisions and understanding their most probable outcomes, he said – visibly agitated – that they sometimes reminded him of five years' olds who would like to learn about the effects of electricity and accordingly put a finger into an electric socket to observe what happens.

His statement was all the more interesting as the IQ level of the Jaruzelski-led *politbureau*, and even more of his closest circle of decision makers, was undoubtedly higher in comparison with earlier *politbureaus*, led by other first secretaries of the Polish communist party. And, superficially, all the more surprising, since at one point he accepted the offer to become a *polibureau* member himself.

I used the term: "superficially," because his decision undoubtedly was professionally justifiable. He certainly learned a lot as a psychologist! More importantly, I am sure he believed that he can do something positive in the public policy area. And he, indeed, have contributed something positive. Certainly not in helping to build late communist castles on the sand that all failed to materialize in the second half of 1980s, but – I am sure – in making the systemic change in 1989 somewhat smoother than it might have been otherwise. Even if the plans of communist party and military superiors were different, the transfer of power was accomplished successfully and – by and large – with good grace.

I am moving ahead of the story, though. The crisis management seminar was disbanded if I remember correctly in early 1984 (when Reykowski decided to change roles). At the same time I was fired from my job in the Polish Academy of Science and was trying to find for myself some niche of sorts. No more intellectually challenging scenarios of the type I presented in the Institute of Management Science – I decided. My knowledge of both economic systems was to be presented first of all in my publications in the West, which began to appear more and more frequently there. My international recognition was rapidly on the increase. Simply speaking, I needed a job to earn some money and, no less importantly, to get the ration cards. Rationing was ubiquitous in 1980s and without ration cards life was even more difficult.

I got my ration cards, an array of them, for various food products, for vodka, for soap and detergent, for sweets, etc., as an unemployed. It was an unusual status under the communist system, where there were officially no unemployed. Each month, on a certain day, we queued in a district office of Warsaw administration to obtain the cards. It was a motley crew. Three different groups were distinguishable there. The first and the largest were the usual bums and beggars, spreading the foul smell of dirt mixed with alcohol. The second group was in stark contrast with the first as far as their external outlook and smell were concerned. They were pretty, nicely dressed, somewhat excessively made up ladies of pleasure. And the third were the people like me: the dissidents, critics of the regime, and some Solidarity activists fired from their jobs for continuing union activity after martial law, who were unable to find another job.

Originally, according to the severe, announced martial law regulations, those who shirked their obligations to work were to be sent obligatorily to the forced labor camps in the Zulawy region in northern Poland, to the east of Gdansk, if they were below 45 years of age. There were not any such camps then operating and they were to be established in the future. Yet, as with many other severe regulations, the ruling group (the *junta* as it was then called, given the strong representation of the military among them) did not intend to follow all their severe threats.

That was a refreshing change. All the previous ruling groups did not follow their promises of better future. Not following also the threats was a positive change. A behavior kept in the style of the merriest barrack in the communist concentration camp.

My search for a niche succeeded at one point in 1984, and the way it had been arranged was in sharp contrast with what happened with my most recent job at the Institute of Management Science. The then head of the Institute of Labor and Social Research, Prof. Antoni Rajkiewicz, stated openly that he could not employ me as a full time professor because at the professorial level he would have to – according to the rules – obtain an approval from his ministerial authorities. He added that there might be problems with obtaining such approval in my case. However, he is in a position to offer me a half-time job for in such case the approval from above is not necessary.

Soon, I obtained next half-time job in another, rather unique academic institution, namely the Catholic University of Lublin (KUL). The University, established right after the World War I with the rebirth of Poland, survived the worst period of communism and by 1980s played an increasingly important role.

Firstly, it was administratively independent from the state. Secondly, in its academic curriculum it was, from the very beginning, completely independent from the higher education authorities.

By the 1980s the communist leadership, facing increasing problems and declining legitimacy, looked for various props – in the first place from the hierarchy of the Catholic Church, undoubtedly a nationally important institution. So, it closed its collective eyes on the fact that quite a few students, politically active during the "Solidarity picnic," relegated from the state universities found the place, where to continue their studies at KUL. Moreover, in a give-and-take-bargaining, communists for the first time allowed KUL to open a department of economics. With a sharply limited number of students to be admitted for the first year of study, but it was an important concession nonetheless. For it was obvious that what would be taught there would not be the socialist political economy!

And indeed it was not. The people who joined the department (a unit within the school of social science) were convinced that it was necessary to prepare students to cope with economic problems of the future by supplying them with the knowledge of normal economics. The term "normal economics" when used by me in public debates, was raising the blood pressure of the – not so numerous, but important – economic believers in the centrally planned and administered economy.

Those who decided to join the economics department at KUL, and they were academics from all over the country, believed that students should learn normal economics from normal, that is Western, textbooks. The textbooks we got were mostly American ones. Given the near complete lack of normal economics textbooks in Polish, one of the requirements to be admitted as a student at the economics department was therefore a decent knowledge of English.

Instructors had obvious problems with lectures that we tried to offer in Polish, while the textbooks were in English. The terminology was often created *ad hoc*, and each lecturer used at the beginning his or her own terminology. I remember that, while teaching money and banking course, in order to give students an inkling of what it all meant in Polish I reached for the respective textbook and books on monetary economics from 1920s!

Maybe it is at this point that I should explain why I and quite a few other fellow economists, including all my colleagues at the department, were convinced that the future was that of a systemic change, not a treadmill of communist reforms. And why that future was not seen as a very distant one. Let me do it, again, in a Voltaire'ian manner. Voltaire once defined history as philosophy taught by examples. So I would like to explain my philosophic approach to the future by referring to two stories from my personal history.

The first example concerns columns I began to write in 1984 for an underground "Solidarity" bulletin *Wola* (distributed in the industrial district of Warsaw of the same name), with the circulation of some 30,000 copies a week. One of the columns called: "Rura nie wybiera" ["A (broken) pipe is not selective"] dealt with an issue relevant for these considerations. I wrote there that with the ever more dilapidated municipal infrastructure in a stagnant economy (see the previous chapter for the Soviet story in this respect!) there would be more and more pipe breakdowns. And their impact would be felt equally strongly by, say, an old ex-worker, now pensioner, in his small apartment, as well as by a police colonel or some middle level communist party *apparatchik* in his much larger apartment, all living in the housing complex in an area where the pipe broke down.

An *apparatchik* or a policeman may have had a larger apartment than a pensioner, but both would shiver from cold, when the central heating pipe broke down in winter. The pipe would not be selective. Everybody was to be "democratically" affected within a given area covered by the breakdown. Over time, with each subsequent pipe breakdown, the representatives of the ruling stratum may one day start wondering, whether they still benefit from continuing to prop up a system in obvious decline. Evidently, the Brezhnevs, Ceausescus, Honeckers, or Jaruzelskis – to name but a few communist leaders – did not feel directly the effects of the decline, but their underlings inevitably did.

The second example refers to a one-off case, but with important implications for the ruling stratum in communist countries. A year or two later I visited an academic friend of mine, an already mentioned political sociologist, deeply involved in underground "Solidarity," to discuss with him some issues of the day. Since his apartment was taped by security police on permanent basis, we agreed to meet at his apartment and then take a walk. Right after my arrival a phone rang and my host, Jacek Szymanderski, talked – to my surprise – quite openly about accepting an invitation for an early evening of the same day. The conversation referred to some "Solidarity"-related issues, but nonetheless the agreed time and place of their meeting were explicitly mentioned (without any code).

Thus, when we left the apartment, I inquired about the issue that looked to me like a display of the nonchalance vis-a-vis the police taping his apartment. Jacek laughed and said that he knows how the security police operates. There is a shift change at about 10:00 p.m. The tapes for the whole day are being collected and new ones put into the recorders. Only then the security people start reviewing the tapes and listening to what has been recorded. So, it is safe to talk without any camouflage about the arrangements for that day; when they learn about it, it is already over. Of course, he added, with respect to arrangements for the future we are much more cautious.

Therefore, it was easy to imagine that after coming back from his conspiratorial activities, my friend could go to sleep and slept like a log. By contrast, the security policemen, working on his case, were yawning and trying to overcome sleepiness, while listening during the night to his taped conversations.

To generalize from these examples, I would like to quote again from my *Economic Prospects: East and West* book, which in the Eastern part dealt with the diagnosis and the scenarios for the future in Poland and elsewhere in the communist world:

> The late XIXth century black educator, Booker T. Washington, stressed the futility of slavery by pointing to the amount of power that would have to be expended, saying that "the only way the white man in the South can keep Negro in the ditch is to stay in the ditch with him".[10]
>
> After the pointed quote from Booker Washington came my own comment: With falling living standards and ever more discontented people, ruling elites may find it so effort-consuming to control the sullen or rebellious societies, while getting less and less in terms of their own welfare, that, after some time, they may find it convenient to enlarge the power base and (gradually or radically) relinquish the system-specific controls.

In both scenarios envisaging systemic change, I wrote in the same book that "it is possible that after the initial successes in terms of economic performance, and resultant increasing wealth, the system would continue to evolve in the democratic direction".[11] Readers may note that the scenarios envisaged either gradual or radical abandonment of system-specific controls. History tilted to the latter direction, supported by the American strategic challenge to the Soviet Union at the time and fumbling new Soviet leadership reactions. But I, again, am getting ahead of my story. We were still in the mid-1980s and what I wrote then was only an informed guesstimate about the future.

Some loose ends also required my attention. Once I decided to become an independent analyst and the signs of my independence in the form of a growing stream of my critical publications in the West started to be visible to apparatchiks in all levels of institutions for communist control, I could expect a number of unattractive developments, typical in such a situation. The first would be the 6:00 a.m. visits of security police and searches of my apartment. The usual outcome was a confiscation of some "suspect" manuscripts and literature.

Following the experience and reactions of others, I established a certain routine pattern of behavior. Every second morning I took notes I wrote in the preceding 48 hours, went to one or two libraries, borrowed some books and journals, marked pages to be copied, and visited a copying service of one of the two bureaucratic organizations, where I developed some earlier personal contacts.

To make it clear to the western readers, there were no publically available copying services under communism! Copiers were under strict control, like everything associated with the "threat" of copying and publishing some uncensored material. They were only for official use. Copying something privately was strictly prohibited by the higher-ups.

Real life had, however, its own demands. People needed copies of some documents. Academics needed copies of articles, quotes from various books and papers, etc. So, the demand was there. And when demand emerges and legal supply is not possible, black market supply comes to the rescue. After all, those working in copying and printing services of various official organizations wanted to earn some extra money – and they could do it under communism only by working "in the black." The black market helped people like me.

Thanks to the ability to copy what I wrote, the most I would lose after a morning visit from security police would be the product of my latest 48 hours, not the whole manuscript on a given subject, which had been hidden prior to the search. Thus, after getting the copied materials I visited my Mother's apartment and stashed there copies of my handwritten notes, typescripts, etc., and came home. Operating in that manner, I could continue my work with some, but without much disturbance.

But soon not only my workload, but also a variety of activities increased considerably. By the mid-1980s the rapidly growing stream of my publications, primarily academic, but over time also in the Western dailies and weeklies, resulted in a growing number of people knocking on my door to discuss economic issues of communist, or as they were more often called at the time, Soviet-type economies. Interestingly, I was much better known abroad than in my own country. The foregoing was true also with respect to the "Solidarity"-related opposition. Nonetheless, more and more journalists, analysts, academics, politicians, and diplomats contacting various "Solidarity" advisers and other activists indicated they would also like to get in touch with me.

The number of Westerners contacting me multiplied as a result of these inquiries. But the quantitative change in terms of interactions with the interested Westerners became also a prologue to the qualitative change. I was on the verge of changing the status from a lone ranger, a dissident analyst, to something different. I was offered a choice and there should not be any doubt which side I was ready to choose.

Chapter 5: Communism – Game Over!

My growing interaction with the outside world had yet another, domestic policy-related effect. Some of the "Solidarity" intellectuals came to the conclusion that I could be a valuable addition to their advisory activities. The idea was accepted and at one point I was invited to take part in the *conversatorium*. This innocuous Latin term covered a group of about thirty people, who advised an underground "Solidarity" leadership (*TKK: Tymczasowa Komisja Krajowa* – Temporary National Commission). It was headed by Professor Bronislaw Geremek, an internationally recognized medieval historian and even more widely recognized political personality among the "Solidarity" advisers from the emergence of the "Solidarity" movement in 1980.

The group met secretly in various safe houses in Warsaw, in fact in safe apartments for there were few old houses left after the World War II (in particular after the disastrous Warsaw uprising). *Conversatorium* participants discussed current political and other developments, considered propaganda measures and countermeasures against those taken by Jaruzelski regime (the latter aimed at undermining the standing of opposition in the eyes of the population), and last but certainly not least prepared and discussed position papers on issues of more than transient importance. Occasionally, a small group from the *conversatorium* was selected to meet secretly with the members of the TKK in order to present our opinion on a given issue of interest to TKK members and answer the queries coming from them.

Clearly, I was moving away from my status of a loner, an independent analyst, known mostly abroad to a rather small number of economists, specialists in the field of Sovietology, comparative economics, journalists covering the Soviet system developments, etc. I indeed was turning over time into a -h-i-g-h-l-y -p-o-l-i-t-i-c-a-l -e-c-o-n-o-m-i-s-t.

As usual, with greater recognition came added duties, also in the analytical sphere. I relatively quickly realized that journalists and politicians were not always convinced by my sophisticated arguments about the distorted world of Soviet-type economies, formulated more often than not in theoretical terms. The lack of conviction in my arguments was especially visible among those who displayed certain sympathy for the socialism system. In turn, very detailed empirics of my arguments seemed to bore a majority of journalists.

Thus, a greater and more varied demand on my knowledge should be met with new – and also more varied – supply. I decided to change the style of my presentations for non-economists and over a period some 12–18 months created an index card system on command economies, based primarily on a series of case studies, referring to a specific issue or issues. I made hundreds of clippings, notes, and quotes from newspapers and economic journals from Poland, Soviet Russia, Hungary, Czechoslovakia, and Bulgaria. I left out Romania primarily for linguistic reasons, but also because their numbers were plainly incredible. I by and large disregarded also communist East German sources because of their extremely tight censorship. They did not present any numbers, even in the so-called academic quarterlies, and therefore East German stories that could feed my index card system were few and far between.

The change in the style of presentations turned out to work quite well. For example, when I wanted to prove to my visitor(s) that these economies not only performed inefficiently, but -i-n-c-r-e-a-s-i-n-g-l-y inefficiently, I presented them with an array of cards from the section: "Investment." They contained clippings and quotes from journals from five communist countries proving that (a) completion periods of comparable investment projects were much longer than in the West; and (b) that the completion periods in the East were getting longer over the last 10–20 years. In actual fact I even prepared from time to time short pieces on this or that subject of interest and sent them by safe channels to Western journals, more often than elsewhere to *The Economist*, with which – thanks to contacts with its deputy editor, Norman Mac Rae – I had for years the best interaction.

The sore spot of communist economies was of course the satisfaction of consumer needs. This was something nearly everybody knew about in the West (even the sympathizers of socialism!) and therefore such topic came very often in our conversations. But here I decided to show something unusual so that my guests would recognize that they knew that the situation was bad, but did not think that it was so bad. Thus, I pulled out of the index card section called "Consumption/Shortages" and showed them notes and clippings from four countries showing the existence of perennial shortages of … toilet paper. It was obvious that the output per head (economists always calculate production and consumption per head!) was much too low for decades.

To the above I added a clipping from an underground opposition weekly about the happening group calling itself "The Orange Alternative" from the city of Wroclaw in Western Poland. That group organized happenings on the streets that looked outwardly like pro-communist demonstrations. On the banners they carried they lauded the authorities for the achievements the population should be grateful for. In this particular case the banner read, "We heartily thank our authorities for the fact that they were able to raise the status of such an insignificant product as toilet paper to the ranks of important affairs of the state!"

The people on the street were laughing their heads off, the authorities were furious, but the police – although ordered to act – was unusually tolerant. One could understand their attitude, when they were approached by say a dozen or two of very pretty girls and well scrubbed, pleasantly looking boys – all with the flowers in their hands. I found very often that joke, or jocular story, was quite a weapon (as well as a shortcut to – faster or better – understanding of the issue).

But I would like to turn now to the *conversatorium* itself and its participants. It was a group of very diverse characters, no matter what criteria one would like to apply to classify its participants. Thus, there were among them utopian leftist critics of the socialism as practiced by the communist authorities in 1950s and 1960s. Among them were Jacek Kuron and Prof. Bronislaw Geremek, the *conversatorium* chairman. There were members sailing from various Catholic clubs in Warsaw and other cities; they were often also important as go-betweens during various negotiations between the communist side, the Catholic Church hierarchy, and "Solidarity" leaders (I would mention here Tadeusz Mazowiecki, later the first non-communist prime minister after World War II, Andrzej Wielowieyski and others). There were also quite a few invited in a personal capacity, like myself, especially economists.

The range of views presented by economists during various meetings spanned the whole mainstream theoretical spectrum – and then some. I even found there the same fellow who in 1981 refused to discuss the obviously faulty consumer market balancing program and demanded its unconditional implementation. His ideological *naiveté*, combined with the ignorance of the outside world (to say nothing about international professional literature!), were appalling.

Once I presented at a group meeting a paper on the starting point and the prospective evolution of the Polish enterprise sector during and after the systemic change. I stressed that at the starting point we would have an overwhelming share of state-owned, but workers' council-managed firms, then a large number of cooperatives and an increasing number of small private firms. All would be operating under the same regulatory regime (in contrast with communist times when state firms were heavily privileged in many respects).

However, I added, I had no doubts that under the same rules of the game the most efficient ownership arrangement, that is private ownership, would soon prevail over other forms of ownership and we would observe quick ownership changes both in the case of state firms and cooperatives. Privatization would become the name of the game. The fellow I mentioned, Mr. Bugaj, protested hotly and stated that there were "strong expectations" that workers' self-management would become the dominant institutional arrangement in our economy.

I did not intend to quarrel with him on the basis of expectations based on ideological preferences and ignorance of the real-life economics. I restated drily that, with a level playing field, I expected private ownership to prevail, and prevail rather soon. Besides – I added – it would be a good idea to look at Yugoslavia and its decreasingly attractive reality (it was at that time close to entering a period of hyperinflation) to assess the efficiency of such arrangements as those preferred by my opponent.

Believers in workers' self-management were an obstinate and quarrelsome lot. Quarrelsome at the *conversatorium* and quarrelsome in other quarters of the anti-communist opposition. Among a growing number of activities at the time were my economic commentaries I supplied to another underground journal, a biweekly called *The Self-Managed Republic* (*Samorzadna Rzeczpospolita*). A person, whose code name was Lukasz, appeared at my institute at two week intervals on an agreed day, took a cassette with my text, and disappeared. Two weeks later he came with a copy of the journal with my article, returned the old cassette, took one with my new text prepared for them and disappeared again.

They usually accepted my choice of a theme but sometimes asked for a specific topic. Lukasz inquired at one point whether I would be willing to write for them something about workers self-management of state enterprises and compare that with other ownership arrangements. I said O.K., wrote a critical text on the topic and that was the end of my cooperation with *The Self-managed Republic* – and contacts with Lukasz. He never appeared again and I never got a word of explanation from the journal why they broke the collaborative arrangement, either. It was a clear case of ideological zealotry.

On most occasions, however, economic discussions at the *conversatorium* itself were more fruitful intellectually as the differences were not that great. Nonetheless I noted that believers in a wide range of interventions in the national economy – even after the hoped for institutional reforms (or changes) – were in the majority within our group. In fact, in our debates I could rely most often on only one participant, Prof. Janusz Beksiak, from the intellectual stable created in early 1960s by Aleksy Wakar (see Chapter 2 above).

Let me tell readers a short story, associated with the functioning of *conversatorium*, even if it did not concern the substance of our discussions. For I regard it as a poetic justice of sorts. I mentioned earlier that the group headed by Prof. Geremek met a few times in a selected apartment and then – for safety reasons – changed the apartment for another. Each of us got usually a small slip of paper with the new address and the time of arrival (that we were expected to memorize and then destroy the paper). When I received such a piece, I usually went a day or two before the meeting in order to locate the place without drawing undue attention to myself or to the group as a whole, whose participants were expected to arrive in about five minutes' intervals.

The next safe apartment was located in the Ochota district of Warsaw. I found the proper house, then the apartment – and smiled inwardly. For a nameplate on the door of that apartment was: Helen Dzierzhynski. The idea that anti-communist conspirators were to meet in the place belonging to somebody bearing the name of the first head of the dreaded Soviet communist secret police (the *Cheka*) was amusing, indeed.

But that was to be only the beginning of the story. The apartment belonged to a recently widowed lady in her 60s. After two meetings in a row, conducted in the largest room there, the library, I noted that the family photographs were displaying features of two men not unlike those photos I knew from the communist history books. The only difference was that the two gentlemen on their photos in the library looked much more benign than the mastermind of Soviet terror. For the record, Feliks Dzierzhynski, the head of the first Soviet secret police, was a Pole by origin (coming from a gentry family). I inquired Helen about the striking similarity of the photographs. Her answer was that she was a widow of a son of Feliks Dzierzhynski's brother. Even more of a poetic justice, indeed.

Incidentally, I met Helen Dzierzhynski a few times after the communist collapse, in the 1990–91 period. It was a sheer pleasure to look at her. I could not find a happier looking person in the whole of Warsaw. She seemed to fly over rather than walk on the pavement. I regretted that I was not a painter, able to record forever the human happiness which emanated from this woman and resulting from the fundamental change of the economic and political system.

Over time analytical activities and debates on position papers within the *conversatorium* group became increasingly problem-oriented. Various papers concerning desirable reforms were presented by economists, among them also by Prof. Jerzy Osiatynski and Dr. Leszek Balcerowicz (both later, after the fall of communism, became ministers of finance). But the group headed by Prof. Geremek, although most important in political terms, was not the only discussion outlet for me at that time. I also had been attending the so-called reform seminar headed by Leszek Balcerowicz since late 1970s at the Main School of Planning and Statistics.

Somewhat later the Catholic University of Lublin (KUL) became increasingly active in the area of reform and change. A group of economists there was overwhelmingly free market-oriented. Moreover, we were a group of optimists, convinced that the *mane-thekel-fares* was already clearly visible on the walls of communism. With the end of communism expected rather soon – as a matter of years – we thought that it was worthwhile to concern ourselves with the emergence of a normal market economy.

One of the outcomes of such optimistic thinking was a series of seminars conducted by our economics department at the KUL guest house in the holiday resort town of Kazimierz Dolny, where we tackled two major issues: an inevitable expansion of the new private sector and the necessary privatization of the communist state enterprise sector, in that order, respectively in 1987 and 1988.

The sequencing was rather obvious. The pressure for the change of rules hampering the expansion of new private firms was easier to apply and less censored than any recommendations for the scrapping of the mainstay of communist economic inefficiency, that is the state ownership of enterprises. After all, even communist governments were (insincerely) stressing in 1980s the need of more market-oriented institutional arrangements. And markets without private firms were an oddity.

The 1987 discussions about the regulatory set-up with respect to new private firms centered on two issues. The first was the rule of equality with respect to all ownership sectors (state, co-operative, private) and the second was the liberalization of the existing rules, that is moving toward the freer – and, finally, free – market regime.

The 1988 seminar dealing with the changes in the ownership structure of state firms concerned a politically and ideologically tougher nut to crack. Our early autumn seminar took place before the political breakthrough and the announced round table between the ruling communists (as well as their forced allies) and the opposition. Thus, any call for privatization as the only efficient ownership arrangement would be met with outright hostility. Moreover, as I stressed already above, even among the *conversatorium* participants there was no agreement on privatization as *the ultimate* solution for the state firms.

Some of my department colleagues, as well as myself, were acquainted with certain proposals coming from within Poland and from without, such as those of a committed Italian leftist, Prof. Nuti (*inter alia* a scientific adviser to the communist weekly *Rinascita*), who proposed some statist arrangements, which did not tackle in any meaningful way the efficiency problems inherent in state ownership. One of such proposals, that was presented at about that time was the transformation of state firms into shareholding companies (corporations) and creation of the stock market, where these firms would try to obtain capital. It is about such "state somethings," that a leading light of the Hungarian economics profession, Janos Kornai, wrote in 1990, that they all amount to the economy, financial markets and their corollary, the stock market, "all made of plastic", like toys imitating the real things. They were a poor substitute for really efficient arrangements on "the road to free economy".[12]

In the Kazimierz Dolny 1988 seminar we were offered a range of various proposals, but neither of them came out in favor of state ownership. Some arrangements were variations on the theme of workers' self-management, with the state ownership as a base, but the majority were individual or team presentations, whose authors primarily concerned themselves with the ways and means to transform the state firms into the privately owned ones.

The one that later became a widely debated institutional arrangement was a proposal of two economists from Gdansk University, Janusz Lewandowski and Jan Szomburg. They proposed privatization based on property distributed across the citizenry. That is privatization based on coupons distributed to all citizens in the country, with which to buy shares of the privatized state firms. (The largest such program, called there *kuponovka*, was introduced after the fall of communism in the Czech Republic.)

It is at this point, I think, that it is necessary to enter into the contentious issue of "shortcut" changes in the state ownership of firms. I wrote in the late 1980s about the major differences between the forthcoming privatizations in countries still under communist rule, or turning already into post-communist countries in transition to the market, and privatizations in the West. Two such differences should be stressed here.

The first was the scale of privatization. In the West, the share of state firms in the enterprise sector, measured by the share in aggregate output, amounted with few exceptions to 5–15% of the total. In the still communist or post-communist East it amounted to 80–100%! Quite a difference! The second such difference concerned the overwhelming concentration of to-be-privatized firms in the "classical" production of goods, in industry and agriculture. Such firms were rarely state-owned in the West and it was obvious that they should be privatized in the first place. It was a necessary step for the shift from *mal*development to development. And relatively easily done at that! No natural and quasi-natural monopolies in the physical infrastructure sector, no human capital-intensive, sophisticated services, generating complicated issues.

It had been obvious to many reformers that privatization pursued in accordance with the Western procedures – and in the absence of Western sophisticated financial markets in the East! – would stretch privatization over many years, maybe decades. Some ways should, therefore, be found to shorten the procedures – and Lewandowski-Szomburg proposal was one of such (quite imaginative and reasonable) "shortcut" arrangements.

Not everybody, even among those convinced that privatization was a must, were in favor of such proposals. The already quoted Janos Kornai was skeptical, stressing that the creation of the middle class, based on private firms' owners, could not be accomplished through a "cavalry charge." Expansion of the private ownership and the creation of the business class – he said – is a lengthy historical process.[13] The forthcoming privatization should be pursued by standard capitalist market economy measures. In Poland, economists who were later to lead the economic team of the future non-communist government were equally skeptical.

However, the reality forced future reformers to face, without exceptions, the importance of the time factor. More state firms kept in state hands for longer periods meant lower efficiency of the national economy. Thus, the issue to be debated in late 1980s was reformulated: which "shortcut strategies" had the more advantageous costs/benefits ratio. Clearly, the citizens-based privatization had an advantage over employees-based privatization. The structure of incentives in the latter was definitely disadvantageous, for example, when issues of productivity increase without simultaneous output increase would be considered by management. For employees-shareholders would be against such measures, fearing redundancy.

Just like workers self-management in state-owned enterprises, employees-shareholders were another institutional blind alley as a solution to the ownership issue in the forthcoming capitalist market economy. Free marketeers among economists were deeply convinced that our future was going to be associated with the normal Western economic institutions with its hundreds of years of unbelievable success, both in the shape of economic freedom at home (free market) and across the world economy (free trade). In our private discussions and underground publications we were talking about rejoining Western civilization.

There is an interesting question to be posed. Namely, whether politicians in Western Europe had been aware of the ongoing decline – or more properly degeneration – of the communist economic system. And whether they were concerned with what may happen in declining communist world. However, the conclusions some of them drawn were purely opportunistic and defensive. So, like former French president, Valery Giscard d'Estaing, they proposed a "new Marshall Plan" for Eastern Europe (including the Soviet Union). Thus, fearing the turbulence, Giscard d'Estaing and others proposed to shore up the declining communist world!

The worst fate that could be imagined for the East-Central European Soviet dependencies! To prolong the agony meant more years in decline with both consumption levels and wider understood living standards getting worse and worse. And with freedom prospects fading away into the future. I reacted to these proposals with a full page article in the very well known *Neue Zuercher Zeitung* daily, sharply criticizing the misguided and opportunistic "new Marshall Plan" ideas.[14]

However interesting were the debates on the shape of things to come, both internal and external, I was able from time to time to help in shaping the ongoing developments in the Polish (still communist) economy. But to explain how, requires the prior evaluation of the economic policies of the communist government of Prof. Zbigniew Messner in the second half of 1980s (until summer of

1988), as well as the economic ideas of the undisputed leader, General Jaruzelski. Communist strategy *vis-à-vis* Solidarity was also of importance in this respect.

Their economic policies were in fact a continuation of a failed centrally planned and administered economy, peppered with some injections of economic liberalization measures that did not fit into the general economic model prevailing from the beginning of the communist rule. Some spectacular decisions were taken, such as rejoining the International Monetary Fund and the World Bank, but these steps had little influence on institutional changes at home. Rather, the rejoining of international financial institutions was seen, by and large, in a similar manner as the opportunities to borrow money on financial markets that emerged in 1970s in the Gierek era.

The way the World Bank loans were to be used was to prop up the antiquated structure of the semi-stagnant Polish economy. For although official statistics showed substantial economic growth in the range of 4.0–5.0%, estimates by some economists from the Planning Institute pointed to meager growth in the range of at most 1.0–1.5%. Thus, Poland was a part of the general stagnation trend in the unreformed – and visibly unreformable – communist economic system (see Chapter 4 above, with its statistics showing near stagnation of annual economic growth rate at 1% or less in the Soviet Union since mid-1970s).

The projects to be financed by the World Bank and its offshoots were often senseless in economic terms as they were intended to strengthen the role of industries that should shrink considerably if the economy were to change into a much more efficient market-based one. With a string of World Bank experts visiting me more and more often, as an internationally recognized expert on communist economies, I saw my role in the process as somebody who tried to shoot down the nonsensical government proposals – at times with success. Convincing experts was much easier than convincing politicians, diplomats, and journalists. For the former, hypotheses, supported by numbers, mattered a lot.

To give an example, I once entertained two or three energy experts on the occasion of Poland's application for $250 million loan for coal mining expansion. I had little trouble convincing them that it was harmful, not helpful, to expand coal mining. Our hard coal was already costly to mine, given Poland's geology and very high labor costs. But even more important for my negative opinion were my earlier calculations.

I presented them diagrams and tables from my earlier study, showing that Poland just as other communist countries of the region used 2–3 times more energy per $1 of GDP produced. I said that if the authorities really wanted to introduce market economy reforms, as they proclaim they intend, then we should expect the demand for energy to fall to the level similar to that in middle-developed countries such as Portugal, Spain, or Ireland (and demand for energy indeed fell sharply with the beginning of post-communist transition in 1990). My arguments were clear for the energy experts; the project was shelved by the IBRD and never reappeared in negotiations with the Polish communist authorities.

Governmental thinking in the economic categories of the distorted world of the past was – I suspect – reinforced to some extent by the no less distorted thinking of the semi-dictator of the period. However strange it may seem, General Jaruzelski, even after his formal departure from the position of the President of independent Poland in December 1990, still maintained that "socialism was reformable." It could be saved if – and here he listed a number of (rather unrealistic) "ifs." "If we were able to offer the share of power [to the opposition - J.W.]. If we were more systematic in pursuing economic reforms... If we were able ...to include in the power structure some people from different political structures who were thinking differently. If we succeeded in doing so I think that socialism with a different face, maybe closer to the Swedish model (although with a larger share of the state economic sector), could survive the test of the times".[15]

It was obvious that Jaruzelski, in spite of his undoubtedly high intellectual calibre, was a prisoner of his personal history, and especially of his military career. Military is a hierarchical service and, with such a background, it was easier to believe in a centrally planned and administered economy than in the market arrangements with their self-correcting and equilibrating capabilities. The pipe-dream about Sweden – present also, *inter alia*, in Mikhail Gorbachev's thinking and pronouncements – was simply the result of economic ignorance on the one hand and the disbelief in the paramount importance of private ownership for economic efficiency on the other. Sweden, regardless of its oversized welfare state, had an enterprise sector that was 90% private.

Moreover, the attitude of government and a large part of the communist party (PZPR) apparatus toward the Solidarity opposition was both insincere and opportunistic. They hoped to use Solidarity's reentry into legal politics – and may be an offer of some minor positions in the government – as a measure of acceptance of the (clearly collapsing) political-economic system, not as a first step toward systemic change.

Such an unhelpful situation existed until late summer of 1988. The change of the Prime Minister was also a change of thinking about the future of Poland. Things could not go on as they did in the past. Not even as they did in late 1980s. Thus, general Jaruzelski and his generals in the government prevailed over the dissatisfied apparatchiks in the Central Committee of PZPR and extracted from them the (reluctant) acceptance for the Round Table talks with Solidarity. A part of the changed political attitude was also the ascendance of Mieczyslaw Rakowski to the top governmental position of the Prime Minister.

Rakowski was for decades regarded as a party liberal, distrusted by the die-hard communist majority, but his post-1988 behavior was marred by his attitude to the Solidarity opposition. He wanted an agreement -i-m-p-o-s-e-d upon Solidarity. He wanted his personal choices from among Solidarity leadership to be appointed to the governmental positions from the ranks of the opposition. Thus, his appointment and his later political behavior generated a lot of mistrust from the side of the opposition and slowed down the march toward the expected reconciliation, embodied in the announced Round Table talks.[16]

In contrast with the political problems he created, his economic choices were on balance sensible. First of all, his government abolished the remaining price controls of consumer goods. They applied to the most socially sensitive processed food products and agricultural produce. Price liberalization is always a difficult and contentious decision. Although beneficial in the longer run, it is resisted by the beneficiaries of such controls, as well as by those afraid of future uncertainties. Rakowski's government abolition of food price controls undoubtedly helped the forthcoming reformers that took over the reins with the choice of the first non-communist Prime Minister, Tadeusz Mazowiecki, in the summer of 1989.

An even better move in terms of the longer term effects was the appointment of a private sector entrepreneur, my former tennis partner (see Chapter 2), Mieczyslaw Wilczek, as a minister of industry, in communist times the most important economic portfolio. His appointment is an attractive political conversation piece. It just happened by chance that both Wilczek's private business firm and his personal retreat were located in the area where Mieczyslaw Rakowski had his (modest) country cottage. Wilczek often invited the future Prime Minister for evening drinks and inevitable conversation. Given my former tennis partner's outspokenness, he undoubtedly made a laughing stock of communist economy in numerous conversations with his guest.

When I met Wilczek after many years at the Polish Business Council, I asked him why he who was so critical of the communist nonsense decided to accept an offer to become a minister. It was the year 1992, already after the collapse of communism in Poland. My former tennis partner said that he just could not refuse the Rakowski's offer. After becoming a Prime Minister Rakowski came to Wilczek's retreat and put it in the following terms. You laughed at me and at the whole system for years – said Rakowski. – Now you have an opportunity to offer remedies and not only offer, but also introduce them into the economy. Somehow, said Wilczek, I thought I could not refuse the offer.

Wilczek is remembered most for his draft of the rules of the economic game, where for the first time since 1945 and the imposition of the communist rule in Poland, the regulatory regime was formulated in economic freedom terms. What is not expressly prohibited in economic activity – run the rule – is legal and can be pursued without fear of being prosecuted. "Wilczek's law," as the regulation was popularly called, is remembered fondly and referred to with nostalgia even today. Then, it gave a strong impulse to the rapid expansion of the new private firms whose number doubled in comparison with the year preceding the introduction of the rule.

It is worthwhile, however, to put the change in the government and general shift in the direction of the greater political and economic accommodation with the opposition in the international framework. I stressed often in these memoirs the need to look carefully at what was going on in the Soviet Union as an indicator of the things to come, more often than not constraints, but at times also opportunities. The second half of the 1980s was a period of the latter. The successive deaths of three octogenarian general secretaries of the Soviet Communist Party convinced the remaining *politbureau* members that they should appoint somebody who would be more than a stopgap, rule for longer period and, hopefully, be able to pull the country's economy – and not only an economy – from the stagnation and decline increasingly visible in 1980s (and taking place even earlier, see above, Chapters 3 and 4 above).

Mikhail Gorbachev was to be the answer.

His dual strategy of *glasnost* (transparency) and more vague *perestroika* (restructuring) was pursued nonetheless by fits and starts – and not without contradictions and tensions. Transparency was to be the recipe for the reinvigoration of the congealed Russian society, while restructuring was a more general (and, therefore, vague) prescription for everything associated with the economic system: necessary reforms, attempts to increase the innovative capacity of the economy (in order to close or at least reduce the growing technological gap *vis-a-vis* the United States), etc. Such aims suggested the far reaching relaxation of the existing rigid rules of the game and created a political environment markedly different from that of the *Brezhnev doctrine*, which dominated the period from late 1960s to mid-1980s.

It was dawning upon the Soviet leadership that the Soviet Union itself was in need of serious reforms. Tinkering was not an option anymore if serious improvements in economic performance were to be achieved! Moreover, attempts at such reforms should be allowed also in Soviet dependencies. With the center of the empire in stagnation and decline they could depend less and less on Soviet economic support in case of economic troubles and the threat of collapse.

What the Soviet leadership, even with Gorbachev at the helm, did not understand was the implications of the deep malaise and *mal*development experienced by the Soviet Union. As Jacek Szymanderski and I stressed in an article written in 1987 for *World Today*, a Royal Institute of International Affairs journal (and again published with a lag), the process of change forced upon the Soviet Union by the reality of stagnation and decline, and reinforced by President Reagan's challenge of technological military competition, was an internal process, driven by the self-destructive nature of the system. We were of the opinion that "its dynamics cannot be much influenced from outside. But there is a strong probability that, in the longer run, it is going to be carried much further than both its proponents and opponents … perceive at the moment."[17] And it was.

Both Rakowski-Wilczek reforms in Poland and Gorbachev reforms in the Soviet Union failed in the end. The popular explanation of failure was the verdict of "too little, too late." This was, however, a too simplistic explanation. Systemic reforms could not succeed where systemic -c-h-a-n-g-e was necessary. The communist economic system could not survive, to say nothing about winning the competition with market capitalism. The often stressed self-destructive nature of political/economic system of communism made the accomplishment of these goals completely out of reach for any reformers, however well-intentioned.

Doomed to fail or not, the political and economic changes in Poland inaugurated in 1988 were in line with what had been happening in the Soviet Union under Gorbachev's rule. Before the change in government, the search for a more efficient economic arrangement looked more dynamic in the Soviet Union than in Poland under the Messner government, a situation historically rather unusual in our part of the world.

While reforming the communist economic system ultimately failed, the new dynamics of Rakowski-Wilczek team gave another impulse to popular expectations of change. – C-h-a-n-g-e rather than reform hoped for by the ruling communists! Behind the scenes negotiations leading to the announced Round Table with the opposition were slow and difficult. Therefore, the much touted event took place – with loud propaganda fanfares – rather late, in early spring 1989.

The political part, or the political "table," was a real breakthrough in comparison with the orthodox communist past. Accepted changes in the political institutions (partly free elections to the parliament, 35% of contestable seats in what was to be its lower chamber, restoration of the senate with completely free elections, as well as the establishment of the powerful position of a President of the country) ensured that major changes were impossible without the consent of the opposition. At the same time the strong presidency with wide-ranging competencies – tacitly in the hands of the communists – were to ensure that changes would not be too drastic or introduced too rapidly. So, it was to be a "refolution" (a term coined by the Timothy Garton Ash), a hybrid, something in between reform and change.

By contrast, the economic part, or economic "table", was a real disaster. And, however strange it seemed for the economically uninitiated, the burden of guilt had to be put on the Solidarity side. I stressed a number of times in these memoirs the strange attachment of leftists in the Solidarity movement to the ideas of workers self-management, so damaging if ever turned into reality (as evidenced, *e.g.*, by the increasing problems of the Yugoslav economy during the 1980s).

Personally, I expected such an outcome, judging by the composition of the Solidarity team selected for the economic "table." Some time before the start of the Round Table talks, I got a phone call from a team leader appointed by Solidarity, an economist strong on theorizing and economic modeling, but weak on character (too well bred to be able to say "no" even to an obvious nonsense). He inquired whether I was willing to join the team. I answered with my own inquiry, asking who were the people chosen so far from "our" side. Upon learning the names, where maybe one or two were economists displaying a thorough knowledge of a normal capitalist market economic thinking, I politely refused. I felt I would be out of place with such a majority.

I still keep the note I made for the Solidarity leadership, evaluating the outcomes of the economic "table." Apart from the resistance of the communist side to far reaching market-oriented changes, even those introduced by Minister Wilczek's law on entrepreneurship (!!), there was little pressure applied by the Solidarity side for market-type solutions. Much energy on the Solidarity side was expended on ensuring the introduction of regulation that would impose workers self-management not only in state-owned firms, but also in private enterprises! Such regulation – I noted – would reduce efficiency even in the ownership sector of the economy, where such barriers did not exist so far. I concluded that "the Round Table did not deliver any positive institutional arrangements, as well as did not create incentives to create wealth."

Fortunately, the dynamics of change, initiated by the political decisions undertaken at the Round Table overwhelmed the developments in the months to come. The partly free elections that were agreed to take place on June 4, 1989, that is in two months after the conclusion of the Round Table talks, turned out to be the beginning of -r-e-a-l change. A Polish historian, Jerzy Eisler, was right when he wrote that "the Round Table appears to be not so much a first chapter of the Third Polish Republic (*Trzecia Rzeczpospolita*), but rather as the last chapter of the communist Poland (*PRL*). It is the historical June 4, 1989, elections that turned out to be the real breakthrough".[18]

The overwhelming victory of the Solidarity opposition that won everything that could be won, given the rules of the game (except for one Senate seat won by a politically unaffiliated entrepreneur), changed not only the dynamics, but also informally the rules of the game. In the non-political area, the nonsensical arrangements, like those undertaken at the economic "table," were simply forgotten. The new government-to-be of Tadeusz Mazowiecki had in practice a clean slate as far as choices in economic institution-building were concerned. But the Mazowiecki story belongs to the second part of these memoirs, while there is certainly a need to tie some loose ends associated with the end of communism in Poland and in a period of three years (1989–91) also elsewhere in our part of the world.

First, it is worthwhile to stress the longer term impact of the generalized stagnation and decline on the changing perspective of the seemingly victorious communists after the imposition of the martial law in Poland on December 13, 1981. Some months later, at the 1982 plenary meeting of the Central Committee, the introductory speech from the *politbureau* warned the rebellious youth, still battling the police on the streets during many demonstrations: "The youth must realize which route has been chosen by the Polish ship. It cannot travel against the course of history. Our country is not aiming to reach the Western shores."

While the majority of the educated stratum was thinking – and at times talking and writing – in terms of returning to the Western civilization, communists repeated the tired slogans of the historical destiny of socialism. Yet even as early as in the 1980s it was clear that socialism has nothing to offer in the ideological, political, and social terms, while its unreformability in the economic area clearly suggested the forthcoming defeat in competition with capitalism. As President Reagan called it bluntly in 1984, communist future was on the ash heap of history.

Even some longtime sympathizers agreed. In 1987 an economic historian Robert Heilbroner, a professor emeritus of the ideologically left leaning New School of Social Research in New York, concluded drily that the Soviet experiment was over. Socialism lost the inter-systemic competition, while capitalism won. There was no doubt about it anymore – he wrote.

> As usual a shortcut to understanding may be offered by the political cabaret. At about the same time as Prof. Heilbroner offered his verdict on Soviet socialism, Polish cabaret author and performer, Jan Pietrzak, said the following: "For decades we read the official slogan: 'The program of the party (that is PZPR, the communist party) is the program of the nation.' Why not the other way round?" Pietrzak comments suggested that the days of the communist party programs for Poland were clearly numbered…

There is no doubt about it that a long distance was travelled by the communist rulers in those seven years between the Jaruzelski-led *politbureau*'s refusal to take the Western course in 1982 and June 4, 1989, elections. It is at the time of the latter event that somebody wrote on the wall of the then renovated Bristol hotel in central Warsaw the terse verdict of history: "**PZPR – game over**."

Continuing with my considerations of loose ends, the following question should be formulated. Why so few experts on the communist system were able to predict the Soviet demise and – more generally – the end of communism as an alternative to the historical Western model of liberal democracy and market capitalism? After all, the *mane-thekel-fares* was clearly visible on the walls of communism at least throughout the 1980s (and for perceptive observers even as early as mid-to-late 1970s). I personally suspect that it was the result of *a dual failure*:

<> The failure of understanding the self-destructive nature of communist system's fundamentals; and

<> The failure of imagination concerning the probability of systemic change.

Let me first tackle the incompatibility of fundamentals with the basic principles of economics. At least since late 1950s the professional literature noted repeated distortions in the command economies and explained their existence in terms of the wrong structure of incentives under central planning. The next step was the discovery that these distortions reemerged again and again, regardless of pursued reforms. As a CIA expert, Gertrude Schroeder, noted, communist economies were on the (clearly unproductive) "treadmill of reforms." For little (if anything) useful happened in terms of an increase in efficiency of the communist economic system. On the contrary, distance between communism and the West in terms of efficiency began to increase at least since 1970s.

I am of the opinion that specialists in the field concentrated too much on explaining the distortions in terms of the analyzed system. Frankly, I have been as guilty in this respect as other analysts, although on occasions I stressed the self-destructive nature of the communist system itself. Too little thought was devoted to institutional fundamentals that must be solved by -a-n-y economic system to operate with a minimum of efficiency if it is to survive in the long run. A list of such fundamentals should be made and the inferiority of the command economy – in fact its outright inability to solve some crucial problems – exposed. I would suggest from my classical liberal perspective four such failures of communism:

1. THE FREEDOM PROBLEM. The tremendous centralization of power over the economy resulted in a near-total elimination of freedom in the pursuit of economic gains. The adverse economic consequences of suppressed individual initiative, innovativeness, entrepreneurship was tremendous. Moreover, they spilled over to other walks of social activities, with similarly damaging effects.

It is worth noting that centralization meant also the rule of a narrow, communist party-based elite, who made almost all economic decisions. Remember the lord Acton *dictum*: "Power corrupts and absolute power corrupts absolutely"? The remaining 90–95% of the educated population (and by the same token no smaller percentage of talents) were kept at a distance from the decision-making processes. The damage to the country's ability to create wealth was no less tremendous as a result.

2. THE INCENTIVES PROBLEM. It was discussed *ad nauseam* in the communist world and repeated attempts made to solve it, again and again. Remember the "treadmill of reforms"? And, yet, in spite of decades of reform measures, the incentives' problem remained basically unsolved until the collapse of the system. The logical conclusion should be drawn that it was not solved because under the institutional framework of communism it was simply unsolvable.

Criticism should concentrate on the fundamental weakness of the structure of incentives in the absence of private ownership. In contrast with private owners, managers of state firms had very much weaker incentives. The damage to efficiency was never remedied under the collectivist ownership regime. Moreover, without private owners in control, the linkages between effort and reward among workers were also severely weakened.

At both levels the problem was aggravated by institutional arrangements under central planning. A world of fiction was created with respect to incentives for managers and workers, who were paid by what they *tell* (report to their superiors) rather than by what they *sell* (pass the test of the market).

The foregoing evaluation of the freedom problem and the incentive problem suggests the extreme difficulties of the communist system in coping with the basics – the efficiency problem. But that was not the end of the story. Even assuming the (miraculous) appearance of communist leaders as uninterested in using power for evil purposes as Mohandas Gandhi, and as brilliant in problem solving as Leonardo da Vinci, who would presumably solve both freedom and incentives problems, the communist economic system would still be a sure loser in terms of comparative efficiency vis-à-vis the capitalist market economy. For the communist economic system would have to cope with two other, this time -u-n-s-o-l-v-a-b-l-e problems:

3. THE KNOWLEDGE PROBLEM. It is a neglected and little understood issue, concerning the nature of knowledge used by economic agents in their decisions. Theorists of the *growth of knowledge* school (Thomas Kuhn, Michael Polanyi, Friedrich Hayek) questioned the existence of knowledge that is purely

additive and communicable. These authors stressed that not all knowledge could be passed on, for example sent upwards to the planning hierarchy. Why?

The growth of knowledge school pointed out that a large part of knowledge used by owners and managers in their market decisions in the capitalist economy is *tacit*, non-communicable. It is the knowledge of time and place. They have it – so to say – in their fingertips. Taking dozens or hundreds of similar decisions they almost intuitively knew what they should do under given circumstances, but were often unable to explain – *ex ante* or even *ex post* – their inner decision-making processes. By contrast, in the highly centralized communist system such knowledge simply did not emerge. For there were no entrepreneurs and managers using their tacit knowledge there. Decisions were taken by planners at the very top.

Furthermore, in the capitalist economy that knowledge is encapsulated in market prices that guide entrepreneurs and managers. But under central planning prices are also set at the top. Therefore, planners can use only a communicable part of knowledge; the only tacit knowledge they can rely upon is their own. Moreover, the communicable part of knowledge is – as stressed earlier – doctored by lower level managers. Central planners' knowledge base is, thus, not only much narrower, but also distorted.

4. THE LEVEL OF RISK-TAKING PROBLEM. For most of human history decisions on economic issues, and associated risk taking, had been strictly centralized. It was true for hunter-gatherer tribes, with their councils of the elders taking the decisions, as well as for kings-gods in despotic empires. Feudal lords in their relations with the serfs were behaving in a similar manner. Since each decision affected whole tribes, kingdoms, or local communities, the risk of catastrophic outcome was reduced by repeating decisions undertaken in the past. An economic progress resulting from experimentation was minuscule as a result.

The commercial capitalism of the medieval Europe changed the inherently conservative pattern of risk-taking. With the growing role of the exchange economy, of money and prices, of commercial credit, of new products and processes pursued by individual merchants, artisans, and financiers, risk taking ceased to be a privilege of the rulers. It became decentralized and radically less expensive.

This decentralization of risk-taking accelerated sharply the rate of economic progress, giving Europe an advantage over other areas of the world. It was a major change in economic history. The communist economic system recentralized, however, the decision-making process – with often crippling consequences (major famines, ecological disasters on a very large scale, etc.). It is for that reason that a Nobel Prize winner Friedrich Hayek called communism a "reactionary" system, rooted in the conservative past.

Intuitively, I think, had Sovietologists, comparative systems' analysts, etc., hammered the basic inefficiency of the symbiotic, political-economic system of communism, the inevitability of failure would have become a household word much sooner. And with it also the idea that THE END may be nearer than it was thought decades after decades.

The failure of imagination I mentioned earlier is more esoteric and therefore less easy to explain in terms of theory and empirical evidence. The best way to approach the issue is, I suspect, to point to the reality. To stress people's resigned acceptance that such a monstrosity as communist Soviet Union had been and still was there for so long. Threatening. Unbudgeable. The idea that it could rapidly disintegrate seemed too daring. Maybe that particular failure of imagination is explainable in terms used by Arnold Toynbee, a historian of civilizations, who once remarked that empires rarely looked stronger, more imposing, than just before their fall.

How absent was such thinking among dissidents and opposition activists in those last moments of communism exemplifies a story from Bulgaria, told by my younger colleague, political scientist Ivan Krastev. With the departure of the communist leader, Todor Zhivkov, who ruled Bulgaria for decades, things began to change faster in that country. It was November 1990, the Bulgarian Round Table was in full swing (with some Polish advisers supporting the dissidents). After the talks, a group of dissidents had dinner at the university canteen. During heated conversations one of the older, better known dissidents, Zheliu Zhelev, turned to his younger colleagues in a visible attempt to shore up their courage. He said, "You are young and you certainly are going to live long enough to see the end of communism".[19]

Two facts should be pointed at with respect to the Zhelev's prophecy about the end of communism. First, it was made at the time, when a non-communist government in Poland operated for more than a year, the "velvet revolution" in Czechoslovakia swept away communism there, and a non-communist government was already in power after the mid-1990 elections in Hungary. And, to make the failure of imagination even more striking, Zheliu Zhelev, who promised his younger colleagues the end of communism in their lifetime, became the first non-communist president of Bulgaria just nine months later!!

Part II: Back to Western Civilization (Or Else…)

Chapter 6: Long Term Economic Trends and Transition to Freedom

I thought so even at the time and am even more convinced today that the popular perception of what happened in the communist world at the turn of 1980s and 1990s has largely been shaped by the – grossly misleading – journalistic and other similarly superficial accounts. Their authors exaggerated the importance of dramatic events and neglected the overwhelming role of long term trends (especially economic ones), as well as the role of distortionary nature of the system itself, in the collapse of communism. In other words it was a success of literary form over knowledge-based substance of systemic change.

Let me add right away that such a situation did not happen for the first time in the modern history of Western civilization. Similar victory was accorded to Charles Dickens and other literary figures describing the alleged sufferings of women and children under the "heartless" early capitalism. Dickensian story was that both women and children had been forced to work very hard and for long hours, with the resultant frequent deaths from exhaustion and associated illnesses. Demographic and economic statistics present, however, the radically different – and highly positive – picture. The period between 1760 and 1830 was the first long period ever in human history, when both population and living standards increased simultaneously (in fact, almost doubled!). Women and children indeed worked long hours, but thanks to the emerging opportunities for paid work (nonexistent before) were able to survive and live longer. This is, however, the knowledge-based perception of the few, not even the perception of the educated population today…

The same pattern of difference between the illusion and the reality emerged in late 1980s and early 1990s. Views of the punditocracy in the printed and electronic media on the collapse of communism centered on dramatic – and easily remembered – events. The Round Table between general Jaruzelski-led communists and the Walesa-led "Solidarity" attracted a lot of attention. So did the half-a-million people demonstration of the Czechs on Vaclavske Namesti in Prague in November 1989, inaugurating the "Velvet Revolution", with its first outcome of the purely communist Czech parliament electing the dissident Vaclav Havel the President of Czechoslovakia! Dramatic pictures of East Germans leaving their communist "paradise" via Hungary, whose (still communist!) government decided to open the border with the West, were also a part of that memory. It is worth adding that an important – and positive! – side effect of the decision of Hungarian authorities was the erosion of power of East German ruling communist *Betonkopfs* ("concrete heads", a German term for obstinate ignoramuses).

Another misleading part of the picture was a no less popular impression that Gorbachev genuinely wanted -s-y-s-t-e-m-i-c -c-h-a-n-g-e in Soviet Russia and East-Central Europe. And, in consequence, former Soviet dependencies owe him their political and economic freedom. Anti-Gorbachev Yanayev putsch strengthened that impression considerably.

The perception of changes that culminated in the 1989–91 period has been based on the memory of dramatic events, not on the understanding of long term economic, technological, demographic, and other trends. Some of these trends were global in nature, external to communist world, but nonetheless strongly affecting their economies (and communist rulers' political decisions). However their impact was barely noticed by analysts, like for example the long term decline in fuels and industrial minerals' prices in 1980s and 1990s.

Even more often long term trends emerged within the communist world itself. They were consequences of the operation of its self-destructive or – at a minimum – highly distortionary institutions. Growing impact of both types of trends began to be visible already since mid-1970s, but at the time the *mane-thekel-fares* on the walls of the communist system was noted only by a few.

The seeds of self-destruction were intrinsic to the system and largely economic in nature. For those, who would object to such economics-centered thinking and would stress, for example, that such a cruel, barbarian -p-o-l-i-t-i-c-a-l system as communism could not last long, my answer is as follows. The no less cruel – and barbarian – Assyrian empire lasted thousand years (with a brief interruption) because economic change was then so slow as to be imperceptible at the time. Therefore rulers usually knew how much output they could take away from the peasants, so that most of the latter would survive until the next harvest. They were rarely bothered by other, more complicated economic questions.

They did not even think about issues such as technological change that in 1970s and even more in 1980s pointed to the inability of the Soviets and their dependencies to reduce the technological gap with the West. In fact, the gap has been on the increase even if the Soviet Union spent on R&D a larger part of GDP than the United States. I proved the point myself in one of my early publications.[20] To repeat, the Soviet empire collapsed primarily because the system could not cope with economic change.

And yet, the global picture was misleading in 1970s and 1980s. In early to mid-1970s it was America that seemed to have been exhausted, morally and economically, after the Vietnam debacle. The Soviet Union and its empire looked stronger than ever (as I remarked earlier, Toynbee had been right in stressing that empires appear strongest just before their fall!).

How the rot began? At the beginning, without being noticed as a problem for the Soviet world, global shock waves were generated in early 1970s by the first oil crisis. Oil price explosion (as well as that of other mineral resources) exacerbated a long standing weakness of communist economies, namely the fact that they used 2–3 times more of basic resources (energy, steel, cement, etc.) to produce the same volume of output than normal, *i.e.* capitalist market economies. The oil price jumps became immediately a serious problem for communist importers of fossil fuels, and in a few years also for their producer and exporter – the Soviet Union itself.

Yegor Gaidar, an economist and for a very short period the Prime Minister of Russia's only systemic change-oriented government, noted in his 1999 book that Brezhnev and his *politbureau* decided in early 1970s to use the windfall profits from exports of oil and (then much smaller) profits from exports of gas to shore up the existing spending patterns of increased military expenditures and increased imports of consumer staples in order to at least maintain the living standards of the population. Such decisions took place – Gaidar pointed out – because the economy already exhausted its potential for further economic growth under the wasteful command economy regime and windfall profits were treated by the rulers as an alternative to economic growth as a source of growing wealth.[21]

For years it became increasingly obvious that the communist pattern of economic performance could not last forever. But a shift to a more efficient system required systemic change, both political and economic. Since there was no support for such a daring move, growth should be expected to decline. And it did (sharply), although doctored official figures did not reveal the depth of the real fall in economic growth rates.

As I stressed already in early 1980s, yet another feature of the Soviet system became increasingly costly at about the same time. Since late 1960s, or early 1970s at the latest, a shift in the economic growth engine role occurred throughout the world economy, but primarily in the developed Western economies. Industries based on the economy of scale were pushed aside by those based on flexibility, entrepreneurship and innovation. I stressed that the change in question proverbially pulled the rug from under central planning. Dramatically higher demands for smooth management of complex coordination processes became too great a burden for the slow-moving, inefficient planning hierarchy. Signs of strain multiplied.

Of course, little would have happened if the Soviet empire decided to continue producing, symbolically speaking, rails and nails. But they in all their ignorant arrogance (God bless it!) wanted to "catch up with and surpass" the West! In consequence the Soviet economic growth slowed down to 0–1% rate. Moreover, the rot spread far beyond the economy.

It is under such circumstances that the Soviet Union was challenged by its *Nemesis*: Ronald Reagan. President Reagan had an excellent team of advisers, who (fortunately for those living under communism!) did not belong to the usual bunch of left leaning sympathizers with the socialist ideas. These advisers stressed the rapidly deteriorating economic and other conditions in the Soviet Union and its growing lag vis-a-vis the West. They pointed out that the thrust of American policy toward the Soviets should be based on the large scale technological challenge, primarily in the military area. Such challenge would soon reveal all the weaknesses of the communist economic machinery that needed more and more resources to produce less and less of sophisticated products (military, as well as non-military).

I am sure that it is to President Reagan and his advisers that we owe the choice of Mikhail Gorbachev first as a *Gensek* (the general secretary of the Communist Party of the Soviet Union), and later as a Soviet President. Trying to respond to the Reagan's challenge, the octogenarians on the Soviet *Politbureau* realized that they need somebody who would stay in power long enough to be able to radically modernize the Soviet economy – even at a high cost (excluding, however, systemic change!). But neither the octogenarians, nor Gorbachev himself realized that an adopted economic/technological strategy of simultaneous *perestroika* (restructuring) and *uskoreniye* (acceleration) was doomed to fail.

Both aims cannot be pursued at the same time. Figuratively speaking, if the car driver puts his foot on an accelerator and tries simultaneously to turn the car to the left or right, the crash is almost inevitable. Such expectations were all the more justified in the case of the creaking Soviet economic machinery. And, indeed, the machinery fell to pieces, very much like inspector Clouzot's car in the final scene of the one of most popular films in the "Pink Panther'" series…

It is within such a framework of accelerated decline that we should consider Gorbachev's strategic thinking and his specific decisions taken in late 1980s. The abandonment of the Brezhnev Doctrine was a part and parcel of the reassessment of the Soviet reality. The new *Gensek* realized that the much weakened Soviet Union did not possess enough resources needed to shore up not only the Soviet Union itself, but also decaying Soviet dependencies. In consequence, he willy-nilly encouraged them to pursue their own reforms, even the far reaching ones. As I stressed in Part I of these memoirs, neither Gorbachev, nor the communist reformers in declining Soviet dependencies, realized at the beginning that at the end of the day the outcome of their efforts would not be some – even far-reaching – reforms of the existing communist system, but inevitably a systemic -c-h-a-n-g-e.

Gorbachev's contribution to the momentous developments in the 1989–91 period were primarily indirect. Domestically, the political drift of *glasnost* (transparency) created the opportunities for the emergence of various political groups demanding more freedom. It is primarily under such circumstances that Boris Yeltsin emerged as a leader of Russia's reformers. Domestically Gorbachev's economic blunders in simultaneously pursuing restructuring and acceleration turned stagnation into an accelerating decline. Internationally, as far as Soviet dependencies were concerned, Gorbachev's inept fumblings did not create strong, reform-oriented groups within the communist *politbureaus* in more orthodox dependencies, but – fortunately – undermined the position of Czechoslovak, East German, and Bulgarian *Betonkopfs* in their respective countries.

These were beneficial, but -u-n-i-n-t-e-n-d-e-d consequences of Mikhail Gorbachev's hectic, often ill-thought, attempts to solve multiple grave problems, long besetting his country and those of Soviet empire. The fall of the Yanayev's putsch and the emergence of Yeltsin as a political figure number one, ready to offer freedom to all who declared the willingness to embrace it, contributed more decisively to the collapse and dissolution of the Soviet Union than any acts of commission and omission taken by Gorbachev. Moreover, Yeltsin's contribution was an -i-n-t-e-n-d-e-d consequence, while that of Gorbachev's was not only unintended, but also unwanted by the latter. After all, he wanted to create less oppressive political system and more efficient economic system, but a socialist one nonetheless…

Summing up, we may point to three levels of impact upon the collapse of the communist system in the Soviet Union and its dependencies. The first, and the strongest, was what I stress throughout my numerous books and articles, as well as underline again and again in these memoirs, namely the self-destructive nature of the economic system (symbiotically tied with the political system). The second was the deliberate strategic technological challenge posed by Reagan administration that exposed all the weaknesses of the creaking Soviet economic machinery. This challenge and Gorbachev's reaction to the challenge greatly accelerated the timing of the Soviet downfall.

What I am going to stress now is not well received in East-Central Europe, especially in Poland. The exaggerated feeling of the importance of "Solidarity"-related developments result often in sharp criticism of my ranking of the determinants of systemic change. And, yet, I would insist that it is only at a third level – in terms of the strength of impact of these determinants – that we may rank the influence of developments within Poland, Czechoslovakia, and Hungary and, somewhat later, in the remaining East-Central European Soviet dependencies.

The rapidly declining Soviet economy and Gorbachev's vacillations with respect to direction, composition, and speed of intended changes created an encouraging environment both for reformers and "system changers" in East-Central-Europe to tackle system specific distortions – or the system itself. And this is what had been happening from late spring of 1989.

In Poland there was a shift away from the (often confused or downright nonsensical) economic ideas prevailing at the Polish Roundtable to those that were to dominate in the forthcoming Solidarity movement-led government. The process started with the appointment of the first non-communist Prime Minister since World War II in August 1989 and ended with the declaration of the return to economic normalcy, that is to the model of the Western market economy, in October of the same year.

But that was only the beginning. Hungarians and Czechs followed very quickly in Poland's footsteps as far as the direction of change was concerned. Those convinced on the need for systemic change took the advantage of the opening opportunities. Contacts between the ruling communists in Hungary and conservative or liberal dissidents intensified and the contours of the forthcoming institutional, political and economic, change were relatively quickly agreed upon.

The intellectual ferment started a few years earlier, though. A friend of mine, Dr. Zoltan Krasznai (mentioned already in Part I, Chapter 4) told me the story of a group of young intellectuals, of which I assume he was a part, that appealed to an older generation intellectual *cum* political authority, Jozsef Antall (in the not too distant future the first Prime Minister of independent Hungary) to initiate and lead a debate on a general theme: "What the world and Hungary will look like -a-f-t-e-r communism?".

It is worth stressing at this point the existence of a network of contacts between academics (including reformers and "system changers") from these three countries, and to a smaller extent reaching beyond the above trio. It should be stressed again and again that academics played an irreplaceable role in early post-communist transition (their role was also crucial under late, declining communism – see Part I of these memoirs). First of all many dissident academics and other intellectuals knew each other from communist times, personally or from their writings.

But to explain the importance of international academic contacts for the spread of ideas of reform and change, I should make a step backward and explain first their indispensable -i-n-t-e-r-n-a-l role in transition. They were often the only ones who knew – at least at the level of theory – how the capitalist market operated in the West, knew the generalities and details of the regulatory regimes in various walks of social life – from the liberal-democratic constitutional rules to the regime of private property rights in the economy. Under the more stable democracy, they would have largely confined themselves to the advisory roles. However, with no knowledgeable opposition politicians able to fulfill these demanding roles, academics – and other intellectuals – were forced by history to put on politicians' shoes.

Just look at the composition of the first Polish non-communist government. The Prime Minister was a journalist, writing for the catholic intellectual journals. His chief adviser on economic affairs, Waldemar Kuczynski, was an economist and economic journalist, an author of a popular book "*After the Great Leap Forward*" (*Po wielkim skoku*) published in late 1970s as an underground *samizdat* edition. He was also Mazowiecki's liaison with the Deputy Prime Minister for Economic Affairs and Finance Minister, Dr. Balcerowicz, a professor at the then Main School of Planning and Statistics (now Warsaw School of Commerce). Economic portfolios were largely filled with academics. Industry portfolio was first held by a professor of management and next year by a professor of economics at the same school, Dr. Henryka Bochniarz (later a very successful businesswoman and a head of the most influential organization representing the emerging private sector). A Minister of Foreign Trade was a researcher from the Institute of Economics of the Polish Academy of Science. And the first Minister for Foreign Affairs was a professor of international law at the Poznan University. In early 1990s I often met my academic colleagues in ministerial and other high ranking positions in East-Central European governments.

Intellectuals played, as I stressed, various roles. Let me give a few examples from my personal history. I had quite a few friends and colleagues in Hungary with whom I discussed informally over two decades, since early 1970s, various aspects of communist economics and economic policy making. In mid-1980s, with the increasingly obvious signs of the crisis, these discussions intensified – and at times also formalized. We began discussing issues openly, at conferences, rather than informally, over a cup of excellent Hungarian coffee.

Certain conferences clearly had a hidden political agenda. Some Hungarian reformers – reformers, not believers in the necessity of systemic change – used them, for example, to exert pressure on communist leadership in Hungary. One of such reformers, Dr. Kalman Pecsi, explained honestly why I was repeatedly invited to make speeches at subsequent international conferences in 1987 and 1988.

> You know, he said to another friend of mine, Prof. Andrzej Brzeski from the University of California, Davis, your friend Jan Winiecki's views are very useful for our reform debates. His radical, free market-oriented philosophy is well known and after these conferences I give my political interlocutors the following warning: "If you do not introduce far reaching market *reforms* we suggest, the next wave will consist of economists like

> Winiecki who tell the audience that we should build at the main square a large concrete ass, smash all the central planning-related institutions against it and start building the capitalist market in our country from the scratch"...

So, in that case I was clearly positioned as a bugbear to frighten communist politicians into action, while on some other occasions – in Hungary and elsewhere – my writings were rather seen as a source of intellectual inspiration.

The relations with the Czechs were less public than those with Hungarians, given the fact that economists there, were (like everybody else) under a tighter communist leash before the Velvet Revolution. But even there was some vague recognition within the communist establishment that it would be impossible to continue without at least changes in the economic system.

> I remember coming back from the US with my wife in early May 1989. Incidentally, it was my first visit to the West we could enjoy together (earlier she was refused a passport by the communist authorities). We were flying the Czech airline CSA, going to and coming back from New York via Prague. On the way back we sat next to a Czech lady living in the US who came to visit relatives in her native country. After having landed, she pointed out through the window at the military officers in uniforms, with dogs on a leash, circling around the plane and remarked that in contrast to Poland nothing seems to change here.
>
> I answered that this was only a surface view, while in reality changes were under way. And added that when she would come to Prague next year the communist system would be over. In fact, I overestimated rather than underestimated the strength of the *status quo*! We talked on the plane in early May, while in November 1989 the Velvet Revolution began. So communism was over not in a year, but in half a year's time...

That changes were under way I sensed also from my earlier contacts with the Czechs. During the stopover in Prague on the way to the US I was invited to talk at the seminar in the newly established Institute of Forecasting (of the Czechoslovak Academy of Science), where most reform or systemic change oriented economists were, intentionally, grouped at the time.

I met there – apart from the already known Vaclav Klaus, later the Prime Minister and later still the President of the Czech Republic (after the velvet separation between Czechia and Slovakia) – also other economists, whose destiny was to play important roles in the Czech economy and politics. Thus, I met there Dr. Valtr Komarek, the director of the institute in question and soon the Deputy Prime Minister for economic affairs, Prof. Karel Dyba, soon the minister for industry, Dr. Vladimir Dlouhy, soon the minister for foreign trade, as well as Dr. Josef Zieleniec (also an economist, soon to be the minister for foreign affairs and later still the President of the Czech Parliament). I met also Dr Thomas Jezek, who in communist times translated some important works of a Nobel

Prize winner Friedrich Hayek and in the free Czechoslovakia became the first head of the privatization agency.

But let us go back to Polish developments. Some weeks after the creation of the first non-communist government by Tadeusz Mazowiecki, a team, headed by Prof. Janusz Beksiak, was established by the parliamentary representation of "Solidarity" movement to prepare the program of macroeconomic stabilization and systemic change, where I became one of the four full time members of the team and the principal author of the stabilization part of the program.

With the appointment of Prof. Leszek Balcerowicz as a Deputy Prime Minister for economic affairs (and additionally a Minister of Finance) both political and intellectual activities accelerated. Leszek delegated his two close collaborators, Prof. Marek Dabrowski, already appointed an acting head of the Finance Ministry, and Stefan Kawalec, also in an important position of the Director General of the said ministry, to participate in the deliberations of the Beksiak-led team and its invited experts. Thus, although original intentions in the parliamentary fraction of Solidarity were somewhat different, close contacts were established between new, non-communist economic policy makers in the government and researchers working on the details of the forthcoming change. We worked hard, seven days a week, mornings and afternoons, and delivered the detailed outline of the program after barely a month, in late September 1989.

The government program – in much less detail, of course – was presented to the public about two weeks later, in mid-October. In eight pages of the *Rzeczpospolita* daily, the government stressed the need to return to the proven recipe of the market economy institutions of the West. It also underlined – and very rightly so! – that the success of systemic change depends also on stabilizing the macroeconomic conditions of the Polish economy (at that time deeply unbalanced, with accelerating price changes approaching hyperinflation).

Our own outline of a program was published later also in English.[22] We presented therein the necessary steps needed to establish macroeconomic stability and estimated the time needed to reach that stage to be about 26 months. Although we expected certain measures to be taken right away, beginning in November 1989, they were in fact introduced only with two months' lag in January 1990. But we were right, as far as our estimate of the period needed to achieve stabilization was concerned. The correctional recession (eliminating the "pure socialist production", unneeded under the normal economic system) lasted from January 1990 to March 1992 and economic growth appeared a month later, in April of the latter year, while inflation continued to subside.

We stressed the importance of stabilization not only for economic growth, but also – if not primarily - for the expansion of the new, fast growing private sector. The owners-entrepreneurs, as well as those considering to become entrepreneurs, would be much encouraged to take such steps under the conditions of stabilizing prices and more stable value of domestic currency.

We encountered certain problems, however, in evaluating the macroeconomic situation of the Polish economy, because it turned out that the Ministry of Finance before being taken over by a new Balcerowicz-led team displayed a rather weak competence in collecting and evaluating fiscal statistics. It was unable, for example, to calculate the size of budget deficit in the face of near-hyperinflation in the second half of 1989. We made, therefore, our own estimates and expected it to approach 7% GDP for the whole year. And, again, we were very close to the final figure (which we learned with a very long lag, in late 1991 or even early 1992).

In late September 1989 came to Warsaw Vaclav Klaus, who at that time did not yet held any official position beyond that of a researcher in the Forecasting Institute, and conducted a series of conversations with some members of the new economic team in the Finance Ministry, as well as with numerous academic economists, including myself. He told me, he was a bit puzzled by the limited interest of some of his hosts with respect to stabilization-related issues. Macroeconomist by training, Vaclav Klaus was keenly aware of the crucial role of stabilization, even if he understood the paramount importance of liberalization and privatization for systemic change. Besides, we should keep in mind that Czechoslovakia did not suffer from near-hyperinflation like Poland, or even from year after year double digit inflation like Hungary, and most Czech economists I met, not only Klaus, were very cautious not to fall into the – destabilizing – inflation trap. They understood that the price liberalization at the start of transition is absolutely necessary to reveal the relative prices in the otherwise distorted economy and accepted the resultant correctional inflation. But they believed that the adjustment period should be as short as possible to avoid the prolonged high inflation episode. To achieve that aim, they stressed the importance of the policy of macroeconomic restraint.

But let me, again, return to Polish transition developments. Both the detailed outline of the Janusz Beksiak-led team, and the official economic program of the government under Leszek Balcerowicz displayed a well recognized structure that I called in my later articles and books *the Holy Trinity of Transition*, composed of stabilization part, liberalization part, and privatization part (as well as the list of the needed basic market institutions to be reestablished or established to create a fully fledged market economy).

The government program had to be translated into a set of parliamentary regulations to be passed before January 1, 1990. It differed, however, in one important respect from the program of the Beksiak-led team, thanks to the bold idea of a well known Harvard economist, Jeffrey Sachs. Nearly everywhere in stabilization *cum* liberalization programs applied earlier in less developed countries, external liberalization (exchange rate and foreign trade regimes) was seen as a second step in the liberalization process. Domestic liberalization was to start right at the beginning, while external liberalization was to follow after a period. Such ideas were transferred to post-communist transition programs.

I must confess that even in my personal, otherwise bold, draft of the transition program that I presented in a nutshell in *Financial Times* at the beginning of 1989,[23] I envisaged the 12–18 month lag between domestic price liberalization and external liberalization. But Jeff convincingly argued that it makes more sense to subject the firms and individuals to just o n e price liberalization shock rather than two in a row. Interestingly, once Polish program adopted an internal and external price liberalization in one step, Hungarians and Czechs did the same. Hungarians started their program in mid-1990, while the Czechoslovak program started in earnest in January 1991.

Apart from common problems of transition back to the capitalist market economy, each country had its own specific issues to deal with. For a very deeply unbalanced economy such as Poland, the stabilization and rebuilding of trust in the national currency was of great importance. Soon, however, it turned out that for some, also country specific, reasons Poland faced more obstacles to privatization than other leading transition countries (more about it later in Chapter 9).

Hungary tinkered with its command economy since mid-1950s and in some respects was ahead of the post-communist pack in terms of institutional change. Some needed reforms were already in place, sometimes made years earlier, and although they did not bring about expected benefits under central planning, the systemic change was easier with institutions already in place (even if distorted or unused under the old regime…).

However, after the mid-1990 free elections, the government of Prime Minister Jozsef Antall and the ruling conservative coalition became obsessed by an idea that Hungarians suffered so much that they should be shielded at any cost from consequences of transition. I remember my conversations with some high ranking economists, like Professor Bela Kadar, a minister in the first democratic Hungarian government of Jozsef Antall, repeating the mantra at various conferences.

Antall's government failed in that task for obvious reasons. Major economic changes cannot be cocooned and their impact disconnected from the society! The consequences of trying were very serious, however. Within the time span of four years, public – mainly welfare – expenditures reached in Hungary the Swedish level, that is exceeded 60% GDP(!), causing major macroeconomic crisis, with both budget deficit and current account deficit reaching the 10% GDP level!

Swedish social democrats could afford to continue with such high level of public expenditures for two decades before the weight of welfare expenditures reached crisis proportions in early 1990s. After all, the Swedish economy enjoyed the healthy capitalist economic development for almost a century. Hungary's conservatives could -n-o-t, because they were afflicted by almost half a century of the *un*healthy, communist economic *mal*development. The foregoing difference meant that such expansion could in Hungary last a few years at best, before producing imbalances of crisis proportions…

In Czechoslovakia they had two separate problems. First, there was a rift between cautious reformers who wanted to move forward only slowly (the "gradualists" led by Dr. Valtr Komarek) and those who preferred the strategy of rapid systemic change (those, like Vaclav Klaus, preferring the "big bang", "fast track", or "shock therapy" approach, as they were called at the time). A large part of 1990 was spent on such indecisive discussions. The foregoing battle for the strategy to be pursued by the government was won by the latter group led by Vaclav Klaus who, for example, already in December 1989 promised Czechs and Slovaks a major privatization program. As he stressed a quarter of a century later, "we explicitly and very early proclaimed that we wanted capitalism" to be reestablished.[24]

Certainly, nothing like that – the declaration of the institutional preference for capitalism – could Czechs and Slovaks hear from Dr. Komarek. He learned his economics in Moscow in Stalinist 1950s and at that time one could learn a lot in Moscow, but the last thing was good economics! His career had yet another interesting twist, namely he was for a few years an economic adviser to Che Guevara(!). Some of my Czech friends suspected that – given Komarek's Moscow connection – he was delegated there by the KGB.

The choice of Komarek as a head of the Institute of Forecasting – an intellectual reform center created by the communist Czechoslovak authorities in late 1980s – and later even as a deputy Prime Minister for economic affairs in the first post-communist government was suggestive about the extent of changes envisaged by representatives of the old order. Fortunately, the forces of the new – emerging – order prevailed during the 1990 and Klaus superseded Komarek as a Deputy Prime Minister in charge of economic transition issues. In consequence, the January 1991 comprehensive program of systemic change was a classical "big bang" program prepared under the leadership of the former.

The second problem was of a different kind. There was a visible difference in the willingness to consistently pursue transition to the capitalist market between Czech and Slovak elites, with the latter much less ready to move forward at a rapid pace. Clearly, some important seeds of the future "velvet separation" were sown at exactly that time…

Readers undoubtedly noted that I have been referring to transition – or pre-transition – developments in three countries only, but it is these three countries that became the early leaders in systemic change (I use the terms: "transition", "transformation" and "systemic change" interchangeably). Bulgaria and Romania differed from Poland, Hungary, and Czechoslovakia, each in its own way, with the former zig-zagging on transition and the latter just faking in 1990s the transition and trying to preserve as much as possible the past political and economic power structure (dictatorship without the old dictator, sacrificed by his close collaborators in late 1989…).

Communist East Germany differed from the foregoing countries in yet another way. East Germans since 1990 were simply being integrated into the well working institutions of the Federal Republic of Germany. So, instead of establishing or reestablishing the institutions of the market, they simply had to learn how the smoothly working capitalist market economy operates. It was not an easy task, either, but certainly much easier than learning-by-doing about the market economy, taking place during the process of change in other post-communist countries…

I had some limited intellectual contacts also with Bulgarians and Romanians; one lady, a Professor and later a Minister of External Economic Relations in Bulgarian government, even declared, when we met in London in the European Bank for Reconstruction and Development in early 1991, that she was very much my fan and "read almost everything I wrote on communist economies and on transition".

By contrast, neither in communist times, nor in early transition I was able to establish intellectually fruitful relations with East Germans. In fact, in the first half of 1990s my contacts concerning transition in East Germany were exclusively with West German academics and journalists. The place in Germany I visited most often was then Kiel *Institut fuer Weltwirtschaft*, where I participated in a series of intellectually highly stimulating conferences on transition between 1989 and 1993 (as well as published a number of important papers and a book on privatization in comparative perspective).[25] My contacts with East Germans started, in fact, only in late 1992, when I won the competition for professorship and chair at the European University-Viadrina, reestablished in Frankfurt an-der-Oder after almost two centuries, and joined the faculty of economics and management in mid-1994.

And then it turned out why I did not succeed in establishing intellectually fruitful relationship with economists from communist East Germany. Simply there were very few high class theorists there. At the Department of Economics and Management there was only o-n-e economist from East Germany; the rest came from West Germany or, like me, from elsewhere. And the lone economist was teaching stat/math-related subjects. And let me add that during the only visit to communist part of Germany in 1975 I did not find any economist I could talk sensibly (and frankly) on economic theory and policy…

I have left out so far my personal interactions with academics from the Soviet Union. The latter country belonged, however, to a different category, because except for a period lasting less than a year one could hardly call Russia, Soviet or post-Soviet, even a candidate to the role of a transition leader. Intellectual contacts with Russian reformers exploded in the 1987–90 period, when the traditional Soviet policy on attendance of academics in international conferences changed. Before it was only the limited number of old, communist party-trusted fogeys, who were allowed to travel abroad and participate in such conferences. The liberalization under the banner of *glasnost* changed all that and in the 1987 conference in Gyor in Hungary I met a group of reform-minded young scholars (later it turned out that some, including Yegor Gaidar, were in fact systemic change-minded).

Serious intellectual interaction began from which I benefited very much. For those "young Turks" filled certain gaps in my understanding of the Russian reality. The first concerned a relatively very weak position of what they called "*zapadniki*", that is those who believed that the future of Russia is to follow the path taken (centuries earlier) by the West. Even at the height of popularity of the Western path, public opinion polls gave that orientation at most 15–20% of the electoral preferences. Thus, to move the economic system in the direction of the private ownership-based market economy, Russian *zapadniki* had to find allies, some of them not necessarily very attractive ones.

The second problem was not systemic preferences but personal views and concerned e-n-v-y as an obstacle to transition (primarily to privatization). Quite a few of these young Turks stressed that the level of envy, combined with distrust, has reached so great intensity as to be a very serious obstacle to smooth operation of an envisaged private property rights regime. Two factors combined to create such a – systemically harmful – effect.

One was well known to me, given the insightful and extremely well written trilogy by Richard Pipes. In the first volume of that trilogy[26] Pipes stressed the sharp difference between Russia and the West in terms of the acceptance of private property as the economic basis of society. In the latter it was the tradition going back to ancient Greece, more than two thousand years old; in the former private property became law only in the second half of XVIII century, during the rule of Catherine the Great, and even then it did not cover all property (e.g. that of Russian peasants).

The institutional difference was much amplified by the (undoubtedly justified) deep feeling of injustice felt by ordinary Russians who associated individual riches, property-based or other, with the privileged position of the ruling stratum, whether under the Tsars or under communism. In most cases their perception reflected the brutal reality. Under the circumstances, private farming and private industrial or service firms were viewed with envious suspicion – and in the future were often an object of sabotage. The climate for private property, pointed out my Russian colleagues, was a highly unpropitious one.

Having sketched an intellectual landscape from my personal perspective, the next step – I think – should be to consider the options we faced, while liberating ourselves from the shackles of political and economic system of communism. Whether elites preferred more limited reforms or far-reaching changes, they faced everywhere, as I stressed in my lectures at the time, three fundamental issues:

<> What to change first, the political or the economic system?
<> Where to go, or what economic system to choose?
and
<> How to get from here to there, or what path of transition to choose?

In the preface to my book *Resistance to Change in the Soviet Economic System*, that was written in late 1980s, but published only after the start of transition[27] I underlined the importance of -p-o-l-i-t-i-c-a-l -c-h-a-n-g-e. Given the totalitarian nature of the communist system, any serious economic change could occur only after the decisive break with the communist monopoly of power. And this was what in fact happened in East-Central Europe. The early transition leadership of Poland, Hungary, and Czechoslovakia was made possible by an earlier dismantling of communist political system.

Above, I wrote extensively about Poland. Elsewhere, for example in Hungary, the change was as deep as in Poland – if not deeper at the start. The communist party not only accepted *ex ante* the prospect of relinquishing its power after the agreed elections, but also – conveniently – split into two before the election date. Thus, already before mid-1990 elections, Hungarian voters faced a (much larger) social-democratic party and a (markedly smaller) more orthodox communist one. Of, course the menu of parties participating in the first democratic elections was much richer, including also parties of liberal or conservative persuasion.

One might presume that the most animated object of political debate at the time would be the second fundamental issue, namely what economic system to choose. Readers following that train of thought would be disappointed, however.

The elites and societies at large faced a range of options:

<> The return to the (forcibly) abandoned capitalist market economy;
<> The choice of some, more or less unspecified, "third way" between capitalism and socialism;

or

<> Market socialism, that is Lange-Lerner-Dickinson model of "auctioneer"-type system, with state-owned firms bidding to obtain orders for output from the center (a pre-WWII utopia).

However, the elites and most of the politically active population (the one taking part in elections) overwhelmingly chose the return to market capitalism. The Hungarian and Czech elections revealed these preferences in no uncertain way, while in the trend-setting Poland, with its – only partly free – elections of June 4, 1989, the picture was less clear-cut. There was little doubt about the majority of the elite's preferences, while preferences of the politically active part of the population were difficult to fathom. In fact, these preferences were a web of contradictions. *Many Poles wanted capitalism in the shops, but preferred socialism in the factories they worked. In fact, such thinking was quite popular also elsewhere in East-Central Europe*. More about it in the chapters below.

The choices made in the three East-Central European countries considered here were made easier by what Germans call *der Zeitgeist* – the spirit of the times – that is the triumphant return of classical liberal economic ideas throughout the world that began in 1980s and lasted roughly until the middle of the past decade.

Such choices were most bitterly disappointing for Czechoslovak believers in "socialism with human face", who were forced to emigrate after the 1968 Soviet invasion, but returned *en masse* to their native country before 1990 elections. They were, however, cold-shouldered by the population, not only on the right side of the political scene,[28] but also on the left. The new Social Democratic party also rejected the economic institutions of state ownership assumed in such a philosophy.

Everywhere, however, I noted visible hankering of some, often politically very important, members of the elites after the "Swedish model". Economically undereducated and knowing little of the Western world, they gave the "Swedish model" a very specific meaning. For people like "*Gensek*" Gorbachev or general Jaruzelski, the "Swedish model" was also something of an escape route from the admittance of the inevitable return to the capitalist market as the only sensible choice. So, "Swedish model" was a way of dissociating themselves from such full acceptance of capitalism – hook, line, and sinker. Instead, they could muse about distinctive differences in the size of the public sector, or in the share of public expenditures in GDP and pretend that, after all, they opted for a compromise, some "third way" between capitalism and socialism.

The "third way" was not particularly popular, at the time, though. A nail in the coffin of sort was delivered by Vaclav Klaus, not only a good economist and (as it turned out) shrewd politician, but also a combative polemist. His saying that "the 'Third Way' leads straight to the 'Fourth World'" reverberated in many debates on transition.

The remaining issue to be decided at the start to transition – how to get from here to there – is going to be considered at greater length in the next chapter. For it should be considered within the framework of the debates not only on transition's course, but also its early effects, which sharply increased pressure on both policy makers and intellectual supporters of systemic change. In other words it should be considered within the rapidly emerging doubts, severe criticism of both transition theory and policy making practice, a well as increasingly insistent calls to change the course…

Chapter 7: Vanishing Output and Intellectual Invasion of Doubting Thomases

On January 1, 1990, Polish program of macroeconomic stabilization and systemic change became operational, the first such program on the path "from Marx to market". By the way, this is how I called the program in the conversation with a Nobel Prize laureate in economics, Milton Friedman, just before his public lecture in Warsaw in late 1989, which I had the privilege to chair. And it is worth reminding that at the time the Polish program was -t-h-e -o-n-e -a-n-d -o-n-l-y reference point to all discussions on the merits (and presumably also demerits) of post-communist transition.

The first weeks of January were very tense and the kind of information that was flowing from the market was discouraging to many observers. Prices, also those of necessities – bread, butter, cheese, eggs, meat, sugar, etc. – were rising very fast. The governmental *ex-ante* expectations written into its program (frankly: *guesstimates*, as effects of price liberalization after 40 years of severe price distortions could not be estimated with any precision!) was 45% rise in January alone. In fact, consumer price index rose in January by 78%.

Few expected at the time that even in the least economically unbalanced communist economy of Czechoslovakia consumer price increase in the first year of their transition, that is 1991, was to exceed 50% *per annum*! In the absence of either in-depth analysis or reference to other similar programs, the massive public shock and disappointment, plus increased intellectual sniping by the critics of transition, was an important outcome of the foregoing developments on the Polish scene.

But there were also (less numerous) cases of greater reasonableness in individuals' attitudes. When Deputy Prime Minister Balcerowicz was making one of his usual tours of shops to see first-hand the price movements, he was invited to a butcher's shop and kissed on both cheeks by its new owner who exclaimed: "I have this shop only due to changes you introduced. I thank you from my heart!".

But what about views from – literally – the other side of the counter than that of a shopkeeper? An old lady, a pensioner, confessed that she did not adjust to the changes fast enough. When she went to a butcher's shop in early January and it looked very much like before the World War II, that is was full of everything one would expect to find in the butcher's shop, she spent almost all her recently received pension in that one shop!

Generally, however, people were surprised, a bit frightened, and at times showing their anger. Few were thoughtful enough to write – like a pensioned former worker in Gdansk port – to Balcerowicz that his pension is very modest but "thanks to you these are real money for which I can buy whatever I need, even if in modest quantities. I believe that my daughter is going to live in a normal country with a normal economy".

On a personal note, a family friend, a journalist, was expecting a baby in December 1989. Her husband was spending 2–3 times a week a few hours in a queue to buy a washing machine. He did not have his number in a queue written on his palm, as was the experience of another friend of mine during her shopping in Moscow (see Part I, Chapter 3 of these memoirs), but he was on a so-called "social list" and had to mark his presence in a queue during each queuing visit to the shop. Otherwise, he would lose his place on the list.

It just happened that he had to take his wife to the maternity hospital on a day, when he was expected to again mark his presence in the queue, and lost the place as a result. It was mid-December 1989, when the baby was born and for the next two weeks they were washing the diapers at her mother's apartment. After January 1, 1990, they went to the same shop, where her husband was queuing for months, and bought the washing machine. At a higher price than before, of course, but without any queuing or other problems. They spent less than fifteen minutes there.

Goods, in an increasing variety, became available, and available all the time, in a matter of weeks. That was the other side of the "new normal". A man who later became an owner of a coaching firm in a mid-sized Polish city of Kielce, remembered that somebody had brought in news about a newly opened private shop. Younger generation did not quite know what it was. So they went there to see the novelty. What he noted was an attractive colorful material covering an old – not very freshly looking – counter. Moreover, there were many goods available on the shelves, where there was almost nothing before. Well – he thought – private looks fine.

This "new normal" could be contrasted with a well known joke from communist times about an old lady who came to a butcher's shop, almost empty as usual, and inquired about a sirloin (not available), then about a cured ham (same answer), and then about something similarly rare in the communist butcher's shop (same answer). She said politely: "Thank you" and left. The personnel looked with amazement after her and somebody remarked enviously: "What an excellent memory of pre-war times the old lady had!"…

On a wider, social plane, however, reactions prevailed over reflections. Interestingly, reactions of punditocracy, or commentators, were even more critical. And the critique turned into frenzy with the first output statistics. The first were those of industrial output, which declined by about 30% in January alone. It is at that early moment that the term: "unacceptable cost of transition" made its entry into the debate on post-communist systemic change.

The surprisingly large industrial output fall resulted also in a slight attack of panic within the Polish government. When statistics for January were made available in the middle of February, Minister Waldemar Kuczynski (chief economic adviser to the Prime Minister), invited a number of economists, including myself, for individual conversations to sound them out about the surprisingly large size of the output decline. I do not have clear recollection of the flow of conversation, but I retain an impression that it was brief and rather superficial.

I do remember, however, that I told Minister that I did not see anything surprising in the heavy output fall, given the well known propensity of communist economies to generate wasteful "production for production's sake" – of little use for producers or consumers. With the systemic change taking place, cuts in such wasteful production were only to be expected. I remember also making a point that output fall should not be equated in the majority of cases with welfare loss. This thesis I elaborated upon at greater length a year later at a major international conference in Rome. At that conference called *Building New Europe* I offered a paper: "Costs of Transition that Are Not Costs: On Non-welfare-reducing Output Fall".

At about the same time as the brief encounter with Minister Kuczynski I had a much longer phone conversation with the then adviser to the government Jacek Rostowski (much later another Minister of Finance and Deputy Prime Minister). We considered then various types of output, which could or, in fact, should disappear in the early phase of the systemic change.

The first and most obvious candidate "was production that never was", but nonetheless found its way into official statistics. We meant what Russians called *pripiski* (write-ins). Given the fact that under the communist economic system state firms were paid not by what they sold, but by what they told (their superiors in the planning hierarchy), officially registered output figures included output that did not exist physically, but only on paper, in statistical reports. It was obvious that with the systemic change that kind of reporting would disappear immediately for if state-owned firms did not eliminate write-ins, they would have to pay corporate income tax on something they did not produce and did not earn any sales' revenues!

Next, we considered production that did exist, but should not. Cases of the "production for production's sake", or "pure socialist production" as Leszek Balcerowicz called such system-specific waste, were mentioned in our conversation. For example, the excessive number of the means of transportation at state firms, which were accustomed to send their own numerous vans and lorries to bring in small quantities of inputs from their undisciplined suppliers. As a result, transport expenditures in the communist economy per unit of physical output was 3–5 times higher than in the capitalist economy! A much stronger discipline of the market would soon eliminate such behavior of suppliers. The same might be said about the excessive number of metal working machines in state firms to produce in-house – and at a very high cost – some missing inputs unavailable from state suppliers. Again, under the market discipline it would be in the interest of suppliers to deliver good quality supplies and right on time as agreed between the contracting parties. Otherwise they would soon lose their customers.

There were other candidates for output contraction, associated with excessively high inventories, as well as excessively high fixed investment, both resulting from "soft" budget constraint of state firms under communist economic system that we also briefly mentioned in our conversation. We were convinced that the budget constraint would harden over time as state firms learned that the macroeconomic stabilization and systemic change were here to stay. One of the consequences would, however, be the fall in output, unneeded under the new incentive structure of the market.

The foregoing conversations were, however, friendly exchanges among those convinced both about the need for systemic change and the proper choice made of institutional changes and policy fundamentals, regardless of differences with respect to some details. Very vocal were, however, those who were against transition to the capitalist market, those who were simply afraid of the future, as well as those who had different ideas how to get from here to there. Representatives of all those ways of thinking were less sympathetic to the pursued transition path. Worse still, they were often more emotional and judgmental than analytical in their opinions. Frankly speaking, those emotions were erecting strong barriers to a meaningful intellectual debate.

Thus, there were critics who did not like the systemic change away from communism. They continued to see communist system as a legitimate version of socialism. It was clear that they would object to both the introduction of the market-based system and to privatization. Next, there were those who were ready to accept the Lange-Lerner-Dickinson pipe dream of the market socialism (state firms plus central planner as an auctioneer allocating output among bidding firms). The latter would presumably "swallow" the pro-market arguments, but would strongly object to privatization. The acceptance of the degree of liberalization would also differ between these two camps hostile to the private ownership-based capitalist market economy.

Next came "third roaders". Characteristic for them were opinions of Prof. Pawel Bozyk, former head of the group of advisers to the central committee of the Polish communist party (PZPR), created during the reign of Edward Gierek. Criticizing, like others, the results of restrictive macroeconomic policies Prof. Bozyk did not reject the existence and even expansion of new private firms, but maintained that many areas of economy activity should be "due to their nature" state-owned.

It turned out, however, that these areas were -v-e-r-y -w-i-d-e. According to Bozyk they should include not only the traditional monopolies (alcoholic beverages, tobacco, etc.), not only the technical infrastructure of the economy, but also "strategic" firms in defense industries, and even those "decisive for the directions of technical progress and structural change". If one adds to the above his ideas about the extent of interventions of governmental policies (both regulatory and case-by-case interventions in almost everything) it becomes clear that his "third road" between communist central planning orthodoxy and the capitalist market economy amounted, in fact, to something not much different from reformed central planning. The only novelty would be a greater role of small and middle-sized private firms.[29] Similar, by the way, were views, for example, of another well known reformer Dr. Kalman Pecsi, a Hungarian believer in reforming the communist system (see above, Part II, Chapter 6).

Interestingly, in criticizing transition, and especially its stabilization component, there were no differences in theoretical underpinnings or policy prescriptions between critics historically associated with the communist camp and those identified with the "Solidarity" opposition. The majority of economists and other critics from -b-o-t-h camps were overwhelmingly against macroeconomic restrictions and nearly all among them suggested reversing the policies in part or in full. They clearly revealed their limited knowledge of macroeconomic policy, balanced economy and foreign trade issues. I criticized the theoretical foundations of such thinking as early as spring 1990. I did that at another seminar in Kazimierz Dolny, organized by the economics department of Catholic University of Lublin (KUL). I outlined there the theory, or heterodox theories, underpinning the fast track transition programs, anchoring them in classical and neoclassical *cum* Keynesian economic thinking in a paper called "Theoretical Foundations of Governmental Stabilization Program: Reality and Political Folklore".[30]

Thus, you could find among the critics of the pursued transition strategy one of the advisers to our Janusz Beksiak-led team, and a noted critic of communist economics, the already mentioned Prof. Stefan Kurowski (see Part I, Chapter 2). He saw in the stabilization program only its fiscal cuts and monetary repression, with their impact on current output, but not the aims and expected outcomes of such policies.

These aims were obvious from the vantage point of the governmental program, and were clearly stated in the outline prepared by our team. The macroeconomics of stabilization policies should be well known to -a-l-l economists. No liberalization is possible without freeing prices. Freeing prices lead to changes in absolute but also in relative prices. Changes in relative prices lead in turn to changes in demand for various goods and services (fall in demand for and accordingly output of previously underpriced goods and increase in demand and output for previously overpriced goods). Moreover, in a situation of excessive wage growth, combined with extensive shortages of goods and services (typical for communist economies), prices would rise for -a-l-l goods to balance supply with demand. Thus, demand and in consequence also output would have to fall. I return later to the issue by how much it should fall.

However, there was also a specific reason for macroeconomic restraint. Systemic change assumed an increased role of the private sector, not only through privatization, but also through the increase in the number of new and expansion of the already existing private firms. As stressed in Chapter 6, it was an overwhelming conviction among the supporters of the idea of returning to the capitalist market economy that private owners would be much less willing to both start new firms or expand the scale of activity of the already existing private firms in the face of the near-hyperinflation, facing the Polish economy in the second half of 1989. Thus, both macro stabilization arguments and systemic change arguments combined in stressing the urgent need for macroeconomic restraint. This, in turn, would lead to the decline in inflation and restore trust in the national currency (a currency in which they earned their revenues, profits and kept their working capital accounts).

And, let me add, the trust was restored rather quickly. In late 1989 only 34% of aggregate savings of households were kept in national currency. The remaining two third were kept in convertible currencies, mostly in US $. Dollarization of the economy was in full swing. However, some time after the introduction of macroeconomic restraint to slow inflation and restore the normal role of domestic currency, these proportions began to change. Nothing like that would have happened without the introduction and steady pursuit of the stabilization program.

Unfortunately, neither Kurowski, nor others, regardless of their theoretical persuasion and political preferences, accepted the foregoing argumentation. They were, in actual fact, ready to abandon the macroeconomic restraint program altogether.[31] So, he and his co-author suggested Keynesian style increase in money supply through the reduction of interest rate (to the level much below the inflation rate!), combined with price controls and – to make things worse – with the abandonment of wage controls! They even maintained that such monetary policy … would reduce inflation(!?).

Stefan Kurowski and another professor, Jerzy Zyzynski, co-invented a curious "sponge theory" to justify the (*de facto*, unlimited) increase in money supply. Why? Because they thought that the economy had been shrinking primarily due to the decline in money supply. They compared Polish economy to a dry sponge that was able to absorb an unlimited amount of the much needed money.

Apart from strange macroeconomic thinking, Kurowski and Przygodzki in their "Program of Revival" suggested a number of measures that would separate the emerging Polish market economy from the world economy. Like radical leftist party Syriza in the recent Greek crisis, they suggested the renegotiation of the Polish program with the IMF and added trade and other policy proposals leading to near autarchy. For they envisaged an import ban on all semi-manufactures that could be produced by domestic firms! It would restore their monopoly on the Polish market and we should always keep in mind that the monopolistic spirit – as Adam Smith reminded us in his writings – is narrow, lazy, and oppressive.

The separation of domestic economy from the world markets, that is elimination of the opportunities created by trade liberalization, has been very often proposed by various critics of the Polish transition program. Even those who at that time called themselves economic liberals (without much understanding what it meant in terms of economic theory) formulated at times, like Adam Glapinski, the thesis that the process of opening up of the Polish economy should be gradual. He suggested also the need for governmental structural policy. And, true to the pattern of rejection of macroeconomic restraint, he stressed that there was one policy move that was absolutely necessary. Namely, general easing of the monetary policy, combined with a plethora of targeted low interest rate credit programs.[32]

Interesting in those and other critical opinions was the missing reflection on the interest of domestic and foreign investors in the economy with at least stabilizing, if not already stable, prices as a condition for getting involved in establishing and expanding operations in Poland. Furthermore, all those foreigners whose investments were seen as important by critics would be thoroughly discouraged by an avalanche of protectionist propositions, suggested by the large majority from among the critics.

I have been presenting above some details of various critics' proposals, concerning the Polish stabilization and systemic change program, to get the Reader interested in the kind of thinking that was quite popular in early months and years of post-communist transition. Moreover, the kind of criticism was, by and large, repeated with respect to all future fast track (or big bang, or shock therapy) programs, from the earliest like Czechoslovak one to other programs similar in scope and direction. Only the "sponge theory" became – a rather curious – hallmark of the purely Polish debate…

Without the usual academic modesty, I should point out that no other economist devoted so much time and effort to the issue of the "vanishing output" at the start of the post communist transition than myself. Between mid-1990 article of mine in the *Welwirtschaftliches Archiv* and the final, conclusive article called: "An Inquiry into the Early Drastic Fall of Output in Post-communist Transition" in 2002 I returned many times to this highly relevant issue.[33]

Let us shift back, however, to the start of Polish transition. Had I been asked in late 1989 by how much would GDP decline after introducing in Poland market rules of the game, I would have, probably, refused to offer one precise number. I would stress, however, that the probable range of output fall could go as high as 20% to 30% GDP for the whole correctional recession period, the period of major shedding the output legacy of communism. And would expect an even larger fall in the most distorted sector that is in industry. The size of output unneeded under the proper structure of incentives of market capitalism was very large in communist economies, and was the largest in the case of industry.

In conversations with my friend, the late Prof. Beksiak, who for about a month was also my boss during our work on the outline of the stabilization and systemic change program for the parliamentary representation of the Solidarity camp, we often discussed the output fall throughout the first (correctional recession) phase of transition. We were both of the opinion that it had to be overall v-e-r-y – l-a-r-g-e. Less obvious were annual figures, depending on the degree and length of the macroeconomic stabilization-related restrictive policies. In the transition program itself we did not offer any numbers with respect to the size of output fall. We warned its Readers, however, about the consequences:

> "(T)he Polish economy is abandoning the Soviet-type economy, a creation of historically unparalleled wastefulness. The costs of bidding utopia farewell are less than costs of forty years of utopia, but unfortunately they are still high."[34]

What we wrote in our program in September 1989 stood in sharp contrast with (rarely explicit) and frequently implicit assumptions of all those who were soon to join the chorus of both domestic and foreign critics of Polish and later other post-communist transition programs and pursued policies. They neither looked at the stabilization/liberalization programs in less developed countries, nor compared the institutional and policy distortions in LDCs with the dramatically larger distortions in communist economies.

In fact, I did not notice much analytical thinking based on serious theorizing behind the critics' assumptions. I suspect critics were first and foremost just shocked by the reported scale of output fall. That was a regrettable development from the vantage point of the much needed debate. For if they looked more carefully at the performance of communist economies, that is economies – as we stressed – of the "historically unparalleled wastefulness", they could reach similar conclusions with respect to the scale of the decline of output unneeded under the structure of incentives of market capitalism. Let me offer two examples:

<> Earlier studies revealed that the level of inventories in the communist enterprises were at a minimum twice as high as in developed capitalist market economies: above 60% GDP in the former vs. above 30% GDP in the latter. Even assuming that differences in the level of economic development explained half of the difference, the remaining half amounted to about 15% GDP to be eliminated during the early, correctional phase of transition.

<> Other calculations showed that to achieve 1% GDP growth rate communist economies needed approximately 2% growth rate of gross fixed capital investment vs. 1% growth rate in developed capitalist economies. There again the difference between the countries under consideration amounted to some 10–15% GDP.

Changing from "soft" to – the usual – hard budget constraint of enterprises under the capitalist market system would necessarily eliminate both types of distortions of the old communist system. And they were the largest and most conspicuous distortions, but not the only ones! We were, of course, not alone, but – frankly speaking – the number of economists who stressed similar causes and consequences was not high, either at the time or even now.

Among these few was, for example, Prof. Ljubo Sirc from Glasgow University, then also President of the Centre for Research into Communist Economies. Reacting to lamentations about the drastic output fall, he stated already in early 1990 that Polish output fell and -s-h-o-u-l-d fall. "Communist economies, on the whole, produce goods, valued at about 10% of Gross Social Product (communist measuring rod used instead of GDP – J.W.), that go straight into inventories never to reappear..." He added also to the above some investment that does not produce things that anybody wants, evaluating it at another 10% GDP (see his introduction to an English version of our stabilization and systemic change program). Please, note the similarity to the estimates presented above (even after correction for the difference in the size of country's GSP and GDP). A number of German economists, mostly from the Prof. Herbert Giersch' school of thinking about the political economy, shared these opinions as well.

The foregoing should have been rather obvious to those well acquainted with the communist economic system. Yet they were largely ignored in between the clamor about an "unacceptable cost of transition" and numerous scholarly interpretations pointing to all possible, mostly marginal or downright irrelevant, causes of the steep output fall in early transition.

Nonetheless these rather obvious (communist) system-specific causes did not seem to have convinced many analysts in early 1990s. Massive criticism of steep output fall continued. Interestingly, we then observed also some intellectual attempts at splitting successful transition leaders into "bad guys", following big bang strategy, Poland and Czechoslovakia, and "good guys" (in fact: a good guy, in singular), that is Hungary. It started, I think, at the Cambridge, Mass., conference I attended in February 1992. There, two authors from the World Bank, Kemal Dervis and Timothy Condon, suggested such approach.[35]

A few words of introduction are needed here about "gradualism". A road from here (that is from communist economic system) to there (capitalist market economy) could be travelled basically at two speeds: rapidly or slowly. With many speed variations in between, of course. The slow road was at the start of post-communist transition called "gradualism".

It was relatively easy to define what the fast track, big bang, or shock therapy stood for. The capitalist market economy is a set of intertwined variables. If the transition economy were to operate with at least tolerable efficiency, the rules of the game concerning these variables should be compatible with each other. Meaning: rules should come, if possible, from the same system. Thus, the fast track suggested that a critical mass of change, that is as much institutional change as possible, should be introduced right from the start to reduce the degree of malfunctioning of the economy in transition.

Gradualism was more confusing for two reasons. First, "gradualists" quite often did not say much against rapid liberalization (or privatization). Those calling themselves gradualists were in numerous cases economists and others who were simply dead set against the restrictive macroeconomic policies that should be pursued from the start of transition. Such gradualists were associated with "bleeding heart" attitudes, combined often with left wing political views, which moved them to oppose policies requiring elimination of excess demand since it implied the reduction of output and employment. Thus, they were against *standard macroeconomic prescription* in the case of excess demand and inflation. The existence of such gradualists who cared only about the level of output and employment in the short run (for it was obvious that the elimination of imbalances in the short run would accelerate growth rate in the long run!) added to the confusion about gradualism itself.

The, so to say, gradualists in good faith who contested the fast track, or big bang, or shock therapy approach had more relevant concerns about the speed of transition. According to *bona fide* gradualists, slow changes in the rules of the game were to help economic agents to more easily adjust to the new economic system and its rules. The pay-off from the slow learning process was (presumably) to be greater ability of both employers and employees to adjust to the changed rules of the game – and the resultant better economic performance.

The problem gradualists faced was that they could not find cases supporting such reasoning. It was not surprising. After all, if the economy started with the larger set of changes in the rules of the game, it was assumed to reach the minimum tolerable level of efficiency earlier than the one with a smaller set of changes under the gradualist approach.

There were also other arguments – of political economy type – against the efficacy of gradualism. The first concerned credibility of systemic change. A critical mass of changes at the start of transition signals economic agents that those in power are serious about change. Reneging on a large set of changed rules of the game is definitely more difficult than on a small one. Thus, economic agents willy-nilly begin to adjust to new rules, whether they like them or not. The same cannot be said, however, about a much smaller gradualist set. Agents may, then, hope that such small changes will be called off at the first sign of malfunctioning and, in expectation of such a course of events, might altogether refuse to adjust to the new rules.

Another political economy type of argument refers to the well recognized phases of reforms or changes. There is a period of early enthusiasm and, then, comes fatigue, when the level of resistance to introduced measures increases sharply. This historical pattern also militates against gradualist approach because it obviously reduces the probability of completing transition (or at least a large part of it) during the phase of enthusiasm. The argumentation used here is presented in a graphic form in Figure 7.1.

Figure 7.1: The usual pattern of interaction between the dynamics of institutional change and the enthusiasm or fatigue with reforms or systemic change. Fatigue comes sooner than the positive effects of changes and resistance to change goes up sharply

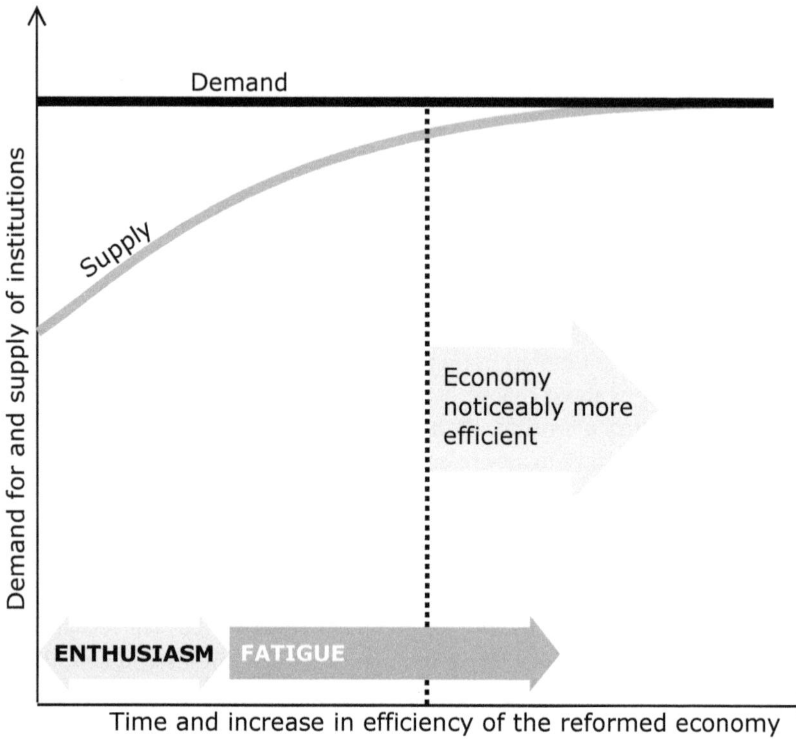

The elevation of Hungary to the role of a gradualist success story by Dervis and Condon was intended to come to the rescue of the gradualist approach. It was, however, a complete misunderstanding, resulting from the very limited knowledge of communist economies among economists not involved in the study of comparative systems, Soviet studies, etc. And these two authors, World Bank experts, were outsiders in this respect.

Communist Hungary, as I stressed already, was a country that tinkered more than other communist countries with its economic system. Thus, when looking at specific changes, those who knew very little (or nothing at all) about the system itself and the "treadmill of reform" could imagine that if Czechoslovakia liberated, say, 100% of its imports, Poland 90%, while Hungary liberated only 30% of imports, the latter country pursued "gradualist" approach. Nothing was further from the truth, though. Hungary made many reforms earlier, when a substantial part of imports was liberalized. What mattered in this and other cases was not the scale of changes made since 1990, but the overall scale of changes with respect to various economic measures, like the degree of import liberalization used in the above example. And with respect to the *overall scale of changes* Hungary was at about the level of the other two leaders in transition (or in some respects even ahead).

Nonetheless, the invention of Hungary as a gradualist success story added to the ammunition used by critics of transition. The left-leaning British daily *The Guardian* wrote then a critical story, with the finger-wagging title like: "The Big Bang Gang Should Listen!", sounding the note of triumph, but there was, in fact, little to triumph about! At the depth of correctional recession industrial output of Czechoslovakia was 46% below its pre-transition level, in Poland 41% and in Hungary 40%. The differences were small, indeed. In terms of the overall industrial output loss in early transition associated with macroeconomic restraint they were not larger, either. Moreover, Poland, not Hungary registered the lowest overall decline: 28.3% (Hungary 30.7% and Czechoslovakia 31.3%). The GDP loss also put Poland minimally ahead of the pack. Anyway, a similar degree of systemic change was reflected in a similar degree of output losses during correctional recession, eliminating "pure socialist production". There was no gradualism in the Hungary's case…

All this was becoming statistically obvious by late 1992. In 1993 one of the best observers of transition, Janos Kornai, noted that output declined markedly -e-v-e-r-y-w-h-e-r-e in the post-communist world. It fell in countries pursuing big bang strategy and those moving forward slowly (what passed then for gradualist strategy…), in highly indebted countries like Poland or Hungary and in debt-free countries like Czechoslovakia, in those following systematically a transition strategy and those pursuing it in a haphazard way. Finally, output fell in countries that followed no transition strategy whatsoever, like Ukraine.[36]

With Kornai's interpretation of output changes after the collapse of communism, the accusations about the "cruelty" of big bang (shock therapy, etc.) subsided. A kind of near-consensus emerged that output fall at the start of transition had been all but unavoidable, as formulated by Laszlo Csaba in 1998.[37] It was a fragile near-consensus, however, as a large number of unrepentant critics continued, or – more precisely – reverted to their rant about high costs (that could, miraculously, be made lower) at the first opportunity.

Nonetheless, both authors like myself, regarding large output fall as an inevitable consequence of leaving the highly distorted world of communist economic system, and those who regarded such fall as a result of effects of the transition strategy agreed with respect to the unavoidability of large output fall. At the same time they "agreed to disagree" with respect to specific causes of such fall. Thus, whenever the debate was re-ignited in later periods, old arguments from early 1990s were often dusted off and repeated again, without much added data or theoretical reflection.

Let me add an extra reality check on my comments on transition and its critics. I would not like to create an impression that transition programs in countries that became the transition leaders were impeccable. Nor the impression that their implementation was faultless all the time.

Errors were made repeatedly, although more often with respect to the implementation than to the design of the strategy. They came primarily from the fact that those in charge had no experience as policy makers. Moreover, their knowledge-building process was difficult, uneven and left a lot of gaps. I have experienced that myself (see Part I, Chapter 2 above).

Thus, for example, both Czechoslovak reformers and "system changers" lost a lot of time quarreling in 1990 about the proper path to the capitalist market economy, that is whether to choose "gradualist" or big bang strategy. Moreover, the view was popular among gradualists that the Czechoslovak economy – without large macroeconomic imbalances – could undergo institutional changes avoiding the introduction of restrictive fiscal and monetary policies. It was an obvious error with respect to the theory of policy-making. Even with a perfect macroeconomic balance, distorted relative prices in Czechoslovakia (no less distorted than elsewhere in communist economies!) required price liberalization to reveal how much they were distorted. Such knowledge is the basis for any specialization effort for it tells producers what they should continue to manufacture and what they should stop producing (and stop making losses at the same time). Therefore, price liberalization, combined with restrictive fiscal and monetary policies, was needed also in the Czechoslovak economy.

Furthermore, nearly everywhere those in charge of post-communist transition underestimated the complexities and, accordingly, the time needed to accomplish privatization. Let me say, however, that on this issue Czechoslovakia, or more precisely Czechia after the "velvet divorce", offers a counterexample with respect to the time required to reach privatization targets.

> There is another example of a straightforward approach to problem-solving worth reminding in the case of the Czechs that took place before "velvet divorce". My Czech colleagues told me about the confrontation of the then Minister for Industry, an older colleague of mine, Prof. Karel Dyba, and the miners. He flatly refused to establish a very costly program of support for the long time loss-makers – Czech coal extracting enterprises. Miners

(more combative than other workers also in Czechia) were angry and decided to stage a demonstration in the Czechoslovak capital city, Prague. They came in large numbers there, reached the ministry for industry and loudly demanded that minister comes out to see them.

And a silver-haired gentleman came indeed, greeted them, and said – in a nutshell – the following. "Germans could offer in late 1960s a costly support program for both the mines and the miners. But they had at that time the history of more than two decades of a highly efficient capitalist economy. And they could afford it. By contrast, we had almost half a century of a highly *in*efficient communist economy and we cannot afford such a costly program, continuing for more than the two decades. Our restructuring cannot last longer than five years and no support can be offered afterwards.

I am very sorry to bring to you such an unpalatable truth" – he said at the end, bowed, and left the gathering, which reacted by a deep silence. Incidentally, I am not sure that such a sincere presentation of the unpalatable truth would be similarly received by, for example, Polish miners, brought up in a highly combative "Solidarity" style…

Coming back to errors in the implementation of transition strategy, some errors were much simpler and stemmed from haphazard economic training under communism and the lack of policy practice before taking over the reins of the economy. Poland also offers here some examples. Polish inflation was subsiding rather fast since the start of liberalization in January 1990 (a reminder: consumer price index increased by 78% in January and then began to decline rapidly). In June monthly inflation rate declined to 3.4%. Low June and, next, July numbers seemed to have convinced the Polish economic team that inflation is low and under control and they decided to relax restrictions a bit (especially wage restrictions). What they forgot was simply the existence of seasonal price changes, with falling food prices reducing inflation in summer (sometimes even to monthly negative numbers, that is to absolute price declines).

When consumer price inflation increased again in autumn to about 5% per month, policy makers pressed the brake even harder than before. This extra tightening was, however, an additional error, given the forthcoming developments. At the beginning of 1991 the trade with the Soviet Union was to change from settling accounts in inconvertible ruble to those in dollar as a means of payment. Such change would inevitably reduce imports and exports of both countries. Thus, the Polish economic team should expect resultant decline in external demand and, in consequence, a decline of domestic output. Such decline would obviously add to the level of economic restraint in the Polish economy.

I was, at the time, apart from my other duties, active in the foreign media and – after the fall of communism – also in Polish media, not (as earlier) only in the underground ones. Thus, I was giving interviews and writing comments on the foregoing and many other issues. I hasten to add that in spite of my whole-hearted support for transition, I was not always praising policy makers' specific decisions, as for example in the case considered above! Yet my usual diligence, this time as a commentator of Polish transition, had a somewhat curious side effect. In autumn of 1990 I was invited by Prof. Bronislaw Geremek, still head of the Solidarity club in the parliament and newly appointed head of foreign affairs commission of Sejm (the Parliament's lower chamber). After the small talk about current affairs, Prof. Geremek – whom I have known from his earlier leadership of the underground *conversatorium* of which I became a member at some point – stated that in recognition of both my knowledge and active participation "on the side of the angels" he would like to offer me an important position of an ambassador to Japan. That is to one of the largest and most important economies of the world.

I got the true meaning of the message. Although Japan had indeed been the second largest world economy at the time, my knowledge and diligence in applying it to the problems at hand would be more useful here, in Poland, not there, in Japan. As I was to learn later (during my private visit to Japan in 1995) my arguments were quite well received by Japanese policy makers and bureaucrats in my lectures and long conversations with the hosts. They were, however, concerned with the post-communist transition in general, not specifically with Polish affairs.

The real motivation of Prof. Geremek's offer was clear. Some people wanted me to be as far away as possible from Poland, hoping that I would – as the most important side effect – disappear also from the Polish media. And although I mostly supported the transition policies and its specific policy measures, these people were presumably too thin-skinned to suffer occasional criticism from someone belonging to their own ranks…

I couched my negative answer to Geremek's offer in a friendly manner. I thanked heartily for the offer of such an important diplomatic position, but then explained my intellectual problems. Firstly, I regarded some parts of the ambassador's job as extremely boring and moreover time consuming. I had in mind all those introductory meetings with my ambassadorial counterparts accredited with a foreign ministry and then after a few years all those farewell meetings with my counterparts (in Japan it would amount altogether to about 300 such, polite and roughly meaningless, encounters!).

Secondly, for an active scholar like myself it would be something like being forced intellectually to retire and I feel I can still contribute a lot to economics, now especially economics of transition. And I was right by the way. Since late 1990 I authored and co-authored 18 books, most of them in English, for an international academic market. Being far away from the "battlefield" of transition and burdened with often boring duties, my productivity – even with my usual diligence – would have suffered very much during the ambassadorship period.

After the meeting with Prof. Geremek I did not bother to start an informal inquiry to learn who – in fact – wanted me out of public debate (in fact, I did not care!). I do not know that even now. What I do know is who joined at some point the process of tempting me to leave Poland and, as they suspected, also to leave the public debate here. Besides, those who wanted me out of Poland underappreciated my diligence. For over the next 13 years I was formally out of Poland, working in turn in Denmark, England, and Germany. Yet the fact of working there did not prevent my active presence in the Polish media.

I won, first, a competitive professorship at Aalborg University in Denmark. But at one point in late winter 1990/91 I got an unexpected call from an Irish economist, an adviser to the then Prime Minister Jan K. Bielecki, with an offer to become an Executive Director in the just established European Bank for Reconstruction and Development, created to support post-communist transition to the market. I consulted that offer with my wife who hoped to improve her fluency in English that suffered in 1980s partly due to the burden of being the wife of a dissident and, as such, being consistently refused a passport to travel. I mentioned above, in Chapter 6, that we went together to the US in late April 1989 and it was her first trip to the West in a decade.

A few days later I answered the offer in the positive, was officially made a candidate to the position, then approved of at bank's first General Meeting, and joined the bank the very next day after approval. As far as the motivation of the offer at hand was concerned, I had no doubt it was the same as with the offer of ambassadorship in Japan. It was also obvious that the PM at least approved of the offer, meaning: he agreed with its intention. It was somewhat inconsistent with his earlier decision to ask me to become a member of his unofficial advisory group (that consisted of four professors: economist and financier Tad Rybczynski from London, Janusz Beksiak and Urszula Grzelonska-Libura from Warsaw, and myself from Aalborg-Warsaw and later London-Warsaw).

At the EBRD my knowledge of communist, Soviet-type economies as well a large network of contacts in Poland and beyond, was much more useful than it would have been in Japan. First, in spite of the traditional firewall between the operational management and the supervisory council, the fact that I was an executive director of the council, that is one taking part in the decision-making process of the management board, created greater opportunity to influence the course of events.

Second, my academic standing as a Sovietologist was generating a continuous stream of requests for an informal inquiry about the state of affairs in the post-communist world and in particular countries – on the side of both merchant bankers, operating in the confines of the private sector, and development bankers, interacting primarily with the public authorities in the member countries. And every interaction is a give and take process that enabled me to influence – to some extent at least – the thinking of the operational staff of the bank.

Third, a newcomer to political practice, I learned the difficult art of coalition-building. An analytically well grounded argumentation is often not sufficient to generate action. One needs to create a coalition of those willing to support a given position at the managerial meetings to overcome the power of inertia of the "established position" on the issue. Let me give one example.

I was the first to raise the issue of the inappropriate – in my opinion – activities of the banking section in EBRD operations in the transition countries. The strategy was to contribute handsomely (in terms of the volume of money involved) to the established Western banks that opened representative offices or, much less often, divisions in the transition countries. However, in a somewhat exotic, and fast changing, regulatory environment, they were at a loss how to evaluate forthcoming loan requests (even if the environment was changing in the right, capitalist market direction!). The outcome was that after a year of more since the opening they had yet to show at least one loan on their books…

I argued that much more effective in the medium run would be to invest much smaller sums in the newly emerging small private banks. They would need also a technical assistance because the knowledge of banking in the post-communist world was even scarcer than that of financial capital. I got the support from the Hungarian Director and the Czechoslovak, and later, after the "velvet divorce", Czech and Slovak Director, but the group was too small to make a dent in the thinking of operational staff. I remember an American head of the merchant banking division in EBRD stating that these small private banks do not have the "track record". Sure they do not! – I retorted – but please note that the whole post-communist transition does not have the "track record" long enough! In Poland it started on January 1, 1990, and in other early transition countries somewhat later. But to no avail.

So, our small group of three directors started looking for allies. I drafted into the group the Spanish Director, who years earlier had been a commercial counselor of Spain in Poland. Then, we were able to convince the Scandinavian directors to our cause. With more West European, not only East-Central European members supporting or suggesting on their own the proposal to prop up small private banks, a change – or, rather, enlargement – of strategy took place finally and a limited number of such banks in post-communist countries was included into EBRD range of supporting activities.

Sometimes a joke came to the rescue. When a $ 100 mill. loan for the Polish telecommunication industry was considered – and contested – I told the Management Board the following story. I said that the Prime Minister was highly unsatisfied with the performance of his telecommunications' minister and decide to fire him. But first he, understandably, wanted to announce his decision to the minister himself. However, due to the frequent technical failures, he could not get him on the phone (please remember it was pre-cell phone era!). There was a wave of smiles, queries subsided, and the loan was approved.

Sometimes media blitz helped the particular issue. In 1993 the President of the Bank, Jacques Attali, resigned under pressure and the issue of his successor came to the fore. The French expected new President to be again a Frenchman, but Scandinavians had another idea and suggested a Danish candidate. Then, Italians joined the fray, proposing an Italian, the acting Vice-President of EBRD (a high class professional, by the way).

I saw that as an opportunity for Poland to propose a very appropriate Polish candidate, Prof. Balcerowicz. By mid-1993 the barrage of criticism subsided to a considerable extent (see above) and Balcerowicz, heading an economic team of the first success story of transition, was well regarded in both the world of politics and the world of business.

Having convinced the Polish Governor of EBRD and the President of Polish central bank (NBP), Prof. Hanna Gronkiewicz-Waltz, about the probability of success, or at least of a greater recognition of both the candidate and Poland itself, I started phoning journalists I had been in contact with during my dissident years under communism. The result has been an impressive string of positive comments on the Balcerowicz candidature in *The Economist*, *The New York Times*, as well as in German, Swedish, Dutch and Swiss press.

An interesting development took place then. West Europeans who thought that the EBRD presidency was a purely West European affair (after all they had more than 50% of the votes) quickly patched up their quarrels in the face of the challenge in this respect from an East-Central European transition country upstart. First, an Italian candidate was withdrawn, then a Danish one, and the French candidate was appointed in place of Mr. Attali. Nonetheless it was a sensible initiative on my side as far as the status of post-communist members of EBRD was concerned. They ceased to be perceived as second class members, by and large mostly consumers of aid extended through the bank.

Foreign media helped me also in my last operation in the EBRD, that is in my resignation from the executive directorship – and from the bank. Again, some background explanation is in order. Polish politics became increasingly quarrelsome since 1992. It was not helped by the creation of the Policy Advisory

Council to the President Walesa (I was appointed a member of that body). The members of the council held too wide a range of views to come up with a sensible, consistent view on any important issue. And, no less importantly, the view supported by a sizable majority. It differed in this respect from the underground *conversatorium* I took part in 1980s. Moreover, President Walesa turned out to be unwilling to consider the issues he disliked or thought that tackling them could reduce support for him among the population. After a shouting match I had, when explained that he could not dodge forever a difficult issue of at least a moderate support for anti-inflationary governmental policy, I found the reasons of participating in the Council to be rather limited (although I decided not to rock the boat by leaving that quarrelsome body!).

Polish politics was becoming increasingly fractious within the large Solidarity-leaning camp. A more or less natural division between left and right, or between believers in more involvement of the state in the civic, economic, and social issues, and those who preferred less, leaving much more space to civic initiatives and private business activities, did not occur (in fact, it did not occur to these days…). Splits took place mostly along personal sympathy or animosity lines and (limited) differences of opinions on issues and tactics of their promotion.

A more important problem, not well perceived at the time, was the combativeness displayed by the majority of participants in those quarrels. Its natural consequence was ever higher walls dividing people who were close, at times very close, in the not too distant past. An extra discordant note was the combativeness of the "Solidarity" trade union representatives who entered directly national politics. In fact it was their spiteful voting that undermined the last (fourth in four years!) Solidarity camp-related government led by Mrs. Suchocka, a Poznan University lecturer at the Law School and a person of Christian Democratic political leanings. Solidarity MPs, who belonged to the pro-government coalition, turned out to be in favor of no confidence vote against the government. The no confidence vote won, the Suchocka government resigned and this development led President Walesa – erroneously, I think – to forgo further efforts to create a more stable Solidarity camp-anchored government and to dissolve the Parliament.

Egregious quarrels, fragmentation of parties, and finally the aggressive behavior of Solidarity trade union representatives estranged a part of the natural non-communist and anti-communist electorate. Moreover, recently introduced electoral reforms, aimed at reducing the excessive number of mini-parties in the Parliament (17 of them participated in the Sejm elected in late 1991!), did not reward fragmentation. Thus, although the reduced electorate of the Solidarity camp gathered about 35% of the vote, they received only less than 15% of the seats in the most important lower chamber of the parliament.

Let me stress one more – an even greater – error President Walesa made at the time, driven by the selfish personal considerations. His chancery came up with the good idea of creating Non-Partisan Block of Cooperation with the Government under the political umbrella of the President. They used the Polish abbreviation BBWR, to remind the historically conscious part of the population about Josef Pilsudski's similar interwar initiative to create a political block supportive of the post-1926 string of governments. The Walesa camp initiative turned out to rapidly grow in popularity, exceeding at one point 40% of those ready to vote for BBWR. And, then, Walesa, fearing that BBWR popularity would exceed his own, started rapidly dissociating himself from the idea. People who expressed their support for BBWR counted largely on the President to lead such a block from above. With such an option being rapidly undermined by Walesa himself, they lost faith in the venture. The net result was that orphaned BBWR barely crossed the (recently established) 5% vote threshold.

The debacle was complete. Post-communist coalition calling themselves Allied Democratic Left (SLD), consisting of the reformed ex-communist monopolist (former PZPR) and a string of smaller parties, as well as a former communist satellite, the peasant party (renamed PSL), got the majority of the seats. In fact, it got the constitutional majority (over 2/3 of the seats in the lower chamber).

Post-communists behaved reasonably on many issues both in the transitory Parliament of 1989–90 and in the highly fragmented Parliament of 1991–93. However, to keep them out of harm's way, continuous pressure should be applied, I thought. Especially after reading their first post-election comments, for example, about the need to change the president of the central bank(!!).

Besides it was "a question of taste", as Zbigniew Herbert, a Polish poet hovering for decades over the Nobel Prize in literature, once wrote. I just could not bring myself to represent on the EBRD board the government led by the same people whom I remembered from the pre-1989 past. The fact that they behaved reasonably when they were an insignificant minority was not a guarantee of the same reasonableness when they gained an overwhelming majority! Please note also, that it was the second post-communist electoral victory since the collapse of communism (the first took place in Lithuania a few months earlier).

Thus, I decided to resign, but in a manner that would make an impression – also on the forthcoming post-communist government. I used again my old, but recently renewed contacts with the Western media – moreover, extended during my stay in London. I explained my arguments in a following way. I said I did not believe that they would try to restore communism, either politically or economically. Communism is dead. But, given post-communists' habits of governance and their intellectual mindset, they could undermine, partly reverse, or, at a minimum considerably slow down, the necessary systemic changes and the stabilization policies.

My arguments were accepted by many in the Western media. I sent them my public statement of resignation with the above arguments, explaining the rationale of my choice, the very next day after ex-communists formed the government in late November 1993. Comments based on my statement were then very frequent in the Western media. And I gathered from the opinions coming to London from Poland, it stunned the new ex-communist rulers (as I hoped it should).

Let me add an interesting aside. Just before elections I got an offer from the leadership of Liberal Democratic-Congress (KLD) to become their candidate for the Senate in Warsaw. And they promised to organize campaign on my behalf as I was at the time busy in London. KLD lost the elections and did not get over the 5% threshold. But since no such threshold was introduced by law for the Senate seats, I nonetheless would have had a chance to win. After all, I was reasonably well recognized by the public, not only from my public appearances in the media and in my presiding over the Adam Smith Center think tank of liberal, free market philosophy, but also from my name being used in political games.

Thus, I was mentioned in the Polish and international press as the first candidate for a Minister of Finance after the late 1991 elections, when the then first candidate to Prime Ministership, Jaroslaw Kaczynski, mentioned his preference for my candidacy (he never came in touch with me, though!). A few weeks later I was also mentioned as one of the two candidates for the Prime Ministership in the "government of technicians", envisaged by President Walesa (an idea aired by his Chancery).

This latter piece of news drew attention of the then head of EBRD, Jacques Attali, who sounded me out whether I envisage leaving the bank. I explained to Attali that I would certainly refuse the proposition if rumors would turn into a firm offer. It was a sheer nonsense – I continued – to create a government of technicians in a country where so much should be changed, and changed as quickly as possible. Technical governments are created in a situation, when there is no prospect of a viable majority. But then government of technicians is obliged to do nothing revolutionary. It is expected to -a-d-m-i-n-i-s-t-e-r the country until the nearest election date, without introducing any substantial, and controversial, change. And transition tasks are controversial enough.

Had I wanted to turn more to Polish politics than to academia, I should have accepted the KLD proposal. But my predisposition was that of a person who in American politics is called *in-and-outer*. An academic who accepts the proposition of a role in the government or in some important body, like the Council of Economic Advisers in the US, when both sides, the candidate and those who make an offer, see the benefits of such offer. In late 1993 I did not see the pressing need of my greater involvement in Polish politics. I refused the KLD offer and never regretted the decision.

After leaving EBRD I continued my, so to say, public economic education activities both through leading the – very active and then well regarded – Adam Smith Center and through my individual appearances in the media, as well as numerous written commentaries. I was also preparing myself for my next academic post. After a brief tenure of professorship at Aalborg University in Denmark I was to join in July 1994 the Viadrina-European University in Frankfurt an-der-Oder, as a professor and chair holder in international trade and finance.

Frankly speaking it was a double advantage for me. In economic terms, my salary was to be 3–4 times higher than an equivalent position in Poland. And, in political terms, it was also safer. In a highly antagonized political relations in Poland, a person who resigns – with a lot of publicity! – due to his disbelief in one side of the major political divide and simultaneously refuses to join the other side (and the side he was associated with for quite some time!) is not particularly welcome in either camp! So, earning my salary abroad and dividing my time between professorship in Germany, my scholarly writing pursuits, and my public appearances and press polemics in Poland looked to me like the safest bet I could make under the circumstances. Moreover, even teaching abroad I contributed to the improved knowledge of capitalist market system of Polish students. Almost 30% of Viadrina students came from Poland.

I regretted very much both the timing and the scale of the defeat of the Solidarity camp in 1993 elections in my country. It is worth reminding the Reader that 1992 was a turnaround year in Poland. Correctional recession ended in spring and the year brought about moderate economic growth, which accelerated sharply in 1993. If it had not been for the quarrels within the Solidarity camp, the return to economic growth, and at an ever faster rate at that (reaching 7% per annum in 1996) would probably allow Polish transition to continue more rapidly and consistently than it did under the post-communist rule between 1993 and 1997. For political parties emerging from the Solidarity camp could presumably win 1993 elections under the rapidly improving economic conditions, although it was not at all sure, given the climate of general political confusion reigning in transition countries of East-Central Europe.

Let me explain that confusion by reference to the split personality syndrome noted by perceptive observers of and in the region. Thus, a journalist of the popular weekly *Polityka* reported in 1991 a TV debate about the fate of the clothing industry within the framework of the Balcerowicz plan. The plan was roundly condemned by trade unionists from clothing factories that were undergoing a difficult period of both the inevitable shrinkage after the opening up of the economy and the adaptation to market competition. However, a perceptive lady noted that all trade unionists were wearing characteristic imported Turkish sweaters, popular in Poland at the time, not sweaters produced in their own factories! And she added that such a split personality syndrome was an everyday occurrence at the time.

Many people enjoyed both shops crammed with a variety of colorful and attractively packaged imported goods, as well as the newly gained open borders allowing them to travel easily throughout most of Europe. However, the same people protested, when their own firms were losing the competition against imports and were threatened with bankruptcy.

Poland was not unique in this respect. A German ambassador to Poland once told a similar story of the "Ossi" in 1993. This is how the "Wessi", West Germans from the democratic Federal Republic of Germany, called Germans from the post-communist East Germany. He stressed, in fact, the same split personality syndrome in Eastern lands of newly reunited Germany. Namely, Ossi working in two car factories in East Germany were nearly all driving the West German Volkswagens, but were demanding that the government continues to subsidize the production of Wartburgs and Trabants they produced but themselves did not even think of buying!

However, I would stress that behind the undoubtedly present split personality syndrome was lurking a serious moral crisis that emerged in communist times. A friend of mine, later a high commissioner in the European Community in Brussels, Dr. Janusz Lewandowski pointed out to such crisis in his perceptive essay on "Capitalism with a Polish Face",[38] referring to the saying he heard in Slovakia in 1980s. Namely that "those who do not steal from the state, are in fact stealing from their own family". I confirm the existence of the above saying, which I also heard from Slovaks more than once!

Deep demoralization of the labor force was a constant factor under communism. I registered that throughout the whole communist period of Polish history, offering in Part I, Chapters 1–4, a string of examples, mostly from the construction sector. Analysts explained the demoralization in terms of the distorted, even destructive, structure of incentives, and rightly so. But the most sophisticated explanation I ever heard dug deeper than that. Prof. Xymena Gliszczynska, a highly appreciated specialist in labor psychology, wrote a paper for Adam Smith Center and later a much shorter article in a daily.[39]

In explaining the depth of demoralization, she used the term *lumpenproletariat* (a well known German term describing the demoralized, marginal groups of the working class). She noted that under communism *lumpenproletariat* shifted from the margins of the working class into the center of the stage. That is to the largest state enterprises, showcases of communism, where they achieved the status of the best paid workers and showered with other privileges – without changing their habits of shoddy workmanship and generally negligent attitude to their duties.

They were supported in this non-meritocratic promotion by the breakdown under communism of the centuries' long link between efforts and rewards. Please, remember, that premiums and bonuses were paid in state firms for what they told (their superiors), not for what they sold! Interestingly, those working in large state firms were often the first to protest if they did not get what they thought they should. Thus, alongside people like Walesa, and his "colleagues-in-arms", one would find in the same large firms many louses from the *lumpenproletariat*, who did not care a hoot. As one, undoubtedly irritated, worker wrote in a questionnaire prepared by Prof. Gliszczynska for employees in large state firms, there were among them numerous "workers-drunkards, visibly swaying already in the middle of their shift, workers often absent from the job, workers-loafers, and the like."

In the capitalist market environment they would quickly have been fired, but under communism they could continue neglecting their duties in the most blatant manner for years, without any reaction on the side of their superiors. And Prof. Gliszczynska concluded that the fall of communism had many causes. Apart from the impact of systemic distortions, it fell also because of both the incompetence of the communist ruling elite and the invasion of the labor force at the center of the economy by the demoralized *lumpenproletariat*.

In my writings of the period I extended the foregoing diagnosis to a large group whom I called – in parallel with Prof. Gliszczynska's definition – *lumpen-intelligentsia.*[40] I had in mind some educated people employed in public administration, health service, education, and the public sector firms, etc., who grew up and later obtained their diplomas in communist times. They neither acquired their moral standards from their families in the process of upbringing, nor in their workplaces from their superiors, nor in professional associations from their peers. The latter part of my opinion requires an additional explanation.

The communist pressure on inherited moral codes, as well as the purposeful destruction of independence and standard-setting qualities of professional associations created a large (and growing) group of people with higher education, but not necessarily with the higher moral standards. They were mostly those who were advancing from lower social strata. Without either standards-setting upbringing or external enforcement of such standards, they often turned into unscrupulous opportunists or – in the opinion of a well known Soviet dissident,

Alexander Zinoviev – followed no moral code, but only the "technical rules of survival".

Such a make-up of the labor force clearly added to the difficulties of restoring the healthy capitalist market economy, historically based on the Weberian protestant ethics. The *lumpenintelligentsia*, just like *lumpenproletariat*, aggressively demanded equal distribution of rewards in the face of the dramatically *un*equal contribution to the wealth-creation and they were ready to get what they wanted by hook or by crook. Both Xymena Gliszczynska and myself stressed it was not a purely Polish phenomenon, but one easily found in other post-communist countries. Even in East Germany, in spite of the long German tradition of good workmanship…

Chapter 8: Coming to the Rescue of Transition: The Power of the Market …

I ended the preceding Chapter on a sober, some would even call it pessimistic, note, pointing to the barrage of criticism of post-communist transition in the face of the registered drastic declines in output, sharp increase in inflation, and some other revealed characteristics of early period of shifting from central planning to capitalist market. The criticism in that period, in fact till 1993–94, was coming not only from those hostile to or distrustful of economic freedom, but no less often from the numerous doubting Thomases, who might have supported transition in principle, but for a variety of reasons (most often due to misunderstanding the role of stabilization in transition) began to doubt in its success. Adding an issue of the corroded moral order increased the range of the pessimistic arguments on the high costs and uncertain prospects of the ultimate success.

In fact, I could add my own family experience as other examples of the presumably intractable problems of transition, had I believed that such interpretation was justified. For the stories just to be reported were only superficially presenting problems. In actual fact, they were pointing to their -s-o-l-u-t-i-o-n-s.

The first family story begins at our new house near Warsaw, we moved into in summer of 1994. It was barely the second week of living there. We have just finished breakfast at the dining room on the ground floor and were about to leave, taking our three years old son, Jerzy, to a private kindergarten nearby. At that moment we heard a sound of the dripping water, splashing somewhere. We looked around and found that water was dripping from the roof just next to our breakfast table – and, worse still, at an accelerated pace at that.

The incident upset the daily routine and was a nuisance for the next few days. The team from the construction company discovered – after ruining a lot on the first floor of our house – that one of the workers have mounted a broken pipe in our bathroom there! I suspect he did not want to wait half a day for the delivery of a good one and decided to mount a broken pipe before moving to another assigned task (saying nothing, I would assume, to a foreman in charge).

Such worker could be reasonably sure that nobody would catch him while doing so and his brazen negligence would be revealed long after turning the house over to its owners. In consequence it would be impossible to establishing precisely who did what at a given moment at the building site. Obviously, the firm was already private, but the mentality and moral standards of the worker in question continued to belong to the demoralizing statist/collectivist past…

> Another family story was the experience of my older son, a computer software specialist. He was preparing a software program tracking inventories for a funeral parlor. And the owner of the parlor in question told him an interesting – and relevant – story about his long search for a team of workers who would satisfy his minimum requirements. Namely, do a decent work and stay sober, while pursuing their usual burial duties at the cemetery. He needed eight such workers and he selected them over a long period of two years – he said – changing in the meantime six teams (altogether 48 workers in order to select 8 decent and sober ones!).

In line with what I signaled above, a sense of proportion was sorely needed in the assessment of the ongoing process of transition. Inherited aberrations apart, there were also forces working strongly in favor of the systemic change. And the strongest among them, not well appreciated at the time, was the *tremendous power of the market* (in fact, it continues to be underappreciated throughout most of the post-World War II history of the West).

Returning for a moment to two family cases mentioned above, the firm that built our house went bankrupt. Thus, the selection process, typical for market capitalism, operated well to separate the entrepreneurial wheat from the chaff. Nothing like that was possible under the communist system. If a firm performed worse than the (already very low) average, the worst that could happen to its management and employees was a merger with another state firm. No "creative destruction", via exit of bad firms and the entry of new hopefuls, was allowed in the communist economy.

By contrast, in Poland, operating already under the regime of market capitalism, bad firms went bankrupt and disappeared. And lousy workers – as in the case of a given funeral parlor – were duly fired. The pattern was fast becoming a "new normal" in the private firms. In publicly-owned firms politics helped the incompetent, the lazy, and the drunkards to survive longer (sometimes much longer) but rarely forever!

Thus, the power of the market was not equally strong in different ownership sectors. Nor was it the same in all production sectors of the economy. Where supervision and accounting for individual behavior could be instituted more easily, as in manufacturing for example, the impact was markedly faster. Where it was more difficult, as in construction, the process lasted longer (but again, not forever!).

Besides, there was no "Great Wall" between the ownership sectors in the economies in transition; the performance of the private firms on liberalized markets exerted at times a very strong influence on the performance of publicly-owned ones. A very good example in this respect is the joint impact of early internal and external liberalization in the domestic and foreign trade areas on the adjustment of state-owned firms.

It was a classical *carrot and stick* framework. The entry of private wholesalers into the Polish and, with a small lag, other East-Central European economies had galvanizing effects on the domestic trade-foreign trade nexus. Relatively small private wholesalers were much quicker than the existing state-owned mastodons at identifying the products for which there has been a large, unsatisfied demand. And, also more quickly, they signaled these consumer preferences to domestic producers. In this manner they created positive stimuli for producers (at that time still mostly state-owned in the manufacturing sector).

So much for the "carrot" of early, wide ranging domestic trade liberalization. However, since there was also a wide-ranging liberalization of foreign trade, it created for private wholesalers an alternative to domestic supplies, that is imports from abroad. And the latter liberalization added "stick" to the relations between private wholesalers and domestic suppliers. The domestic state-owned producers understood that if they do not deliver the requested goods, at expected quantity, of expected quality, and at the agreed time, their production would simply be superseded by imports – and they would be threatened with bankruptcy.

The operation of the domestic trade-foreign trade liberalization nexus was particularly important in heavy industries because of the high capital threshold for new entrants to these industries. In light industries (clothing, leather goods, footwear, wood, and furniture, etc.) new private firms mushroomed and after barely a few years were often dominating the landscape. But in heavy industries, be it steel-making, manufacturing of household consumer durables (so-called white goods), automotive industry, etc., the story was different. There, new private domestic producers would appear rather late, given the existing capital threshold. And foreign direct investors would be cautious in making their decisions to enter new, little understood markets. Only foreign trade liberalization ensured that competitive pressure would be applied on the monopolistic or oligopolistic domestic state-owned firms.

It is worth noting in passing that external liberalization allowed distorted post-communist economies to reap both traditional and non-traditional benefits of liberalization. Thus, they "imported" relative prices from the world markets to help firms to learn where they are competitive and where they are not, as well as to start trading along the lines of their (often newly discovered) competitive advantages. However, as pointed out above, the openness to the world markets allowed these economies also, non-traditionally, "import" competition, where it was most needed at early transition to the capitalist market economy!

As far as foreign trade liberalization was concerned, the foregoing considerations implied the decisive role of markets in forcing state-owned firms to improve their performance in transition via imports. However, the role of markets was also – or even more strongly – felt with respects to exports.

Please, remember that exports to world markets were an Achilles heel of communist economies, given their perennial problems with both quality of their output and technological obsolescence (in fact, -g-r-o-w-i-n-g obsolescence over time!). In consequence, except for raw materials, exported manufactured products fetched low (in consequence, increasingly low) prices on world markets or were simply unsalable there. Export structure of communist countries differed little from that of less developed countries, except for exports to other "brotherly", that is communist, countries.

One of major positive surprises, already in early transition, was the sharp acceleration of exports – and please note that exports in early to mid-1990s came largely from the same state-owned firms that faced allegedly insurmountable problems with increasing exports in communist past. The reality surprised many pundits in the West who were mostly convinced that the ability to compete on the world markets would continue to be a major weakness even under post-communist transition.

Yet countries pursuing the stabilization and systemic change on the way to become fully fledged capitalist market economies, surprised nearly everybody, by rapidly changing their pattern of trade in line with the basic dictates of trade theory. The so-called gravity model of trade stresses that the geographic direction of exports has basically two determinants. Exports tend to flow, first, to rich countries and, second, to countries that are geographically close. And to a largest extent to those that are both rich *and* geographically close.

Pre-World War II trade pattern of East-Central European countries reflected the impact of the gravity model very well, with exports of Czechoslovakia, Hungary, Poland, as well as Romania and Bulgaria, concentrated predominantly on Western Europe. But almost half a century of communist rule changed markedly the geographic pattern of trade flows. Both Soviet pressure on trading first of all among the communist countries (with the, failed, hope for collective self-sufficiency) and the reality of much lower quality requirements in communist markets and resultant ease in unloading low quality goods on these markets, contributed to the rapid emergence of dominant shares of exports going to other "brotherly" countries.

However, just a few years of post-communist transition were enough to eliminate completely the trade impact of half a century of communist economic system. Already by 1994 – after barely 3–4 years of transition!! – geographic export pattern reverted to that from 1920s and 1930s as prescribed by the gravity model. In all five countries mentioned in the preceding paragraph share of exports to Western Europe returned to the pre-WW II shares or even exceeded them markedly.[41]

Thus, freed from the political shackles and from imposed distortions of central planning, exports returned to the pattern expected by international trade theory. The *tremendous power of the unshackled markets* revealed itself once again.

Moreover, as expected, empirical studies supplied the evidence that good export performance was strongly correlated with the successes in pursuing what I was calling the "Holy Trinity" of transition. Countries that were more successful in institutional change and in pursuing disciplined stabilization policies were also registering better export results.

So far I stressed the successes in reorienting the geographic structure of trade, that is shifting exports toward nearer and richer clients. However, these countries succeeded – albeit more slowly – also in changing their product structure toward better, more value adding products. The research proved that the shift away from the product structure displayed in the communist period was the most important driver of export dynamics, much more important than growth of global trade.[42]

It is also worth noting that the dynamics of exports of successful transition countries was greater than the dynamics of world exports. This was the case not only in the early years of transition but also throughout the next 15–20 years of political and economic change in the region. Excellent results in exports to world markets in the case of economies notorious in communist times for their dramatic export underperformance should undoubtedly be added to the list of indicators of success of transition to market capitalism.

There were many other indicators of success visible already in the mid-to-late 1990s, that is the period considered primarily in this chapter. However, before I turn to them, a few other reminiscences of the period are in order. In the preceding chapter I pointed at the growing empirical evidence that all transition countries were affected by large output declines, regardless of whether they pursued the so-much-disliked fast track/big bang/shock therapy strategy or not. An excellent paper by Janos Kornai brought that evidence to the attention of the critics of the dominant transition strategy. Largely under the impact of Kornai's paper – I think – they ceased to criticize output losses, allegedly generated by the big-bang strategy, accepting (however reluctantly) the idea that such losses were all but inevitable.

Nonetheless they never ceased to believe that these output losses were real and led to large – at best only temporary – declines in living standards. The scale of these declines was seen as roughly equivalent to the scale of output losses. The conviction that early transition led to large declines in living standards was widely accepted not only by many analysts, but also by large segments the population of countries in transition. If one leafed through the pages of dailies and weeklies of East-Central European press (leaving aside the press of the post-Soviet countries of Eastern Europe), one would draw the conclusion that the disaster of sort affected living standards of these societies. The conclusion that was grossly erroneous, I would like to stress.

Pro-transition economists in Poland and elsewhere tried to change that prevalent view. One of the steps undertaken to that effect was a series of discussion panels and conferences devoted to transition. At this point I would like to refer to the conference organized in 1999 by the Polish Society of Economists (Towarzystwo Ekonomistów Polskich – TEP) under the thought provoking title: "*Snatching the Defeat from the Jaws of Victory*". There, a number of authors presented the evidence that the propaganda of defeat measured by the decline in living standards was based more on distorted perception than on reality.

In a paper presented at that conference I myself stressed, for example, that we should look not only at current consumption, but also at the changes in the level of wealth. In the economies impoverished by communism it made no sense to look at the level of savings and other financial wealth indicators. A more accurate picture would be presented by changes in the ownership of household durables between late communist period and the transition years. Accordingly, I presented the statistics, showing that in the ten years period, 1988–98, employees' households sharply increased, *i.a.*, their ownership of:

<> passenger cars from about 30% to 50% of such households;
<> color TV sets from about 40% to over 80%;
<> automatic washing machines from less than 60% to over 90%;
<> audio towers from 20% to over 40%; and
<> video tape-recorders from less than 5% to over 70%, etc.

Pensioners' households and farmers' households also recorded advances in this respect. Some other durable goods such as personal computers, compact disc recorders, film cameras, and even microwave kitchens, were such a rarity in communist times, even in late 1980s, that comparisons with the transition period made no sense whatsoever.

An important part of my message was that increases in the households' ownership of various consumer durables in Poland were larger in the 1988–94 than in the 1994–98 period. Thus, these large increases took place in the period of (statistically) large declines in real wages and, presumably, in living standards! It seemed obvious that we should change our views on economic outcomes of the early transition period.

To begin with, the registered 10% decline in food consumption in Poland in early transition (three times lower than the decline in food production, by the way!) was not necessarily, and certainly not wholly, the result of declining real wages. For a large number of Polish households it looked more like a *conscious choice*. These households, facing for the first time in half a century the large increase in the supply of much desired durables, decided to forgo some food consumption to increase their ownership of what they desired more.

Was Poland an exception? My conclusions about Poland were supported by a comparative survey of transition countries, made by another friend, Prof. Laszlo Csaba, who wrote that the "consumption in the region has not fallen as sharply as circumstantial evidence … would have suggested".[43] My tentative conclusion would be that the widely understood living standards, including current consumption, ownership of consumer durables, etc., suffered much less than the propaganda of defeat tried to make everybody to believe in Poland and elsewhere.

The criticism of transition and its (perceived) outcomes, stressed in Chapter 7 above, appeared quite often at the conferences organized in early 1990s by the Polish Economic Society (Polskie Towarzystwo Ekonomiczne – PTE). The problem with that criticism was that from the beginning of transition until mid-1990s it was the only association of professional economists in existence. Thus, the criticism of transition – emerging from their conferences and public pronouncements of their members – was often, mistakenly, perceived by the general public as *the official position* of the body of Polish professional economists.

For many economists thinking along the lines of classical economics and supporting transition it was a dangerous distortion of the reality – and one that might be harmful for further developments in transition as such. To eliminate the lopsided institutional set-up and change the balance in this respect, a group of these economists decided in late autumn of 1993 to establish another association. In this manner an organized countervailing power to that of the doomsayers from PTE would be created. Representatives from the group in question came and asked me to chair the organizing committee of the forthcoming association.

Why they came to me? It was days after my – very loud! – resignation from representing the newly formed government, headed by ex-communists, in the European Bank for Reconstruction and Development as an executive director of the supervisory board. Thus, apart from my academic and public policy debater's performance, many economists supporting the initiative were convinced that my presence at the head of such a committee would also send a message suggesting a policy choice as far as an attitude to transition was concerned.

The then existing association (PTE) was full of old-style communist reformers, quite sympathetic to the new government. The new association, which took the historical name of the Society of Polish Economists (the first was established in 1916), was to be seen as distancing itself from *systemic reforms* and unequivocally supporting *systemic change.*

Society of Polish Economists (TEP) was duly formed and under the chairmanship of Prof. Waclaw Wilczynski, an older generation free-market economist from Posnan, became very active in support of the systemic change in the years to come. Prof. Wilczynski chaired the society until 1999 and I succeeded him in that position, chairing the TEP in the next, 1999–2007 period.

While referring to transition debates I and other TEP members participated both at home and abroad it is worth stressing that the second half of 1990s was the period of empirical verification of various, often exotic, economic theories and policy prescriptions. I mentioned in the preceding chapter an exotic macroeconomic "sponge theory" of the unlimited amount of money Polish economy could – and should – absorb. The severe undersupply of money was seen by its authors as the one and only cause of output decline. Polish policy makers rejected the "sponge theory". By contrast, Russian central bank rulers were very active in printing money, simultaneously undermining the position of systemic change-oriented Yegor Gaidar government and contributing strongly to three-to-four digit hyperinflation in the 1992–94 period.

Csaba in the already quoted survey pointed out to a more general confrontation between standard classical *cum* neo-institutional, as well as neoclassical prescriptions on the one hand and some unorthodox alternatives to both strands of economics on the other. As far as the latter were concerned, it is worth stressing that, indeed, many economists of various theoretical backgrounds and different political affiliations joined the chorus of vehement opposition to institute macroeconomic restraint at the start of transition (see Chapter 7 above).

The foregoing issue was put in a comparative perspective by Prof. Csaba in his 2002 survey. He contrasted two broad approaches to stabilization, as far as disinflation and the resumption of economic growth were concerned. The standard, that is classical and neoclassical approaches, by and large proved to be successful. Wherever the transition proceeded along the lines of the "Holy Trinity" (stabilization, liberalization, and privatization), once inflation declined – either sharply or more slowly but systematically – the economies sooner or later registered the return to economic growth. Moreover, other signs of successful performance could also be observed (he stressed, as I did above, a much better export performance of the foregoing group of transition economies).

By contrast, the performance of countries whose policy makers found intellectual basis in the so-called structuralist economic ideas rejecting the imposition of macroeconomic restraint, generally registered higher inflation and for longer periods. Economic growth was, in consequence, coming later, sometimes -m-u-c-h later. Laszlo Csaba's conclusion was that it is stabilization, and especially its disinflation component, that leads to economic growth, and not the *vice versa.* Dash for growth in order to reduce inflation in such an – allegedly more benign – economic environment generally failed. Thus, unorthodox approaches to stabilization failed the historical test of their validity in post-communist transition.

One could not agree more with his reasoning and conclusion. However, to me, although it was an important step forward, it did not end the contentious debate on success vs. failure of transition. As the 1990s went on I became increasingly dissatisfied with the explanations that classified countries purely in accordance with their successful or unsuccessful pursuance of what I called the "Holy Trinity" of transition. In my opinion something else must have intervened as well.

Ever more numerous comparisons made within various international financial institutions, as well as those made by individual analysts, invariably suggested the split of post-communist transition economies into two different groups. Success stories, or leaders in post-communist transition, were usually – if not exclusively – countries belonging to one group, that is countries of East-Central Europe. They were Hungary, Poland, Czechia, Slovakia, and Slovenia, as well three Baltic countries: Estonia, Latvia, and Lithuania that caught up with the group somewhat later. The lag stemmed from the fact that they not only had to cope – like the first five countries – with political and economic transition, but also underwent (economically painful) separation from the Soviet and later post-Soviet economy. In contrast to the eight success stories listed above, less successful countries, or laggards in transition, were mostly post-Soviet countries (with the exception of the three Baltic countries belonging to the former group).

An explanation of sort – more in the nature of an unsystematic noise – was offered during 1990s. It was put in personal rather than in institutional *cum* policy terms. "You were lucky – I often heard – because you had Balcerowicz in charge", or the Czechs heard that they were lucky, because they had Klaus at the helm. The list of such lucky exceptions could be made longer, of course.

I rejected such personalization of history by using two counterarguments. Firstly, I answered that I did not believe that talents were distributed across nations in such a capricious way that you did not see them to the East of the line drawn between Estonia in the North-East and Slovenia in the South-West. One should look for more systematic answers as to why to the East of the said line there had been few if any undisputed leaders. Statistically capricious talent distribution was a false trail in this respect.

And, secondly, I argued that, yes, Poland had Balcerowicz, Czechia had Klaus, Estonia had Laar and Slovakia had (with a lag, at the turn of the XXI century) Miklos in charge. However, Hungary, for example had a succession of politicians from both left and right without anybody towering over the transition process as much as those mentioned above did. Lajos Bokros was a "hired gun" to clear the macroeconomic mess left by the first non-communist government of Jozsef Antall; he did his job well and left. And, yet, Hungary became first the leader and later a part of the leading group of countries in the post-communist transition. Slovenia and Lithuania were offering – by and large – a similar story to tell.

I have been of the opinion that what really separated groups of countries was, first of all, the different institutional heritage, affecting countries and whole regions throughout their history. In considering institutional heritage the impact of communist institutions looked like an obvious first choice. After all, we dealt with countries undergoing transition away from the communist system. Classifying countries in terms of success or failure, or their belonging to the group of leaders or laggards, on the basis of differences in their communist past seemed almost natural.

And, indeed, if we looked at the line drawn between Estonia in the North-East and Slovenia in the South/West, then societies in countries to the East of that line indeed have been living under the communist system longer than those to the West of that line. As transition laggards were also countries located to the East of that line, while transition leaders were located to the West of it, it seemed that we found another differentiating variable. Societies living for a shorter period of their history under communism had a better chance to succeed in transition – and the vice versa. At first glance, the search for an additional variable – alongside the variables making the "Holy Trinity" of transition – was satisfactorily concluded.

However, before shouting "*Eureka!*", I argued that we should also look at the remaining transition countries, mostly to the South of both East-Central European and post-Soviet countries. A look there undermines the thesis that the length of the period of living under communism is the differentiating variable we were looking for. Let us consider Bulgaria and Romania (to say nothing about Serbia and other countries involved in the post-Yugoslav civil war). Bulgaria and Romania were under the communist rule for a much shorter period than post-Soviet states, no longer than were eight transition leaders. And, yet, even if the two joined – with a lag – the European Union, they could hardly be presented as transition leaders! Thus, my perception was that the search for an additional variable helping to differentiate between success or failure of transition should continue.

The thesis that I signaled first in 1996 at the Vienna Mont Pelerin Society meeting was that we should look for that differentiating variable between leaders and laggards in transition primarily by looking not so much at the communist past, but rather at the *pre*-communist past. History casts a long shadow, often creating different sets of mutually compatible institutions that I prefer to call civilizations. I pointed out that the existence of different *civilizational fundamentals* across groups of post-communist countries has been an important factor shaping their responses to the challenge of transition.

What else, apart from being for a shorter period under the communist rule, did these eight countries – commonly regarded as leaders of transition – share in terms of civilizational fundamentals? In contrast with post-Soviet, as well as Balkan countries (apart from Croatia), they were a part of the West, or Western Christendom, sharing its institutions. And we all know that Western civilization offered through the ages more economic, civic, and political freedoms than other civilizations, past and present.

One may object that Eastern Christendom is just a part of Christendom and, as such, a part of the same civilization, but such interpretation can easily be refuted. Let me start with the relationship between temporal and transcendental authority in both branches of Christendom. Economic historian, David Landes, observed that "Christianity … early made the distinction between God and Cesar. To each his own…This did not preclude misunderstandings and conflict…", but the benefits for the evolving civilization were considerable. "(W)here authority is divided, dissent flourishes. This may be bad for certainty and conformity, but it is surely good for the spirit and popular initiatives".[44]

As I stressed at about the same time (see my 1997 article on "The Transformation to the Market… Ibidem", p. 263), this characteristic applied only to -W-e-s-t-e-r-n Christendom. In the Eastern Christendom patriarchs never criticized – or quarreled with – the emperors, neither earlier in Byzantium, nor later in Moscow. To use the somewhat more modern (communist) terminology, patriarchs were emperors' "deputies for ideological affairs" of sort. Divided authority would be unthinkable in the two successive despotic empires of Eastern Christendom…

Even more important, I think, were differences in the extent of economic freedoms between Western and Eastern Christendom. Ancient Greece's political and civic freedoms, combined with the foundation of economic activity on private property, and the elaborated rule of law created in the private (civic) sphere in ancient Rome, survived primarily in Western (including Central) Europe.

The revival of economic activity in Western and Central Europe from the Xth century, CE, onwards, built further progress on these foundations. This progress was primarily due to the revival of the cities that step by step expanded economic freedoms and, to buttress these, bought or wrestled from their political masters civic and, conditions permitting, also political freedoms. Nowhere else in the world an institution called *commune*, a city government elected by the burghers, from among the burghers, and run in the interest of the burghers, has ever been established.

The economic and civic expansion of medieval cities was an unusual phenomenon, contrasting sharply at the time not only with the rest of the world, but also with the world beyond expanding cities. For even in Western Europe, beyond cities, feudal system, characterized by vertical relations, dominated.

By contrast, in the self-governed cities, horizontal economic relations between equals were the norm. Moreover, craftsmen, merchants, and financiers participated in civic and political life of the cities, *e.g.*, by electing officials of guilds and merchant associations, and – as a political corollary – officials of city governments. Moreover, cities needed rules that would govern such relations between equals, as well as judges to apply such laws. Feudal laws, solving the problems of vertical subordination, such as those between seigneurs and vassals, were useless for the purpose of judging commercial and other disputes among equals. So, were the individuals, who applied feudal rules of subordination, because they were also immersed in the vertical subordination structure (for example, the disputes between serfs and their lord were decided by the lord himself…).

Decentralization characterizing Western world helped in enhancing and extending freedoms at the level of the individual. If a craftsman, or merchant, or financier felt oppressed by regulations or taxes, he could easily move from one city to another, where the extent of economic freedom was greater. Since such departures reduced the tax base of the cities left by the departing burghers, their self-governing authorities were under pressure to liberalize the offensive rules or cut taxes. Such developments gave rise to the phenomenon called by some authors *institutional competition*. So, in the West the dynamics of change was in the direction of greater freedom (and as a result, greater efficiency).

The reverse was true in the Eastern Christendom area. There was nothing like *communes* in Byzantium. And the two centuries of subjugation of Russian principalities to the Mongol/Tartar rule deepened the despotic streak in both the institutions and the style of governance of the emerging winners, Moscow kings (and later emperors). The self-government of a few autonomous cities, remnants from the pre-despotic past (with Novgorod in the lead) was brutally repressed. Russian empire was very much like despotic Asian empires that are called by some historians *patrimonial*, that is states, where the ruler decides about everybody and everything, including life and property of his subjects.

By contrast, Tallin and Riga enjoyed the self-government as did all Hanseatic cities already in the early to middle medieval period. Their craftsmen, merchants, and financiers pursued economic activities on the basis of their private property under the rule of law, characterized by a large degree of economic (and civic) freedoms. The foregoing applied also to East-Central European states, such as Czech Kingdom (latter part of the Hapsburg empire), Hungarian kingdom (*ditto*) and Polish and later Polish-Lithuanian kingdom. There was less self-government in the cities in these kingdoms, but the system of private property was well established and protected. A smaller or greater degree of the rule of law (including civic freedoms) was present there as well.

By contrast in Russia, as stressed already, everything was owned by the emperor (the *tsar*) and everybody, even the highest officials of the state, was at the mercy of the tsar's whim. The foregoing was true even under the "Westernizing reformer", Peter the Great. In actual fact private property was first officially guaranteed by the law of the Russian state under the Empress Catherine the Great as late as in the second half of the XVIII century. And even then for the upper and middle class owners only. Peasants had to wait yet another century.

The foregoing contrasting histories of Western and Eastern Christendom, with hundreds of years of living under the rule of law, as well as established and protected private property in the countries belonging to the former civilization, made a lot of difference in post-communist transition. In, say, Prague or Budapest, or Tallin or Riga, return to the dominance of private property and its more or less strict legal protection, was seen after the 1989–91 collapse of communism as the return to normality.

Not so, however, in, say, Moscow or Kiev. There, the private property was looked at with suspicion and the unwillingness to accord to it proper legal protection by the bureaucracy was palpably visible. The same applied generally to capitalist market rules of the game, better appreciated and applied in East-Central Europe than in post-Soviet states.

My Russian colleagues told me some horror stories concerning competition. The absence of capitalist market rules of the game not only under communism, but in fact for most of the history of Moscow kingdom and then Russian empire, created the perception of competition as a game without rules. So, hearing about "ruthless competition", Russian entrepreneurs (of sort…) understood it not as an economic game, where a loser who cannot cover his costs by his revenues is forced by the losses to exit the market. For them "ruthless competition" meant eliminating competitors not from the market but from the face of the earth. It quite often happened that they sent to the competitor's office a few *Mafiosi* with Kalashnikov guns, who subsequently finished off the competitor, as well as all his close collaborators...

In such a frame of mind, where suspicion of something perceived as alien institution (private property rights) or something that seems to threaten one's livelihood (no less institutionally alien economic competition), the general rules of the capitalist market or some specific rules will not be applied properly and consistently. Or if they will, they will be distorted in their applications to suit prejudices and/or interests (viz. the infamous Magnitsky case in post-Soviet Russia).

Thus, different civilizational fundamentals play an important role in the process of transition. Some sets of mutually compatible institutions (including law enforcement procedures) contribute to the smoother systemic transition, while other may have the opposite, detrimental effects. Let us explain the difference by stressing that some general and/or specific rules may be well designed, but their application in a different framework of civilizational fundamentals may end in the resounding failure.

To begin with, the economy of a post-Soviet country such as Russia would not be helped much by the fact that the regulations on entrepreneurship or those on property rights have been very well designed. It mattered infinitely more that the weak or missing *general law and order* of the despotic, corrupt, and inefficient regime created conditions, where average entrepreneur perceived a high threat to both his life and property. Under such circumstances even routine business transactions were perceived to be dangerous and – if undertaken at all – they were usually very short term-oriented or took pathological forms.

We can conclude that due to the lack of the *Rechtstaat* (rule-of-law) tradition and – more widely – in the absence of law and order in general, even the best designed specific rules will not generate much entrepreneurship. So it is not surprising that entrepreneurship indicators, for example a number of new firms per 1000 inhabitants, were in the second half of 1990s an order of magnitude lower in Russia than in Hungary, Poland, or Czechia.

The interaction between economic freedoms and other – civic and political – freedoms is important also in the wider sense than the entrepreneurship and property rights-related issues. In liberal democracies and capitalist markets such interactions build trust among individuals. And it is not the narrowly defined business trust, built in the process of repeated transactions between the same parties, but the trust in the fundamental institutions of the state. To be more precise, the trust in the *continuity of fundamental institutions* of a given country.

Individuals living under such civilization, also entrepreneurs and business people in general, learn over time to trust that they do not wake up one morning under the rule of institutions inimical to what they learned to trust in and observed over long periods. The probability of such an inimical change is greater in countries, where the continuity of such fundamentals was already broken, as in post-communist transition leaders from East-Central Europe. However, the probability of inimical institutional change is even greater in countries, where good institutions did not take roots at all, as in post-Soviet or in Balkan states.

The foregoing considerations find their support in the history of that part of Europe. It is presented graphically in Figure 8.1A and 8.1B. Figure 8.1. A presents the transition leaders, eight countries: Czechia, Estonia, Hungary, Latvia, Lithuania, Poland, Slovakia, and Slovenia (marked) and the remaining countries of the region (unmarked). A brief note: I presented the eight transition leaders on that map at many conferences and nobody ever questioned that one or another country did not deserve to be included into the leaders' group.

The Figure 8.1B shows the religious border between Western and Eastern Christendom in the XVI century in the same region. An interesting feature of these two figures is that if one puts one map on another, he or she would discover that it is -t-h-e -s-a-m-e -b-o-r-d-e-r. Thus, the maps are at least highly suggestive that civilizational fundamentals matter in the post-communist transition process.

I presented these ideas in a number of places, among them at two Mont Pelerin Society meetings in Vienna and Potsdam, Germany. They generated mixed reactions among the participants, also among the then present Nobel Prize winners. I remember Prof. Gary Becker being cool to the idea, while more institutionally-minded Prof. James Buchanan was markedly more interested. These ideas I elaborated in a number of articles and books of mine.[45]

Frankly, the idea that different historical civilizational fundamentals were no less important in transition than the "Holy Trinity" of transition were not well received by the majority of those following closely the post-communist systemic change. I was disappointed, but not surprised by such a reaction. I noted it already during an earlier debate on the causes of large output declines in early transition. If some author stresses something both rather obvious (or at least something that -s-h-o-u-l-d -h-a-v-e -b-e-e-n -o-b-v-i-o-u-s for those studying Soviet-type economies) and undermining dominant views on the subject, such negative reaction is only to be expected.

After all, I pointed out in an earlier (output fall) debate that many other specialists missed the important role of inventories, which were in communist economies 30–40% GDP higher than in capitalist economies. What I did might have been seen as a rebuke to those who missed the importance of such a significant factor! The same happened, I suspect, with respect to the impact of civilizational fundamentals. Here too, what I proposed was in fact a proposition to add a level

Figure 8.1A: Leaders and laggards: East-Central European and East European economies

Figure 8.1B: XVIth century border between Western and Eastern Christendom. Leaders are only to the West of the border

of analysis. Most of the time the analysis of post-communist transition was pursued largely at two levels. At the level of general rules (see my "Holy Trinity" of transition: stabilization, liberalization, and privatization) and the level of specific rules. The introduction of history of institutions and institutional change and their impact on the present added an important third level. But, it again, could be seen as a rebuke by those who disregarded so far the impact of the long run on systemic change!

This chapter deals primarily with the power of the market, its rules of the game and its operations, as well as with my intellectual and (more rarely) political engagements during, roughly, the second half of 1990s. From the perspective of the power of the market it is worth pointing out that successes in transition, both with respect to building (or rebuilding) the institutions and economic performance, are highly supportive for the thesis on the strong impact of the market on the countries that have been widely regarded as transition leaders. The stress on the long term civilizational foundations only underlines what, for example, Janos Kornai wrote in his 1990 book *The Road to a Free Economy* that "*embourgeoisement* is a lengthy historical process".[46] Precisely. All those burghers (craftsmen, merchants, financiers) both benefited from economic freedoms of the market and expanded them. The rule of law as applied to the civic sphere, especially economic transactions, created the foundations, upon which merchant capitalism thrived in medieval Europe and later, during the Enlightenment era, evolved into industrial capitalism.

It seemed obvious to me that the *restoration* of the capitalist market institutions in East-Central Europe – from Estonia in the North-East to Slovenia in the South-West would be easier than building these institutions almost from the scratch in post-Soviet countries of Eastern Europe. For even if many of capitalist institutions were abolished during the communist rule, the knowledge and – more often – the memory of these institutions, passed to younger generations by their fathers, grandfathers, and great grandfathers who lived under these institutions, continued to exist in East-Central Europe.

An interesting contribution to the point considered here was made by Prof. Sirc during the panel chaired by me at the 1990 meeting of the European Economic Association, its first meeting after the collapse of communism in East-Central Europe (although not yet in the Soviet Union). During the discussion there on causes, dynamics and consequences of communism's collapse we agreed that the turning point from ever slower economic growth to more or less marked decline took place in 1970s. Ljubo Sirc pointed out to other panelists and the audience that there is one more determinant of the fact that 1970s became such a watershed. He explained that 1970s were the decade, when the last generation of those, who learned before the World War II what work (meaning: decent work) was about, had retired. That was a highly perceptive comment concerning East-Central and Balkan economies, where communism was imposed in mid-1940s. Photo in Figure 8.2. shows Prof. Sirc sitting first from the left, next to Prof. Csaba and me.

Figure 8.2: Participants in the "historical" panel on communist collapse and the beginning of post-communist transition in summer 1990 at the Lisbon annual meeting of the European Economic Association. Sitting from the left are Prof. Ljubo Sirc from Glasgow University and Chairman of the Centre for Research into Communist Economies, Prof. Laszlo Csaba from the Institute of Economics, Hungarian Academy of Science, author of these memoirs, chairing the panel, and Prof. Paul Dembinski, University of Geneva, Switzerland. (Photo from personal archives of the author)

However, the last generation of those who learned what decent work was about in the Soviet Union had retired in early 1940s, and died quite soon afterwards. So, when the opportunity to build a capitalist market economy emerged in 1990s there was nobody around to tell younger generation what capitalism and work within such an institutional arrangement was about…

In many a debate, as well as in a number of my publications, I tried to present the view that the power of the market has an impact – and very strong impact at that – if there is a certain level of knowledge of what the market rules of the game are about. For it is not enough to introduce the rules which the "Holy Trinity" of transition consist of, but we should expect some knowledge of these rules among market participants, as well as their acceptance. It was much easier to find both in those countries, where the intergenerational transfer of such knowledge and acceptance was at all possible. It clearly was not possible in Russia and other post-Soviet states for two reasons. Firstly, there was little to transfer in the first place (see above) and, secondly, whatever positive in these respects could be transferred, was not transferred because there was nobody around to undertake the task of such intergenerational transmission. Thus not only there was no institutional continuity of the rules of capitalist market, but also no interpersonal continuity of the transfer of the knowledge of such rules.

I started this chapter with personal stories from the family. And it makes sense to end it in a similar manner. The second half of 1990s was a period of continuous institutional changes for the better, slower than at the start of transition, but substantial nonetheless. By contrast, improvements in living standards tended to accelerate toward the end of the decade (and the century). The latter changes were the most impressive in the latecomers to the group of transition leaders, that is in Baltic countries. Once they successfully coped with separating their economies from that of the former Soviet Union – at a cost of the largest fall of output among transition leaders – their economies accelerated and in the decade 1998–2007 were the fastest growing not only in Europe, but also among the fastest growing in the world.

A success in terms of large aggregates is always a sum of individual successes. Thus, individuals in Estonia, Latvia, and Lithuania learned – like their counterparts in Hungary, Czechia, Poland, Slovenia and Slovakia a few years earlier, that *sky is the limit* if one finds one's own exciting career path. And career was not always a corporate career, but also a career in doing what one likes best, combined with the feeling that one has an influence on the course of events.

Some such (Polish) careers may be worth recalling here. A young girl started on that path on June 4, 1989, when – still a student at the history department of Warsaw University – was delegated by "Solidarity" to the electoral commission in Zoliborz district in northern Warsaw. Next, was a managerial position in the Press Publishers' Association, something excitingly new in the world of freshly liquidated censorship and the end of press monopoly of the communist party.

After a few years Anna Smolka, the girl in question, moved from public to private institutions. In 1997 she became a head of public relations in one of the national investment funds. Why there? Because she believed in privatization and the – necessary – dominance of the private sector in the economy. Two years later she took a similar position in the just forming Polish Confederation of Private Employers (PKPP). Once things started working smoothly, Anna was simply looking for another challenge. When she was interviewed, she was a co-owner of a small public relations agency, worked for herself and continued to be happy.[47]

From the same series of conversations one more such individual career is worth quoting. Also a student at some point of his career, young man in question failed at the exams and started looking for another career. During one of his trips to the West in search of some menial jobs (a few hundred dollars saved was at the end of 1980s quite a sum), he noticed a business area completely absent in Poland. Together with another colleague, both decided to start a firm producing t-shirts with names and logos of various musical groups. That was the starting point; later they offered their services to other clients, business firms, etc.

The first big client appeared in late 1991. Coca-Cola Poland made an order in five digit numbers for the 1992 Olympic Games in Barcelona. Final order was for 40 000 t-shirts with a $ 20 000 cash advance. Problems cropped up, given the lack of technological experience, but they were sooner or later solved. The firm began to prosper. Most of the revenues was ploughed back into the firm. More machinery and more employment.

At the beginning they employed 7 workers. After the change in the name (into Willson & Brown) and the expanded range of offered products these numbers multiplied. In the next decade, by the time of the interview, the number of employees swelled to 450! As of 2001 they started exporting. And participating in international fairs in Berlin, Paris, Moscow, and Duesseldorf. A worthwhile piece of information is that both owners of the firm took their first holiday in 1998, after seven years since the start of the firm.[48]

Leafing through the pages of Czech, Hungarian, Estonian, and other press would generate similar stories of young people who found that under the democracy and capitalist market the sky is the limit…

And what about my own sky? I already decided toward the end of the first half of 1990s that I am not particularly interested in a career of a professional politician. My links with politics were indirect, via public economic education, and occasionally advising some politicians. My public activities first in the Adam Smith Center (CAS) and later in the Polish Society of Economists (TEP) were very much in accord with the above preferences.

And as a scholar I continued writing books and articles for the international academic market. What I wrote in the Polish press was still largely a part of public economic education. When a collection of these writings was published by C.H. Beck in 2000 I gave it a (proper!) title: "Polemics written on the road (to capitalism)".

After 1997 elections, won by the "Solidarity" camp parties – AWS ("Solidarity: Electoral Action") and Freedom Union – I got from the former yet another political proposition. Some people from AWS told me that I was being considered for the post of the Minister of Finance. But under the condition of pursuing the *de-communization* in the said ministry. I answered, a bit flippantly, that I can promise *de-idiotization.* Ministry of Finance requires experts in many specialized areas and there is no place there for idiots. Whether specialist in financial regulation is left leaning or right leaning, or a classical liberal is of secondary importance in the situation of the dearth of high class specialists in those difficult areas. Finance Ministry employees are not policy makers; they are technicians of sort. As Readers might have guessed, after the conversation in question the offer from AWS disappeared in the thin air…

Chapter 9: A Collision of Emotions, Ideology and Economics

I stressed, primarily in Chapter 7, that stabilization had been the most contentious part of the "Holy Trinity" of transition from early to late 1990s. Battles were, however, mainly intellectual and policy-oriented. An average citizen of a transition country was not directly involved and arguments used were way above his or her level of economic competence (extremely low, given the economic illiteracy reigning under communism!).

About the only moment his or her concerns touched the stabilization was when wages were negotiated between a given trade union and state enterprise management (that is in the absence of a real owner!). So, in Poland they protested, for example, against the introduced tax on excessive wages (a part of the stabilization program for a few years). But the foregoing were, in fact, trivial pursuits. Much more depended on the stabilization part; I reminisced at length on the issues involved – and battles about them – in Chapter 7 above.

In parallel with my specific involvement in the stabilization issues (see in particular the work on the "Beksiak Report"), I have always been deeply interested in – and concerned about – the privatization part of the "Holy Trinity" of transition. It pre-dated the start of transition, please note the seminars I co-organized in Kazimierz Dolny on the new private sector and privatization of state enterprises in 1987–88, the years directly preceding the "game over" verdict on communism by history.

True, in preparing the program of stabilization and systemic change in late summer of 1989 (the already quoted report for the Polish parliament) I was mostly working on stabilization. However, I never lost track of the privatization issues and participated very actively in the debates on the shape of the privatization part of our program. I even contributed to some of institutional arrangements finalized in that part of the program.

The reasons of my keen interest in the privatization (from above) issue were obvious. I never had the slightest doubts about where we were to go. The road we should travel was one leading to a capitalist market economy. And such an economy required -p-r-i-v-a-t-e -f-i-r-m-s, with their healthy structure of incentives, to be dominant in the national economy. Economic history knows no case of the well performing market economy with the dominant state firms! "No capitalism minus capitalists!", as I stressed very early in transition on the pages of *the Financial Times.*[49]

It was also obvious to me that *there is a world of difference between privatizing the firm and privatizing the economy*, a point rarely discussed in theoretical terms in the early transition period either in Poland or elsewhere. When these issues became relevant in transition, I wrote, with a colleague from the Beksiak-led team, Prof. Tomasz Gruszecki, an article to that effect that appeared in *Aussenwirtschaft* in 1991.[50] Among the relevant issues at the time were also those concerning the choice of rules to be applied to the just emerging privatization processes. Accordingly, we stressed the different sets of rules needed in the case of each basic form of privatization.

Thus, we pointed out that there exists *privatization "from above"*, the privatization of the state-, or more precisely, publicly-owned firms. It required a wide set of specifically enacted rules, combined with the availability of both public and private organizations, professionally able to get involved in the privatization process (as it was perceived at that time).

However, there existed also – a much neglected intellectually – *privatization "from below"*, the establishment of *de novo* firms, private already from the scratch. The latter privatization did not require any specific tailor-made rules. The general rules, established in the liberalization part of the "Holy Trinity" of transition, would be sufficient to create a level-playing field for all firms operating on the market, including new firms that began their activity during the transition process. Rules of establishment and rules of operation, as well as rules concerning financing and taxation, all should be established as general principles and applied to the economy as a whole, not only to new firms. An important conclusion emerging therefrom was that privatization "from below" was by far the easiest in terms of establishing rules of the game. And the idea was prevalent that if the rules were set right, privatization "from below" would expand rapidly throughout the post-communist countries. No machinery of the state would be required to support – or, worse, command – the process, in contrast with the privatization "from above".

Unfortunately, few in post-communist transition countries noted the importance of the privatization "from below" issue and the conclusion about the relative ease of setting it right. The attention of nearly everybody – employees of state firms, trade unionists, politicians old and new, journalists, even transition experts – was transfixed on what nearly all perceived to be *the privatization*. That is on privatization "from above".

Frankly, it was difficult to criticize them. After all, state enterprises in post-communist countries amounted at the start of transition to some 80–100% of employment in the respective economies, 70–100% of output and 95–100% of their productive assets. Moreover, as transition countries – especially transition leaders – turned into liberal democracies, state firms' employees and their families became also a large part of the electorate in each country! The latter numbers brought into the picture a new factor, namely -e-m-o-t-i-o-n-s, both ideologically-based and those based on envy pure and simple.

The Readers may for the moment put aside ideological emotions, as I was already dealing with ideologies earlier, both in Part I, Chapters 4 and 5, and more recently in Part II, Chapter 7, in considering the structure of ownership. Envy as a prime mover of human action is a thoroughly underappreciated – and even less researched - issue. Yet, in the privatization "from above", envy-based opinions and reactions were quite often dominant. The foregoing applies to most privatizations.

It is enough to remind the Thatcher government conducted privatizations in 1980s. Wherever flesh-and-blood individuals have been offered some preferences in obtaining bits and pieces (usually shares) of a particular privatized firm, blood pressure rose among many who regarded themselves as unjustly deprived of the preferences in question. Protests exploded, supported by opposition politicians who sensed in these protests an easy road to power. Let me add that, quite often, they had also an ideological (i.e. collectivist) axe to grind.

The privatization stories in post-communist transition were not much different in this respect. And following my conviction that a joke is a shortcut to understanding, let me repeat the story of a Polish humorist, the already quoted Jacek Fedorowicz. He based his psychological explanations on the well known story about the frog and the scorpion. His stories were originally presented in the 1993–94 period on the radio (it was "Radio Z", one of the most frequently listened to in Poland at the time).

> Scorpion begged frog to rescue him from the flood. "Give me a chance to sit on your back" – he pleaded. The frog was, however, full of misgivings: "But how can I be sure that you will not sting me during the journey?" – she asked. "But it is obvious – argued scorpion – that in such a case we would both get drowned." He convinced the frog with that explanation. "So, you see the point – she said – OK, get on and I start swimming." Unfortunately, in the middle of the deep water, the scorpion stung the frog. "Sorry – he said (when they were both drowning). – This is in my nature, I am afraid…"
>
> The same story can be repeated with respect to privatization of state firms. People knew, in principle, that state firms had to be privatized. After all, politicians, media, and – last but not least – the experience they earned during visits to the West told them that private ownership is infinitely more efficient. However, when employees of state firms in transition countries learned that some real property was to be privatized, that there would be some owners in flesh and blood, they would sell their soul to the devil to learn that these owners got the property in question through some dirty tricks and it would be taken away from them. Like scorpion, they had it in their nature.[51]

The consequences for privatization (that "from above") of such a concentration of envy was obvious. Few politicians would push for rapid privatization of state firms in such an aura of ill will and envy. The process would slow down considerably. And the longer inefficient state firms continued to operate in the little privatized environment, the worse would be the performance of a given economy as a whole.

Two extra comments. First, if a humorist story does not convince the Readers sufficiently, let me present a concise statement of a philosopher. Leszek Kolakowski, one of the authorities on Marxism, took a broader view of a range of arguments against private property within the framework of revolutionary philosophies of the XIX and XX centuries. In his view "in many (but not all) revolutionary movements, what was justice in doctrinal terms was, psychologically and practically, envy."[52] Kolakowski harbored no doubts that the immediate aim of nationalization was to destroy the existing elites – whether aristocratic, or meritocratic, plutocratic, or intellectual – and to supersede them with a new, propertyless – and therefore much more obedient! – political class. Clearly, the ideology and envy tend to coalesce at some point!

Second, with envy blinding many people's views, they somehow accepted completely contradictory opinions. An extensive survey made by researchers from the Kozminski Business School in Warsaw revealed that the same large sample (about four thousand interviewees) said" "yes" to the following views: appx. 60% of them agreed that privatization is necessary because it increases the efficiency of privatized firms and appx. 70% of the same sample agreed that privatization amounts to thievery and in that process one financial swindle is chasing another. Warm greetings from the scorpion's inner conflict!

The co-existence of such views looks surrealistic, but it is not. It does not matter that "privatization as thievery" is a figment of an envious imagination. It does not matter either that it was so many times empirically proven not to be the case. Let me for a change quote myself from one of my early comments on the topic in 1992: "Falsification of a myth does not eliminate it from intellectual circulation. Myths are fed by beliefs in specific phenomena, not by applying knowledge to explain them."[53]

Thus, given the strong beliefs in such a myth, Dr. Janusz Lewandowski, a Minister of Ownership Transformation in two governments in early 1990s, had more than 60 criminal investigations associated with privatization cases directed against him. He was exonerated in -a-l-l these cases, but his experience has certainly been discouraging for those trying to accelerate privatization in post-communist economies. The other side of the coin was that the state-owned dinosaurs were allowed to survive for years in a row, in spite of increasingly bad economic indicators. For large state firms had something that new, usually small, private firms did not have – namely the political clout.

The politics of privatization "from above" varied across countries. It definitely was much more complicated – and less successful – in Poland than, for example, in Czechoslovakia, and later Czechia. The outcomes were decided by the socio-political environment in a given transition country and by the strategy and tactics pursued by privatizers themselves.

Sticking to the two countries mentioned above, Polish system-changers undoubtedly operated in a much more difficult environment. On the one hand, they had – like all post-communist transition countries – ex-communists, turned social-democrats who instinctively (and to some extent ideologically) were against privatization from above. The same applied to ex-communist trade unions. They all learned how to live off the state ownership and the need to adjust was met with little sympathy, to say the least.

On the other hand Poland was unique in a sense that within the victorious "Solidarity" camp there was strong belief in the economically nonsensical utopia of workers' self-management, with workers (employees) councils managing state-owned firms. Remember my clashes with the believers in the utopia I mentioned in Part I, Chapters 4 and 5? Clearly, the utopia in question discredited itself by the collapsing Yugoslavia at about the same time when transition programs began to be formulated. Workers' self-management in state firms was, thus, indefensible in its practically applied Yugoslav form.

However, the ideological guardians in the "Solidarity" movement unerringly reached for the second-worst solution, demanding insiders' privatization. Firms were to be given for free or at a minimum sold on easy terms to employees. A neo-institutional branch of economics, theory of property rights, explains conditions of efficiency of various forms of ownership, as well as efficiency of varieties of a particular form of ownership. I worked along the lines of the theory in late 1980s-early 1991, applying it to the communist/post-communist world. Thus, in my study: *Privatization in Poland*[54] and in some other publications, I listed certain criteria upon which the efficiency of various ownership arrangements should be evaluated.

Applying these criteria, I stressed the lowest rank of employee ownership among the varieties of private ownership. To make a long story short and easily understandable, I looked at the *control* variable, that is the ease of owner(s)' control over the performance of the firm and found that employee ownership, given its large number of owners, faces severe difficulties in the decision making process. Benefits of combining ownership and managerial functions decline sharply under so many proprietors in comparison with sole proprietorship. Next criticism is that under employee ownership certain types of investment decisions will not be undertaken. For example, in the stagnant market (no output increase envisaged in the short to medium run) owners-employees will not vote in favor of productivity-increasing investment because it must result in redundancies. Furthermore, in closed type employee ownership arrangements preferred by believers in the utopia in question there is no "fresh blood" entering the firm in the form of new, dominant owners with good managerial and technological ideas. Ownership equality is, unfortunately, ruinous for economic efficiency…

Those in charge of Polish privatization program (euphemistically called: program of ownership transformation to avoid the unloved word: "privatization"!)) understood the traps and were dead set against the employee ownership. Their response was to stress the preference for the most transparent form of privatization of state firms. Since trade unionists and others were eager to pin a label of "thievery privatization" or "sale of national treasures" to almost every privatization that the government team, with Prof. Balcerowicz at the helm, pressed for, the government opted for the "cleanest" type, namely the public sale of shares on the country's stock market.

However, their expectations that transparency will reduce the amount of general criticism and – even nastier – specific accusations were unfortunately too optimistic. Envy and ideology (amounting often to one and the same thing!) continued to hold an upper hand. The government saved the largest and most important state firms from gross inefficiency and quite probably bankruptcy in the medium run by pushing through public sale of shares (or, alternatively, direct sale to foreign investors). In that it succeeded, but most medium-sized state firms were privatized as employee-owned firms. Besides, the cost of the foregoing successes with respect to the privatization of large, important state firms was tremendous in socio-psychological terms. Privatization from above continued to be an albatross around the Polish transition's neck.

The wave of envy, although present everywhere, was not so overwhelming in every transition country. And good political ideas could turn privatization into an asset rather than the liability for transition. Such is the story of Vaclav Klaus' approach to the issue in question. Thus, already in December 1989 at the second large gathering at Vaclavske Namesti in Prague, Klaus promised the then Czechoslovak population the restoration of the right of citizens of the country to own productive assets. The right – he stressed – they were deprived of by the communist rule.

It was an excellent approach in terms of social psychology. The *kuponovka*, citizens' privatization program, envisaging the prospect of individuals buying shares of selected state enterprises after receiving coupons from the state at a token price, was presented as an -a-c-t -o-f -j-u-s-t-i-c-e. The property, taken over by the communist state without the consent of citizens, was to be, symbolically, returned to the latter. The program increased confidence not only in that particular form of privatization, but also in the post-communist transition as a whole.

It is worth noting that at the helm of the Czech politics there has not been a complete agreement on the shape of the future economic system. It was a public knowledge that the two Vaclavs did not see eye-to-eye on economic issues. President Vaclav Havel and at first Deputy Prime Minister of Czechoslovakia and later Prime Minister of Czechia, Vaclav Klaus, differed widely even on fundamentals, including privatization. However strange it may seem, Vaclav Havel, a son of a pre-war large-scale entrepreneur, also liberal in his political views, was a socialist as far as his economic thinking was concerned.

Inevitably, intermittent clashes with Klaus concerned mostly economics. They were nonetheless clashes between intellectuals and, regardless of the exchanged barbs between the two leaders, the government operated efficiently. Also in setting up and later operating the promised citizens' privatization program. About a quarter of productive assets of the Czech economy were privatized in that manner, raising the level of goodwill of the Czech population for privatization "from above" in particular and for transition to the capitalist market in general. Quarrels and suspicions with respect to various roads taken by the Czech privatization were present there as elsewhere. But they were rarely so poisonous as in Poland.

Apart from envy and ideology, there were other factors affecting the shape of real life privatization. Probably the most important was what I called – following Nobel Prize winner Friedrich von Hayek – *the fundamental unplannability of social processes*, which evolve spontaneously, undermining the best designed plans and preferences of the ruling elites. I made that unplannability a red thread of my speech to a wider audience in the Japanese International Cooperation Administration in Tokyo in 1995.[55]

I had been asked to make an overview of the privatization (from above) taking place in the region and in return stressed that many factors intervene between ideas, programs, and specific plans of various governments and the privatization outcomes. The most important – in my view – was the unplannability of social processes, which reflects the effects of joint influence of many (often not very well understood) phenomena, both one-off events and longer-term processes.

I used the first three transition leaders – Hungary, Poland, and the Czech Republic – as case studies of the differences between rulers' preferences *cum* practical policies and outcomes in my speech to Japanese audience. Thus, to begin with Hungary, the Antall government had two problems affecting its attitude to privatization "from above".

It was, first of all, very distrustful of the old communist *nomenklatura* and to close the opportunities for privatization swindles, the government highly centralized the privatization process. However, centralizing sales, regardless of whether it is sale of underwear or of enterprises does not work as it slows down sales considerably. So, whatever Hungarian government intended to sell largely continued to stay in the state hands.

If the distrust of the people from the old regime slowed down privatization, there was, in turn, another factor that accelerated the process. Frankly speaking, the ruling conservatives in Hungary did not like privatization as such. However, they were obsessed – as I stressed earlier in this part of memoirs – with the idea of protecting poor, suffering Hungarians from effects of stabilization and systemic change. Therefore, there was little stabilization the first place.

By contrast, the privatization of state firms got a strong tailwind from the foregoing conservatives' obsession. Protection – through a variety of subsidies and other measures – requires a lot of money. Budget deficits bulged in Hungary from year to year and to finance them there was one way only, namely to sell as many enterprises to foreigners as possible. In consequence, not only privatization accelerated, but also it was pursued largely through the most efficient method. For among privatization methods, theory of property rights gives priority to the direct sale of one firm to another. An additional strengthening factor is if the sale is to a successful firm in the same line of business. Thus, the firm is sold to an entity that is both competitive in general (successful on the market) and competitive in particular (in the same line of business). My Hungarian friends, who were mostly in the intellectual camp of system-changers, were joking that the only positive effect of the otherwise costly – and futile – idea of saving Hungarians from adverse effects of systemic change was precisely the unplanned and unexpected boost to privatization…

Czechs, in turn, succeeded in implementing the *kuponovka* program of the near-free distribution of rights to buy shares in state firms by citizens. However, the idea held by many free marketers among Czech economists about creating a shareholders' society did not survive the test of social reality. They often imagined that Czechs would all become shareholders and would keep the shares they bought with coupons from the *kuponovka* program and manage their portfolio on their own.

However, they did not reckon with the well known sociological/psychological reality of the risk aversion's presence in every society. It may differ to some extent. For example, Germans are known to be sharply more risk averse than many of their European neighbors. But the differences mean that, say, instead of

20–25% of members of a given society being ready to take the risk of becoming shareholders (as in Great Britain) only, say, 15–20% or somewhat less, would be ready to do the same in Germany. There, the risk-takers amounted to between 13% and 18% of the population in the last 15 years; and the share was shrinking over the years.

Czechs turned out to be within the normal distribution of risk aversion and risk taking. Out of all those who bought shares within the *kuponovka* program about 25% kept those shares, deciding to manage personally their portfolios. The overwhelming three fourth of Czech participants decided to reduce the level of risk by turning their shares to investment funds to manage.

I am afraid, however, that foregoing comments might have created a false image of the relative privatization performance among the transition leaders. Czechs and Slovaks, and after the smooth divorce Czechs only, were portrayed as the undisputed leaders in this respect. Hungarians, due to idiosyncratic behavior of their first democratic government, also succeeded, but almost by default. They privatized a lot in the most efficient manner, even if for wrong reasons (to finance growing budget deficits). And, indeed, had we defined privatization as privatization "from above" only, their privatization performance would have been much better than that of Poles, with their government being mired in controversies over almost all aspects of privatization and criticized heavily both by the ex-communists and a large number of "Solidarity" collectivists.

Yet, I stressed strongly that what matters for progress in privatizing the national economy is not only privatization "from above", but also that "from below", namely the creation of new (overwhelmingly private) firms. And it is in the latter type of privatization that Poland excelled among transition countries.

The liberalization component of the "Holy Trinity" of transition was more free market-oriented – or, at a minimum, less intrusive – with respect to many issues affecting the decisions to start and/or continue business activity. Both the rights of establishment and those of operation of existing firms were less burdensome in Poland than elsewhere in transition countries (with my friend Wilczek's law, see Chapter 6 above, being an excellent starting point even before transition program had been launched on December 31, 1989).

The results of the regulatory liberty were very impressive, indeed. And they started immediately after the first major steps in liberalization. Already in 1989, after the passage of the Wilczek law in late 1988, the number of newly established firms doubled in comparison with the preceding year. And after the passage of the transition program in the last days of 1989, their number doubled again in 1990, in comparison with 1989, and continued to increase at elevated rates year after year until mid-1990s.

The contribution of the new private firms to output and employment in the Polish economy was markedly higher than that of privatized state firms. By 1995 23.6% of industrial sector's GDP had been produced in new private firms, with the contribution of the privatized sector being about half of that number (12.4%). Comparison of shares in industrial employment looked even more favorably for the new private firms: 36.8% vs. 7.5%. Even toward the end of the decade of 1990s, with privatization from above accelerating, the share of the new private sector was markedly higher than that of the privatized sector: in 1997 the ratio of shares in industrial employment was respectively 44.9% vs. 16.4%.

Moreover, it should be noted that industry (mining, manufacturing and utilities) had been in Poland and elsewhere in post-communist countries the least propitious sector to privatize for both political and economic reasons. In political terms large industrial state-owned firms possessed – as stressed already – a lot of political clout and in numerous cases successfully resisted privatization. And it is worth remembering that under communism the share of large firms was very high, much higher than in market economies of the West. Besides, the "Solidarity" utopians supported such resistance in principle. Especially in those cases, when the government rejected trade unionists' demands for the privatization in the least efficient manner, that is through the insiders' privatization of a given firm.

Economically, industry was the most difficult field of entry for the new private firms in the case of capital intensive branches of that sector. A high capital threshold to establish a new firm prevented the entry of potential entrepreneurs into a large number of industries, where minimum capital requirements were high. And it was especially high under the circumstances of the impoverished post-communist countries, with their very low real savings.

Thus, the numbers shown above, however impressive in relative terms, were in fact the worst if we looked across sectors in the Polish economy. For example, in the construction sector the share of the new private firms was 24.5% of total sales of the sector already in 1990, the first year of transition. And that share increased to 67.6% in 1995 and 73.6% in 1997. Privatization of state firms contributed little, beginning with 3.3% of sales in 1991 and 18.5% in 1997. Thus, construction, with the total share of the private sector at 91.3% in 1998 could be seen as being almost privately owned at the end of the first decade of transition. The story of the trade and repair sector was almost identical. The share of the new private firms in total sales was 28.4% already by the end of 1990. That share increased to 82.4% in 1995 and 85.2% in 1997. By the end of 1998 the share of the private firms in total sales of trade and repairs' sector amounted to 95.0%.

So, it should not be surprising that at the level of the national economy as a whole the shares of the private and public sectors in GDP reversed over the decade from 30% vs. 70% in 1990 to 70% vs. 30% in 1999. At the end of that decade Poland was still slightly behind Hungary, Czechia, and Estonia in terms of the share of the private sector in GDP, but the distance was very small, amounting to a few percentage points only. Exceedingly good performance of the new private firms (privatization "from below") compensated for the sluggish privatization "from above".

In fact, exceedingly good performance of the new private firms -o-v-e-r-c-o-m-p-e-n-s-a-t-e-d for the slow moving, fiercely resisted privatization of state firms. Polish economy was for in correctional recession for slightly more than two years at the start of transition, the shortest period among all successful and less successful transition countries. And its economic growth rate over the whole decade of 1990s was the fastest among all countries in post-communist transition.

Also, in more general terms of relative performance of transition countries, the selection of leaders and laggards in transition was correlated with the performance of the new private firms. Statistics in this respect, showing, for example, so-called entrepreneurial density (the number of employers and self-employed per 100 or 1000 persons of the population) generally showed that entrepreneurs in successful transition countries – not only in Poland, but also in Czechia, Hungary or Estonia – were higher by a factor of ten than in less successful transition countries, such as Romania or Russia.

In a research project, where economists from Czechia, Hungary, and Poland took part, we looked at the performance of privatized firms and *de novo* private firms and its causes. The major question was: wherefrom came faster economic growth of new private firms than privatized state firms and how it affected relative economic growth of the national economies in transition?

I stressed strongly in my early publications the contrast between industrial relations, or more specifically intra-firm relations between owners/managers and employees, across the two sets of firms. Let me start the comparisons with the privatized state-owned firms. In these firms, to say nothing about state-owned, not yet privatized firms, the owners-managers and managers-employees' relations remained for quite some time a carry-over from the communist past. Privatization of a state firm in the post-communist environment meant simply that the relations among the same people (limited replacements in managerial positions notwithstanding) changed rather slowly, regardless of the new owner's pressure for performance within the firm and the impact of the market environment outside the firm.

The change was slow because the same people in nearly the same internal environment did not feel the pressure to get rid of bad habits from the communist past: the unwillingness to take an initiative, pursuance of the leisure on the job, negligence or even non-observance of technological specifications – not to mention the outright theft. Even firms under the control of a strategic owner faced such resistance to change. Of course, things changed over time. Management at all levels was either replaced or adapted under pressure. In the firms under the control of strategic owners the change was faster than in other privatized firms. By contrast, it was the slowest in the cases of insiders' privatization, especially in employee-owned firms. After all, the utopian ideas were invoked also because such privatization promised less – or at a minimum less rapid – changes.

However, the changes generally take time. Time measured in terms of years rather than months. Therefore, the improved economic outcomes in privatized state firms appeared over a number of years. In the short run, up to three years, economic performance changed little. Even in the medium run, that is between three and seven years, such changes were often not impressive.

The performance story is completely different in the *de novo* firms. There, owner-manager relations (if it is not the same person) are set right from the very beginning, in accordance with the rules of the private ownership-based capitalist market economy. The same applies to an even greater extent with respect to the relations between owners/managers and employees. Remember the story of a funeral parlor from the preceding chapter, whose owner/manager completed his staff over a period of almost two years with an annual turnover of employees amounting to 300%? He needed the semi-skilled and sober staff and set the rules of the game within his small firm right from the start. After changing six teams he finally completed the one he needed.

Generalizing on the case, what helped considerably new private firms was the fact that they faced – in actual fact – new employees. It did not mean that these firms employed only new entrants to the labor force (not demoralized by working in state firms…). It meant that even older employees, with bad habits acquired in the communist past, adjusted much faster in the working environment of a new private firm. Facing the much more rigorous rules of the game, with the structure of incentives well correlated with good performance, they performed better than in the "old comradeship" of shirking, cheating, and stealing. And, bluntly speaking, if they did not – as those drunkards in the already quoted case of a funeral parlor – they were sure to face rapid dismissal; it was something very rare in the communist times and, therefore, was indeed a part of the "shock therapy".

Thus, given the foregoing, the larger was the share of the new private sector in the aggregate output and employment of the private sector, the faster was, by and large, economic growth rate. Of course, it mattered how large was the private sector relative to public sector, but intra-private sector proportions mattered strongly. That story was summarized in 2004 in a book *The Private Sector after Communism* by Jan Winiecki, Vladimir Benacek, and Mihaly Laky.[56] In actual fact, I wrote about those issues years earlier and the book in question was just a corollary of many years of research.[57]

The dynamics of the new private sector in post-communist transition proved *ex post* what I much earlier stressed *ex ante*. I hope that the Readers will forgive my short journey into the past and allow me to remind my earlier intellectual battles in this respect. Battles I won, since the course of 1990s proved my point without doubt. In Part I, Chapter 5, I referred to the controversies that emerged in the Prof. Geremek-led underground *conversatorium* with respect to the ownership make-up of the Polish economy after communism. I made then, in mid-1980s, the presentation where I predicted that in the post-communist Poland, with the level-playing field in terms of economic regulations, the ownership structure of firms would be shifting rather rapidly in the direction of the dominance of private ownership.

Such prediction, given the well known advantages of private ownership over all other forms of ownership, seemed to me a safe bet. However, I was criticized by some collectivist utopians among the *conversatorium* membership. Unsurprisingly, I was criticized on ideological grounds as one of the members of the team underlined that there was strong preference within the "Solidarity" movement in favor of the workers' (or employees') self-management as the model to follow.

However, I was also criticized as being unrealistic. After all, if so many state firms were to be governed by the employees' self-management councils, their overwhelming numbers would carry over those in other state firms whose employees were less convinced – the utopians argued. In fact, the thinking went even further! Some opinions were formulated about the expected conversion of other ownership forms, primarily *de novo* private firms, into employee councils' managed firms. Some ideas were formulated also about converting cooperatives in that manner!

The "Solidarity" utopians, indeed, achieved a symbolic victory during the Polish Round Table in early 1989. With the communist side not willing to pursue battles on vague ideological issues (being of little importance for their interests!) and the majority of the participants on the "Solidarity" side strongly in favor of workers' councils, the economic table conclusions contained the recommendation on the compulsory (sic!!) conversion of all firms in accordance with the workers' council model. I criticized the conclusion in question (as well as many other) already in early 1989 and referred to that criticism in Part I, Chapter 5.

Fortunately, as a perceptive comment of a historian, Jerzy Eisler, underlined, the Polish Round Table conclusions were the last chapter of the communist past, not the first chapter of post-communist systemic change. Polish transition was driven by the ideas dominant during the formation of the first non-communist government led by Tadeusz Mazowiecki, that is the ideas of a return to Europe (or the Western civilization) in terms of liberal democracy and market economy. Fortunately, utopians' success at the Round Table turned out to be limited in terms of the longer term future of the Polish economy.

Interestingly, the predictions of "Solidarity" utopians about the wave carrying state-owned (and not only state-owned) firms in the direction of the workers' council model turned out to be based on little more than a large dose of *wishful thinking*. Interestingly, the privatization "from above" – regardless of its variety – eliminated the workers' councils together with the state ownership. Even in the transformation of state ownership into employees' ownership the same process was taking place. Employees indeed exercised their rights, but they were *ownership* rights of capitalist market order – not *employment-based* rights of some, little specified utopia – and voting took place in accordance with the (roughly egalitarian) distribution of shares among employees. As employees' owned firms encountered growing problems, internal and/or new external owners appeared in these firms, changing the ownership structure along the well known lines of dominant strategic owner(s) and his/their right to appoint managers.

The most convincing with respect to changes predicted by me in mid-1980s were developments in the cooperative subsector. Cooperatives were under communism classified as a part of the so-called "socialized sector". Systemic change shifted cooperatives to the private sector, but the change in statistical classification did not save cooperatives from near extinction as a form of ownership. An overwhelming majority of cooperatives changed into classical privately-owned firm (most often as a partnership).

An almost dramatic fall of the share of cooperative firms took place in the trade and repair sector, where in 1989 54.7% of total sales of the sector was accomplished by the cooperatives. By 1997 that share shank to 4.1%!! Cooperatives were not so numerous in other sectors, but during the period in question their share in total sales also shrank considerably, for example in industry it changed from 7.8% in 1989 to 2.9% in 1997 and in construction the same share declined from 2.9% in 1989 to 0.6% in 1997. It was clear to the observers of the process of change that the choice of a cooperative form of ownership under communism was a choice made under the communist system imposed constraints. Given the choice they were offered in transition, they decided to switch to a more efficient classical private ownership.

While considering roads to the private ownership-based market economy, very little, if anything, was said about yet another theoretically valid and historically justified road – *reprivatization.* After all, return to capitalist market should include the restitution of nationalized property to the rightful owners. Embarrassingly, such an option in post-communist transition had never been seriously considered on any large scale, even if in some countries (Czechia, Estonia) quite substantial partial restitution was, indeed, implemented in the early period of systemic change.

Why not reprivatization? The droves of Western experts, advising transition governments, were dead set against it. They explained that half a century – or in the case of most post-Soviet states even three quarters of a century after nationalization, the property had long lost its original characteristic and original value. Such an evaluation applied to all property, but in particular to productive assets: to buildings and even more to machinery and equipment. Experts stressed that these changes would require very long periods of legal wrangling, slowing down privatization (from above) and post-communist transition in general.

The outcome of such evaluations and politicians' decisions were usually the regulations in transition countries that in principle rejected restitution and superseded it with partial compensation for the lost property (usually at the negligible percentage of the assessed value of physical and, in some countries, also financial assets). Poland was different also with respect to reprivatization issues in a sense that it did not solve and regulate the reprivatization issues – a-t-a-l-l. Whatever restitutions took place in Poland were the result of early decisions by local authorities and/or successful judicial procedures initiated by the original owners.

And yet, in spite of the morally embarrassing outcomes there was very little – if any – public discussion in transition countries in question. A group of transition monitors discussed the puzzle at one of the annual transition-evaluating conferences in Bled (Slovenia). The discussion was indecisive. No conclusions enjoying the support of the majority of discussants emerged there. Therefore, I decided to continue the theme in the correspondence with Prof. Ljubo Sirc, former President of the Centre for Research into Communist Economies, and my long time friend.

I wrote a lengthy analytical letter to Ljubo explaining my opinion as to why reprivatization was marginalized in transition. It is true, I wrote, that experts advising transition governments suggested to minimize restitution to reduce its assumed adverse effects on post-communist transition. However, the lack of strong public protests against undertaken institutional arrangements should become a food for thought for further discussion of the issue.

I revealed the gist of that correspondence some years later in my 2012 book "*Post-communist Transition. A Case Study of Institutional Change*" (in Polish), already quoted in my memoirs.[58] I explained in the letter that although I do not see signs of the public debate, nor are there serious public opinion surveys, I sensed a feeling of injustice among many individuals I queried on the issue – in Poland and elsewhere. The feeling of injustice particularly among those who did not belong to the potential beneficiaries of reprivatization.

Thus, almost all citizens were losers under communism (except its ruling stratum), given the extreme inefficiency of the system. There were, then, many categories of losers under communism, not only previous owners of productive assets. A large mass of losers were highly educated and high-skilled individuals, who earned from one tenth to one third of the salary in comparable non-communist Western countries. These losers realized at some point in post-communist transition that a proposed reprivatization process intended to compensate only -o-n-e category of losers under communism.

What was under the circumstances the perception of these other categories of losers? With the post-communist transition now under way, they hoped to reduce over time the salary differentials that existed in comparable Western economies. However, they realized that under the reprivatization schemes they would be, together with all others, paying now the costs of reprivatization. That is some categories of losers will be financing the compensation of yet another category of losers! It should not be surprising – I underlined – that the feeling of injustice among the former was very strong. So, there was little sympathy for the undoubtedly rightful and morally acceptable claims of former property owners; and much more support for the regulations sharply limiting the extent of compensation for the lost property.

I thought it was worthwhile to restore in these memoirs the argumentation contained in the correspondence with my old friend. I knew he would not be wholly convinced, but at least he was presented with a coherent – I thought – view on the causes of the lack of internal support for the large scale reprivatization (external experts' opinions having only limited impact on policy decisions). The scarcity of opinion surveys and serious research notwithstanding, I assumed that the feeling of injustice I described was common in most transition countries. After all, it was only a few countries, where population seemed to be relatively more sympathetic to reprivatization. Thus, in a public opinion survey presented at the first Bled conference in 1992, Prof. Veljko Rus stressed that only in two countries – Estonia and Czechoslovakia – support for the option: "Return property to the former owners" exceeded one third of all opinions (precisely 34% in each country). And, let me add, precisely in these two countries the extent of restitution to former owners was relatively the largest.

In Slovenia, where claims of Prof. Sirc to the property of his parents and grandparents languished so long, such option enjoyed only 20% support. Another option: "Give the productive property to the workers" enjoyed twice as high support (40% of opinions) in that country. In actual fact the latter option – highly inefficient in economic terms as I stressed already – enjoyed in Poland an even higher support (49%). Since in a democracy public preferences matter it is not surprising that such an inefficient option of the employee ownership was turned into law and implemented to a considerable extent (fortunately, in Poland only in the case of middle-sized state firms). Bad economic choices enjoying public support will be pursued in a democracy – even at a high cost to the voters themselves...

By the beginning of the second decade of transition, at the threshold of the XXI century, the privatization of the national economy was by and large accomplished in the transition leaders. The combined share of both privatized and newly established private firms in output and employment fluctuated within the 70%–85% range of the aggregate national economy. Everywhere *de novo* firms enjoyed more or less rapid growth, with Poland in the lead and Slovenia lagging markedly behind others. In fact, the latter country was also lagging to some extent in the privatization "from above". Slovenia was clearly an outlier in this respect.

I remember discussing the "Slovene paradox" at one of the annual Bled conferences in early XXI century (very appropriately, as Bled is a Slovene holiday resort). Slovenia has been undoubtedly a success story. It started its post-communist transition as a country with the highest per capita GDP among transition leaders and maintained its position till the end of the second decade of transition, that is the 2000–09 period. It restored output growth and contained inflation in early transition relatively fast. The economy was well balanced, internally and externally, no current account crises occurred in spite of the highly unpropitious starting point in establishing one's own currency in 1991 (civil war in the disintegrating Yugoslavia). And, yet, the state sector was relatively large, banking remained in the state hands, the privatized sector – given its collectivist ownership characteristics – was performing in a mediocre manner, while the new private firms, compared to other transition leaders, were few and far between.

I was then in a minority (was it not a lifetime characteristics of my views? - JW) by stressing that Slovenes enjoyed so far the fruits of both its communist and pre-communist advantages. Slovenia was already at the turn of XX century the most developed part of the former Yugoslavia, with the thriving private sector in light manufacturing industries. After the communist victory, the status of Slovenia as a producer of quality goods saved it from the worst consequences of the centrally planned economy that is the complete isolation from the world market.

Central government of communist Yugoslavia decided that its northwestern part should specialize in exporting to capitalist market economies, given its manufacturing competence. Thus, a substantial part of Slovene economy continued to interact with the West and in this manner felt at least -s-o-m-e pressure to adjust (with respect to output quality, technological sophistication, etc.) to the high Western standards. Therefore, when Yugoslavia fell apart, beginning in 1991, the extent of adjustment to the standards of the capitalist market was markedly smaller in Slovenia than in other transition leader countries.

Slovenia enjoyed, then, a kind of history-driven advantage over other transition leaders (to say nothing about transition laggards…). However, I stressed during the Bled discussion on "Slovene paradox", its advantage would be shrinking over time as stabilization, liberalization, and privatization progressed elsewhere. At some point of time the unsolved – or badly arranged – institutional problems were going to catch up with the Slovene economy.

And in a few years' time since the Bled discussion in question they did. Unprivatized banks, left in the state hands, created steadily larger and larger portfolio of bad loans they made to big privatized firms, which did very little to change the structure of incentives and in consequence improve the quality, technological sophistication and the product range of their output. Large privatized firms did not feel the pressure – clearly present elsewhere in the transition leader countries – from the underdeveloped quantitatively and underprivileged financially new private sector.

Since the "great financial crisis" of 2008–09, Slovene economy has been shrinking rather than expanding. Its banking sector is under the rehabilitation procedure supervised by the European institutions. And the structure of manufacturing output continues to require upgrading. The GDP per capita distance to other transition leaders has been shrinking for some time.

The second decade of transition – and the first decade of the XXI century – was largely characterized by the process of adaptation and continuation – or even better in some cases adaptation and acceleration. Transition leaders accelerated their catching-up process with the richer part of Europe. I do not like to put too much statistics into memoirs, but an evidence of acceleration was compelling. Thus, exports of the eight transition leaders taken together in the early period of systemic change (1990–96) amounted to 212.4, with 1990 equal to 100.0. However, in the next period, until the entry of the eight leaders into the European Union (1996–2004) aggregate exports accelerated further to 313.6, with 1996 equal to 100.0. All the time, since the start of transition their export growth rates were faster not only than those of "old" EU, but also faster than world trade growth rates – and at accelerated rates at that. Thus, their exports grew faster than world trade by 37.0% in the 1990–96 period, but exceeded world trade by 72.9% in 1996–2004 period!

It became increasingly obvious that these countries on the verge of joining the European Union in 2004 turned into typical middle-developed, middle income capitalist economies, with their normal achievements and failures for that sort of economies. What made them somewhat different, was a higher than usual dynamics resulting from recent institutional change. Above average exports were just one of indicators of their dynamism. Productivity data underpinned such results. Manufacturing productivity growth in eight transition leaders-turned into new EU members in 2004 was about 4.5 times higher in the preceding 1995–2003 period than respective productivity of "old' EU-15 countries. I mentioned manufacturing first as it was linked strongly with export performance. However, the productivity growth rates of national economies of the transition leaders were also about 5.0 faster than respective productivity of "old" EU-15 countries.

The "new normal" status of new EU members could be confirmed in one more way. Namely by the accelerated increase in the foreign direct investment flowing into transition leaders. Firstly, multinational firms recognized the benefits of increasing stability of institutional arrangements and policies in these countries. And, next, recognized the benefits of investing in middle-developed economies with still less then middle level of wages (in terms of West European proportions). Lastly, they invested in countries ready to join European Union, the largest market for goods in the world.

However, with the passage of time the availability of other advantages became increasingly visible. Dalia Marin, a professor from Munich University, proved that the pattern of trade (outsourcing) and investment (offshoring) reveals not only cost advantages, but also advantages of available human capital in the eight new EU countries from East-Central Europe.[59] Human capital not always available in sufficient quantities in investor countries (in the study by Prof. Marin it was Germany and Austria). Thus, not only export capability of investing firms increased as a result, but also the level of sophistication of these exports.

The developments I have been outlining above – the "new normal" of the eight transition leaders – lasted until the outbreak of the so-called great financial crisis in the 2007–09 period. However, it is interesting to note that the crisis itself did not change the opinion on the "class of 2004" of new EU members. Whatever problems they had, were problems of capitalist market economies that one way or another messed up their economic policies. Thus, three Baltic countries and Hungary went through the typical housing bubble and subsequent bust (registered also, *inter alia*, in the US and Spain).

If I were to think about some differentiation between ex-transition leaders, now new EU members, and the "old" EU-15 in the context of the global financial crisis, I would single out Estonia, Latvia, and Lithuania as countries that were, so to say, ready to face the music. That is to accept the need to clean up the mess, even if it entailed quite a high cost. Almost half of the benefits of economic growth in the ten years preceding the crisis were lost as a result of deep recessions, caused by restrictive policies pursued to eliminate the distortions generated by housing bubbles.

However, after a deep fall in GDP – and GDP per capita – these countries regained their vitality and since 2010 belong to fastest growing EU countries. This is in stark contrast not only with the very special case of Greece, but also with other middle-developed, middle-income countries of the EU South. It is interesting to look in 5–10 years from now at the growth and level of GDP per capita in these three countries and, say, Greece, Portugal, or Spain. In fact, it would also be interesting to look from the same perspective at Italy, whose second decade of near stagnation – largely due to a refusal to make necessary institutional changes in the political and economic system – and compare its economic outcomes with those countries of East-Central Europe which showed much greater readiness to make necessary institutional and policy corrections, even at a temporarily high cost.

But what I suggested in the preceding paragraph does not belong to memoirs concerning the period of transition. It was largely over. They are considerations concerning middle-developed market economies put in comparative perspective; a normal way of looking at countries at a similar level of development, regardless of their history.

Postscript: Looking Back, Looking Forward

This is not yet another piece of my memoirs, but rather some considerations on the issues that emerged from the memoirs. There is not much that can be added to my considerations of communism, communist system, centrally planned and administered economy, etc. Except, may be, for one reflection, linking the past with the momentous change taking place since 1989–91. Namely, countries of East-Central and Eastern (including Southern) Europe underwent two major systemic changes in less than one century! First they lived through the forced imposition of a communist system and later they lived – and some are still living – under the largely voluntary departure, or departures, from communism.

One way or another, the region in question, that is East-Central and Eastern (including Southern) Europe may be looked at as an incomparable historical laboratory of institutional, political and economic change. Studying and writing about the changes in question has been a fascinating endeavor. At least it was such for this author.

However, even if writing about systemic change has been a fascinating endeavor, writing polemically about those who tried – and keep trying – to rewrite the history in question is treated by me as an intellectual duty to defend the reality of transition against often tendentious distortions of that reality. Thus, I decided to actively react in this postscript to the three waves of unreason that could have been observed in the transition and post-transition period:

<> In early 1990s;
<> At the turn of the XXI century; and
<> Since 2008–09, that is since the "great financial crisis".

Of the three waves of unreason only that of the first period can be relatively easily explained in scholarly terms. After all at the start of transition in East-Central Europe there was not much widely spread understanding of the issues involved and even less empirical evidence that could be used – for or against – a given transition strategy. Or so was he opinion of the punditocracy. Some even compared the change from communist system to market capitalism to re-creating eggs from an omelet! It was an obvious exaggeration because – as I stressed in the memoirs – stabilization/liberalization strategies, with a dose of privatization, were a common occurrence as far as highly distorted, macroeconomically unbalanced less developed economies (LDCs) were concerned. The difference with post-communist transition was largely confined to the size of the privatization component, which was overwhelmingly larger in post-communist economies. It was a major difference, but the similarity of problems suggested the plethora of experience available for transition's analysis, design, implementation, and evaluation.

Besides, the perception of limited knowledge gave rise to various (largely spurious) alternatives to what I call the "Holy Trinity of Transition", combined with rebuilding or building of some specific market institutions. Among such spurious alternatives one could even find a strategy of creating artificial markets, with the corollary of the artificial stock market, w i t h o u t private firms. I reacted to that fantasy with an article in the *Financial Times* (June 20, 1990), with a title" "No Capitalism minus Capitalists". History knows no case of a successful market economy without dominant privately-owned firms; a quarter of a century later the statement is as true as it was in 1990. The deep decline of the oil rich Venezuela adds to the evidence.

Also statements about the "unacceptable costs of transition" (see Chapter 7) could be more easily understood – even if not accepted as valid – at the early transition time because in LDCs early side effects of reform in terms of accompanying output decline were measured in single- not double-digit terms. However, the knowledge of workings of the centrally planned and administered economy should help here.

Politicians under stress could conceivably be absolved, but not scholars studying Soviet-type economies. The latter should have known about communist system-specific "output that was not" (except in reports to higher-ups), "production for production's sake" (without wealth creation), investments as free goods and other curiosities of the economic system with soft budget constraint of state firms, rewarded for what they tell rather than for what they sell. (There were no capitalists then and there who would have their own wealth in the game and would behave differently than managers of state firms!) Scholars should also know that the higher the level of development, measured by GDP per capita, the greater the cost of getting rid of accumulated distortions.

The second wave of unreason that happened around the turn of the century (and millennium) is less intellectually justifiable – and less understandable if confined to post-communist transition *per se*. After all by the year 2000 it was already clear that those countries that seriously pursued the "Holy Trinity of Transition" plus some specific institutional changes – that is those that chose the theory- and policy-recommended route to capitalist market – recorded higher economic growth, reduced inflation faster, excelled in exports, as well as drew more foreign direct investment on per capita basis.[60]

Yet it is around the year 2000 that we experience the next wave of criticism of transition in almost all its aspects, involving a variety of authors, including a

Nobel Prize winner Joseph Stiglitz. The criticism, missing the most important developments, devoid of comparative perspective, was driven – I suspect – more by the ideological prejudices than anything else.

At this point I would like for a moment to revert to memoir-type recollections.

> I was at that time a professor at the European University-Viadrina in Frankfurt a.d. Oder, where I run a seminar with a strong interest in transition issues. Since I had a batch of Polish students there I suggested two of them to present at the seminar a paper on two books (they should properly be called pamphlets!) published in Poland around the turn of the century by an American professor of Polish origin, Kazimierz Poznanski. They had heavily "loaded" titles: "A Great Swindle: The Defeat of Polish Reforms" (published in 2000) and "Craziness of Reform: The Sell-out of Poland" (published in 2001). Just for the record, Poland was ranked at that time by nearly all international institutions and think-tanks as number one among all transition countries as far as institutional change and economic performance were concerned.
>
> These two (quite good) students came to me at my office hours a week later and asked energetically to give some other transition literature to comment upon. They were visibly offended by my selection of literature and said that they would feel embarrassed to consider seriously and present at the seminar to their colleagues such "trash"...

The foregoing wave of unreason was not understandable in academic, intellectual terms on stand-alone basis. However, as noted by a former head of economics and statistics department at the OECD, Prof. David Henderson, the turn of the millennium was also a period of the "Rise in New Millennium Collectivism"[61] Henderson noted the ever widening scope of anti-discrimination laws affecting labor market processes and housing market developments, the growing single-issue interest groups generally presenting anti-liberal solutions to their pet problems, as well as post-modernist erosion of traditional Western values and preferences associated with liberal democracy and capitalist market economy. It was not an all out attack on market capitalism that we have been experiencing since 2008–09, but the first signals of an illiberal storm. Within the framework of a rising wave of anti-capitalist market feelings and arrangements the "trash" – as my students called Prof. Poznanski books – began to be not so much acceptable, but to some extent understandable as a part of the Henderson's collectivist trend....

Finally, the third wave of unreason affecting the evaluation of transition is taking place somewhat haphazardly, within the ocean waves of criticism of various aspects of capitalist market economy we experience today. The academia in the Western world does not seem to be nowadays concerned with a group of post-communist countries and their dichotomous classification between transition success stories and transition failures (or at best laggards). If they deal with post-communist transition it is more an outpouring of personal frustrations among long-time critics of transition. You can find more criticism among politicians and journalists who have a stake in the blame-game than among academics. Academics from successful transition countries write occasionally highly critical stories – mostly counterfactual, or neglecting facts and figures altogether – but they are welcomed in the present intellectual climate as another piece of "evidence" supporting the wider critique of the capitalist market economy.

I called these waves of criticism waves of unreason, but a harsh assessment is – in my opinion – justified. For it is unreasonable to insist on presenting failure in cases, where success has long been evident. And the difference between the success of East-Central European countries (alphabetically Czechia, Estonia, Hungary, Latvia, Lithuania, Poland, Slovakia, and Slovenia) and the failure or not much more than failure in the cases of post-Soviet and South European countries has been striking, regardless of the indicator chosen.

The eight countries in question have been for more than a decade well performing fully-fledged members of the European Union and if they encountered problems, even serious problems, they were problems of middle-developed market economies, not problems of unfinished transition (Slovene recent crisis is a partial exception – see Chapter 9). In fact, when the great financial crisis came, some of the eight former transition leaders, now EU members, performed better than middle-developed South-Western economies: Greece, Spain and Portugal (Ireland plays in another, higher league and will not be considered here).

A comparison of Greece and Latvia is telling in this respect. Latvia, a newcomer to the of problems of market capitalism, suffered the consequences of a mismanaged housing market bubble, aggravated in the small capital-hungry open economy by a lot of foreign currency borrowing. Latvia aspired to become in the near future a member of Eurozone and Latvian politicians, with the currency board arrangement in force, decided in favor of painful "internal devaluation", that is deep cuts in demand, including public sector demand. GDP fell by almost 20%. Yet the recovery – even in the unpropitious environment of the great financial crisis and its aftermath – was relatively rapid and Latvia almost reached its earlier, pre-crisis level of GDP per capita by the time of writing these memoirs. And the Latvian economy continues to grow much above the EU average.

Greece did the opposite. It also borrowed too much, but above all borrowed recklessly, even to pay bureaucrats salaries and pensions (both most attractive in the EU in relative terms). Greece went bankrupt and its economy came under the supervision of the EU, ECB and IMF. The process of cutting the public sector to size has barely began. Even after five years of the reform program. Greece still has almost four times as many public sector bureaucrats per 1000 of population as, for example, the United Kingdom! And the extent of privileges of bureaucracy (early retirement, etc.) continues to be mind-boggling. The resistance to the needed changes has been overwhelming. No surprise, then, that the outcome in economic terms has been very bad. In 2014 GDP per capita in Greece was lower by a quarter. There was no economic growth until the second half of 2014 and the political change resulted in further GDP decline. Regardless of how the present drama ends Greeks already lost a lot of time – and GDP…

At the other end of the scale, Poland was the only EU country that did not suffer GDP decline at the outbreak of the great financial crisis. There was no such economy among middle-developed South-Western economies. Overall since the start of transition Poland and other seven former transition leaders reduced the distance to the rich, highly developed countries of Western Europe by a third or more. And they continue to grow faster than richer members of the EU so the distance continues to decrease. There is no doubt that these countries are success stories, now catching up with or even surpassing middle-developed South-Western EU member countries, and in the 15–20 years time frame they may catch up with the rich Western Europe.

The convergence with the rich Europe proceeds not only in terms of material progress measured by GDP per capita, but also in a wider life satisfaction (LS for short). A recent study compared LS in the old and new EU member countries in the period between the start of transition and the beginning of the great financial crisis (1991–2008). Taking the European Value Study surveys as a statistical base, the authors – Jiri Vecernik and Martina Mysikova – calculated that the distance in the life satisfaction over the two decades has been on the decrease in line with the decrease in the developmental distance measured by GDP per capita.[62]

It is significant that the only area where the satisfaction has been on the decrease over the 1991–2008 period were East German *Laender*. And this in spite of the fact that GDP per capita in post-communist Germany grew the fastest in comparison with the eight post-communist success stories considered here. My interpretation of the foregoing is in line with my reasoning explaining the half a century of declining economic growth in rich Western Europe (and rich West in general) presented in my book *Economic Futures of the West.*

The explanation is couched in terms of a psychological theory of "learned helplessness", elaborated by Prof. David Seligman. According to Seligman, individuals assume that the world around them is predictable and that acting in line with the perceived rewards and punishments one should expect to achieve his or her goals. Applying his general thesis to socio-economic reality of the welfare state, achievement of economic goals (such as higher salary and promotions) are explained in their minds by their earlier purposeful actions.

However, if rewards and punishments are seen by individuals to be applied at random and effects (*e.g.*, higher welfare payments of various sorts) cannot be linked to individuals' purposeful actions, the outcomes for those benefiting from welfare programs may be a turon to passivity, unwillingness to take an initiative, inability to learn, and even emotional disturbances. The set of these syndromes is called *learned helplessness* to stress the role of experience – the experience of unpredictability of the world around them – in establishing such a syndrome in individuals affected by the unpredictability.

People in post-communist East Germany, in contrast with those in the eight post-communist success stories, got everything so to say "on the plate" – from the institutional framework to higher wages – from West Germany. There was much less linkage between action and outcome among individuals in the former. Some learned helplessness syndromes have been quite visible in Eastern *Laender* of Germany. Hence, the striking decline in life satisfaction and signs of learned helplessness effects, in spite of the fact, that the absolute level of GDP per capita in post-communist part of Germany was higher than in each of eight success stories, where level of LS was on the increase over the period of 20 years under consideration.

So much for looking back, but what about looking forward, that is considering the future of the successful countries of the region? Here, the expectations, based on the trends concerning the pivot of these countries, that is the rich countries of Western Europe, are definitely less rosy than the past. Interestingly, main sources of expected future problems stem from the developments in the same rich Western Europe that were so important for transition's success stories of the same countries of East-Central Europe since the demise of communism in 1989–91.

As I pointed out in Chapter 8, the so-called gravity model of exports under the conditions of free trade helped a lot in reorienting foreign trade of eights success stories from East to West. And since trade flows are largest to countries that are both close geographically and rich, they not only reoriented, but also accelerated their exports to Western Europe, which grew very fast, much faster than world trade. They amount now to about three fourth of all exports from East-Central Europe.

These successful accelerations of exports took place, however, at the time, when rich West European economies used to increase their GDP at the rate of 2.0–2.5% annually. Yet, economic growth of Western Europe has been declining since 1960s from one decade to another. By now it is at best at the range of 1.0–1.5% per annum growth rate. The decline is going to affect adversely export performance of the countries in question. After all, ever more slowly growing economies increase their imports relatively more slowly as well. Thus, external growth impulses for East-Central European countries are correspondingly weaker now and may become even weaker in the foreseeable future.

The continuing economic slowdown is not going to be reversed any time soon. Empirical evidence emerging in the past 15–20 years links declining growth to increasing share of public expenditures in GDP. And that share, especially of welfare expenditures, have been on the increase since 1960s, reducing incentives to work, earn, save, and invest. Redesigning the welfare state and cutting it down to size is going to be extremely difficult. Therefore, any improvements cannot be expected soon (if at all…).

Besides, the welfare state and its expenditures have strongly negative consequences in terms of the "learned helplessness", mentioned above in the context of Eastern *Laender* of Germany. I developed this line of argument in the recent book of mine "*Economic Futures of the West*"[63] Thus, the lasting economic slowdown results not only from pure economic effects, but also from social distortions injected gradually into the system by the expanding welfare state. As such it will be all the more difficult to eliminate.

Next problem, or next external constraint, imposed on the future prospects of East-Central European success stories stems from institutional weaknesses or downright failures in building integrated Europe. The combination of quixotic institutional arrangements of the Eurozone (high barriers to entry, weak execution over fiscal behavior of member countries, and no exit procedure) combined with readiness of member countries to soften the rules of behavior of the members as far as their fiscal discipline is concerned, reduced the credibility of the Eurozone. Unwillingness to take individual countries to task for their lack of such discipline and unwillingness to pursue the needed structural (regulatory plus taxation) reforms shows the indecisiveness of the Eurozone as an integrated whole. That indecisiveness is reinforced by the larger political framework of "ever closer union" and the (crazy) idea that every European country should be on the bandwagon, regardless of its repeated transgressions of the rules.

The embarrassing picture of the indecisiveness, clutching at the straws, and the readiness to make almost every compromise – however rotten – in order to project outside the visibly false picture of united Europe has been again at work in the case of the unfolding Greek crisis. Pretensions of unity and uniformity reduce the already low credibility of European institutions, not only of the Eurozone. I am not at all surprised that John Bolton, former US high-ranking diplomat assessed that the European Union "has produced precisely the opposite of its founders aspirations: a Europe (being) less than the sum of its parts, weaker not stronger".[64] Thus, East-Central European success stories cannot count on integrative arrangements overcoming the deficiencies of national economic and other policies of rich Western Europe.

Yet, I continue to be guardedly optimistic in terms of relative performance of the East-Central European countries catching up with old, rich (and visibly tired) Western Europe. The years of 5% or higher annual economic growth rates are over in the foreseeable future, but with rich West European countries at best growing at the rate of 1.0–1.5% per annum, the economic growth of Poland, Czechia, Hungary, Slovakia and the Baltic trio (Slovenia being to me a question mark) in the range of 2.0–4.0% annually suggests that the latter countries will continue reducing the developmental distance measured in terms of GDP per capita, although at a somewhat lower speed.

However, there is one big "if" – of a rather recent vintage. The if in question is the revisionist Putin's Russia, which has actively been questioning post-cold war order of late by military, as well as by what has recently been called "hybrid" means. Their longer term aims are to divide the European Union, undermine NATO, and reestablish its influence – if not primacy – in the former Soviet Russia's dependencies.

The importance of Russian challenge would have been markedly less threatening if it did not coincide with what I wrote above about weak – and increasingly weaker – economic growth of Western Europe, about internal wrangling and declining problem-solving power of European institutions, as well as weak – if not downright incompetent – current American presidency, unwilling and may be even unable to lead the West as America did until 1990s. In such an inhospitable political/military environment ability to maintain an economic growth at a steady – relatively high – rate could be weakened by the emerging imperatives of other priorities.

And, yet, I assume that Western Europe, or at least important countries of Western Europe, will be able to maintain a modicum of decisiveness in the next few years and the United States increase to some extent their strategic interest and level of NATO-based military presence in Europe. Under such circumstances there will not be much of a retreat from the present *status quo* and no large *de facto* losses are going to be registered by the West, including the most exposed East-Central Europe till the end of this decade.

Moreover, the long-term balance of economic power is slowly but inexorably changing to the disadvantage of Russia – even with Western Europe's problems analyzed above. The mineral commodities' price cycle has been in its price declining phase, which is going to continue for the next 10–15 years at a minimum. The example of how devastating that would be for Russia's ability to expand can be found in Russia's history in 1980s and 1990s.

A the same time there is no chance that the Russian economy – especially manufacturing industry – would reform and perform at the level of East-Central European success stories. Neither Soviet Russia, nor Putin's Russia were able to introduce and successfully accomplish free market-oriented reform. So, markedly higher efficiency is not going to supersede the windfall benefits of the price increasing phase of the mineral commodities' cycle. With Russia's economy getting increasingly weaker in the medium to long run, the window of opportunity for Putin's Russia to do serious mischief in Europe is limited to the next couple of years. May be till the end of the present decade. Thus, Europe, and especially East-Central Europe (closest to my heart) is under serious threat of Russia-incited disturbances for a limited time span only…

References

Chapter 1

1 See J. Muravchik, *Heaven on Earth: The Rise and Fall of Socialism*, San Francisco: Encounter Books, 2002, 31–59.

Chapter 2

2 See my background paper to the report on the state of teaching economics in Poland: J. Beksiak, E. Chmielewska, U. Grzelonska-Libura, and J. Winiecki, Warsaw, 1990, mimeo.
3 S. Kurowski, *Historyczny proces wzrostu gospodarczego* (*Histrical process of economic growth*), Warsaw: PWN Publishers, 1963.

Chapter 3

4 M. Glowinski, *Marcowe gadanie* (*Newspeak in the March 1968' Style.* Comments on Words Used in the 1966–71 Period), Warsaw: Pomost Publishers, 1991, pp. 262ff.
5 J. Holzer, Notatki o humanistyce (Notes on the Humanities), "*Polityka*", no. 14, 1971.
6 The dynamics of such processes was best described after the fall of communism by a Hungarian Janos Kornai, see his book: *The Socialist System: Political Economy of Communism*, Oxford, The Clarendon Press, 1992, Chapter XV.
7 J. Fedorowicz, *W zasadzie – tak* (In Principle, Yes), Warsaw, 1974.

Chapter 4

8 J. Winiecki, *Economic Prospects: East and West*, London: Centre for Research into Communist Economies, 1987.
9 See *Economic Prospects …*, Preface, p. 12.
10 K. Deutsch, *The Nerves of Government. Models of Political Communication and Control*, New York, N.Y.: The Free Press, 1966, p. 115.
11 *Economic Prospects …*, pp. 60ff.

Chapter 5

12 J. Kornai, *The Road to a Free Economy. Shifting from a Socialist System: The Example of Hungary*, New York: Norton, 1990, p. 72.
13 See *The Road to Free Economy …*, p. 54.
14 See J. Winiecki, "Ein<<Marshall Plan>>fuer Osteuropa? Warnung von falschen Erwartungen", *Neue Zuercher Zeitung*, November 26/27, 1988. An English version of the article appeared in *Swiss Review of World Affairs*, February 1989.

15 See *Koniec epoki.* Wywiady Maksymiliana Berezowskiego (*The End of the Epoch.* Interviews by Maximilian Berezowski), Warsaw, 1991, p. 11.
16 See a book by Jerzy Eisler, *Siedmiu wspaniałych. Poczet pierwszych sekretarzy PZPR* (*The Wonderful Seven: The Galaxy of Communist First Secretaries*), Warszawa: Czerwone I Czarne Publisher, 2014, Chapters 6 and 7.
17 J. Szymanderski and J. Winiecki, The Gorbachev Challenge II: A View from the East, *World Today*, 1989 pp. 145–48.
18 Jerzy Eisler, *The Wonderful Seven* ...Ibidem, p. 445.
19 "Czas Balcerowicza minal (The time of Balcerowicz is over). An interview with Ivan Krastev, *Dziennik - Gazeta Prawna*, December 29, 2009.

Chapter 6

20 See Jan Winiecki, *The Distorted World of Soviet-type Economies*, London: Routledge, and Pittsburgh: Pittsburgh University Press, 1988, Chapter 6.
21 Yegor Gajdar, *Anomalie wzrostu gospodarczego* (Anomalies of Economic Growth), Warsaw: CASE [Center for Social and Economic Analysis], 1999.
22 See *The Polish Transformation: Programme and Progress.* By Janusz Beksiak, Tomasz Gruszecki, Aleksander Jedraszczyk, and Jan Winiecki. London: Centre for Research into Communist Economies, July 1990 (the program was on pp. 19–59).
23 See, Jan Winiecki, "How to get the ball rolling", *Financial Times*, January 13, 1989.
24 See V. Klaus, "Czechoslovakia and the Czech Republic. The Spirit and the Main Contours of the Postcommunist Transformation", Anders Aslund and Simeon Djankov, eds., *The Great Rebirth. Lessons from the Victory of Capitalism over Communism*, Washington, D.C.: Peterson Institute for International Economics, pp. 53–71, quote on p. 56].
25 For the latter, see, Jan Winiecki, *Privatization in Poland. A Comparative Perspective*, Kieler Studien, Tuebingen: J.C.B. Mohr, 1992.
26 *Russia under the Old Regime*, 1974, references are made to Polish 2006 edition, published by Magnum.
27 London: Routledge, 1991.

Chapter 7

28 See Vaclav Klaus short note of his conversation with Ota Sik, the intellectual father of "socialism with human face", in his contribution to the *The Great Rebirth* ... Ibidem, p. 56.
29 See, P. Bozyk, "Na skróty – dalej" (Using Shortcuts Makes the Road Longer), *Przeglad Tygodniowy*, no. 47, 1990].
30 See a collection of my papers and articles from the 1990s, written in Polish. The paper in question was "Teoretyczne podstawy rzadowego program stabilizacji: Realia i folklor polityczny" [Theoretical underpinnings of government's stabilization program], in: *Polemiki w drodze (do kapitalizmu)*[*Polemics on the Road (to Capitalist System)*], pp. 55–59.
31 See, S. Kurowski and M. Przygodzki, "Program ożywienia" (The Program of Revival), *Zycie Gospodarcze*, no. 27, 7.07.1991.

32 See, A. Glapinski, "Mam klucz" (I Have a Key), *Zycie Gospodarcze*, no. 27, 7.07.1991.

33 See, *i.a.*, my "Post-Soviet-type Economies in Transition. What Have We Learned from the Polish Transition Programme in Its First Year?", *Weltwirtschaftliches Archiv*, vol. 126, no. 4, 1990, pp. 765–90, "The Inevitability of a Fall in Output in the early Stages of Transition to the Market: Theoretical Underpinnings", *Soviet Studies*, vol. 43, no. 4, 1991, pp. 669–76, "Steep Output Fall and Some Other Alleged Puzzles in Economics of Transition", in: Andrzej Brzeski and Jan Winiecki, eds., *A Liberating Economic Journey. Essays in Honor of Ljubo Sirc*, London: Centre for Research into Post-Communist Economies, 2000, pp. 29–63, and "An Inquiry into the Early Drastic Fall of Output in Post-communist Transition: An Unsolved Puzzle", *Post-Communist Economies*, vol. 14, no.1., 2002, pp. 5–29.

34 *The Polish Transformation: Programme and Progress* ...Ibidem, London: CRCE, p. 55.

35 See K. Dervis and T. Condon, Hungary – Partial Successes and Remaining Challenges: The Emergence of a "Gradualist" Success Story, in: *The Transition in Eastern Europe*. Vol. 1: Country Studies, Ed. by O.J. Blanchard, K.A. Froot, and J.D. Sachs, Chicago: University of Chicago Press, 1994, pp. 123–53.

36 See J. Kornai. "Transformational Recession", Budapest: Collegium Budapest Discussion paper no. 1, 1993, later published as "Transformational Recession: Main Causes, *Journal of Comparative Economics*, vol. 19, no. 1, 1994, pp. 36–63.

37 See his "Transformation as a Subject of Economic Theory", Budapest: KOPINT-DATORG Discussion paper no. 57, 1998.

38 J. Lewandowski, "Kapitalizm z polska twarza", *Gazeta Wyborcza*, 17.05.1994.

39 For the latter, see "Sprawiedliwosc wedlug zaslug czy wedle potrzeb?" (Distributive effects in accordance with one's efforts or with one's needs?), *Rzeczpospolita*, 16.09.1993.

40 I presented these ideas at the Mont Pelerin Society General Meeting in Vienna in September 1996 and later in an article "The Transformation to the Market: At High Cost, Often with Long Lags, and Not Without Question Marks", *Journal of Public Policy*, vol. 17, no. 3, 1997, pp. 251–68.

Chapter 8

41 See in particular J. Winiecki, *Transition Economies and Foreign Trade*, London: Routledge, Chapter 2.

42 See J.F. Francois and J. Woerz, "Shifts in International Trade and Value Added from 1995 to 2007: Insights into the drivers of growth", *Focus on European Economic Integration*, vol. 3, pp. 37–56.

43 L. Csaba, "Convergence and Divergence in Economic Transformation and Integration", in: D. Schorkowitz (ed.), *Transition-Erosion-Reaktion. Zehn Jahren Transformation in Osteuropa*, Berlin: Peter Lang, 2002, pp. 41–69, the quoted passage on p. 46).

44 *The Wealth and Poverty of Nations. Why some are so rich and some so poor*, New York: Norton, 1998, p. 38.

45 See, "The Transformation to the Market ...", Ibidem, 1997; "Three Crucial Issues in Post-communist Privatization. A Polish case in comparative perspective". A paper prepared for the Mont Pelerin Society regional meeting on "Transition to Free Societies"

Potsdam, Germany, 1999; J. Winiecki, V. Benacek, and M. Laky, *The Private Sector After Communism: New entrepreneurial firms in transition economies*, London: Routledge, 2004 (Chapter 2); "Determinants of Catching Up and Falling Behind", *Post-communist Economies*, vol. 16, no. 2, 2004, pp. 137–52.; *Transformacja postkomunistyczna: Studium przypadku zmian instytucjonalnych* (*Post-communist Transition: A case study of institutional change*), Warsaw: C.H. Beck, 2012 (Chapters 6 and 8).

46 J. Kornai, Ibidem, p. 54.

47 Anna Smolka, businesswoman, a conversation with, *Gazeta Wyborcza*, February 2, 2009.

48 See, Dariusz Rutczynski, businessman, a conversation with, *Gazeta Wyborcza*, February 2, 2009.

Chapter 9

49 *The Financial Times*, June 20, 1990. See also another article of mine on the same theme, J. Winiecki, "Kapitalisten Gesucht. Verschiedene Wege zur Marktwirtschaft", *Wirtschafts Woche*, November 9, 1990.

50 See, T. Gruszecki and J. Winiecki, "Privatization in East-Central Europe: A Comparative Perspective", Aussenwirtschaft, vol. 46, no. 1, 1991, pp. 67–100.

51 J. Fedorowicz, *The Great Encyclopedia of Capitalism. The ABC for Beginners and Politicians*, Warsaw: Adam Smith Center, 1997.

52 L. Kolakowski, "Totalitarianism and the Virtue of the Lie," in: *1984 Revisited*, Ed. by Irving Howe, 1983.

53 "Mity polskiej prywatyzacji" (Myths about Polish Privatization), *Przeglad Polityczny* (Political Review), 1992 (quotation on p. 108).

54 See J. Winiecki, Privatization in Poland. A Comparative Perspective, Tuebingen: J.C.B. Mohr (Paul Siebeck), 1992.

55 See "Privatization in Eastern Europe. Lessons and Future Prospects" by Jan Winiecki, Tokyo: ICA, October 3, 1995 (printout of a lecture, as well later questions and answers).

56 See J. Winiecki, V. Benacek, and M. Laky, *The Private Sector after Communism. New entrepreneurial firms in transition economies*, London: Routledge, 2004.

57 See my own earlier publications, such as "The Superiority of Eliminating Barriers to Entrepreneurship over Privatization Activism of the State", *Banca Nazionale del Lavoro Quarterly Review*, No. 198, September 1996, pp. 313–31; "Three Crucial Issues in Post-communist Privatization", A paper prepared for The Mont Pelerin Society regional meeting: "Transitions to a Free Society". Potsdam, Germany, October 1999, later published in *Communist and Post-communist Studies*, vol. 33, 2000, pp. 505–15; "The Polish Generic Private Sector in Transition: Developments and Characteristics", *Europe-Asia Studies*, vol. 54, no. 1, 2002, pp. 5–29.

58 *Transformacja postkomunistyczna* ... Ibidem, pp. 176–80.

59 D. Marin, "The new international division of labor in Europe", In: *Competitiveness of New Europe. Papers from the second Lancut Economic Forum*. Ed. by Jan Winiecki, London Routledge, 2009, pp. 122–36.

Postscript

60 See, for example, the Thirty-first Wincott lecture in 2001, published later in Leszek Balcerowicz, *Post-Communist Transition: Some* Lessons, London: The Institute of Economic Affairs, 2002.

61 See D. Henderson, *Anti-Liberalism 2000. The Rise In New Millennial Collectivism*, London: The Institute of Economic Affairs.

62 J. Vecernik and M. Mysikova, GDP and LIfe Satisfaction in European Countries – Focus on transition, *Post-Communist Economies,* vol. 27, no. 2, 2015, pp. 170–87.

63 J. Winiecki, *Economic Futures of the West*, Cheltenham, UK, and Northampton, Mass., USA: Edward Elgar, 2013, for relevant considerations, see Chapters 6 and 9.

64 J.R. Bolton, "The Agony of Greece and the Crisis of the European Project", *New York Post*, June 23, 2015.

www.ingramcontent.com/pod-product-compliance
Ingram Content Group UK Ltd.
Pitfield, Milton Keynes, MK11 3LW, UK
UKHW041826031026
15587UKWH00002B/587

9 783631 668795